Strategies for Successful Student Teaching

A Guide to Student Teaching, the Job Search, and Your First Classroom

Third Edition

Carol Pelletier Radford

Center for School, University, and Community Partnerships
University of Massachusetts Dartmouth

Boston   Columbus   Indianapolis   New York   San Francisco   Upper Saddle River
Amsterdam   Cape Town   Dubai   London   Madrid   Milan   Munich   Paris   Montréal   Toronto
Delhi   Mexico City   São Paulo   Sydney   Hong Kong   Seoul   Singapore   Taipei   Tokyo

This guide is dedicated to Sean Duarte,
a transformational teacher, who passed too soon.

Vice President and Editorial Director: Jeffery W. Johnston
Senior Acquisitions Editor: Meredith D. Fossel
Associate Editor: Anne Whittaker
Editorial Assistant: Andrea Hall
Vice President, Director of Marketing: Margaret Waples
Marketing Manager: Darcy Betts Prybella
Senior Managing Editor: Pamela D. Bennett
Project Manager: Kerry Rubadue
Senior Operations Supervisor: Matthew Ottenweller

Senior Art Director: Diane Lorenzo
Text Designer: Element-Thomson North America
Cover Designer: Ali Mohrman
Permissions Administrator: Rebecca Savage
Cover Art: Fotolia
Full-Service Project Management: Element-Thomson North America
Composition: Element-Thomson North America
Printer/Binder: Edwards Brothers
Cover Printer: Lehigh-Phoenix Color/Hagerstown
Text Font: Sabon

Credits and acknowledgments borrowed from other sources and reproduced, with permission, in this textbook appear on appropriate page within text.

Every effort has been made to provide accurate and current Internet information in this book. However, the Internet and information posted on it are constantly changing, so it is inevitable that some of the Internet addresses listed in this textbook will change.

Library of Congress Cataloging-in-Publication Data
Radford, Carol Pelletier.
    Strategies for successful student teaching: a guide to student teaching, the job search, and your first classroom / Carol Pelletier Radford.—3rd ed.
        p. cm.
    ISBN 978-0-13-705948-5 (alk. paper)
    1. Student teaching—United States—Handbooks, manuals, etc.   2. Student teachers—Training of—United States—Handbooks, manuals, etc.   I. Title.
    LB2157.U5P39 2013
    370.71—dc23
                                                                    2011050594

10 9 8 7 6 5 4 3 2 1

www.pearsonhighered.com

ISBN-10: 0-13-705948-5
ISBN-13: 978-0-13-705948-5

Preface

The ideas and strategies I share in this edition have been implemented and practiced in real classrooms with novice teachers during their student teaching experiences. Everything I have learned in the last 5 years as I worked with dedicated student teachers in New Bedford and Fall River, Massachusetts, finds its way into this edition in some way. Whether it is my stance on visible learning or new knowledge being utilized in templates, I integrate my learning from these novice teachers and share it with you.

The tone of this third edition is one of transformation. Transformation requires us to hope. To me this means that effective teachers must transform their practices from *control-centered* to *learner-centered* and from *individual approaches* to *collaborative* activities for all learners. It requires transforming expectations from "I don't think that students can learn this," to positive thinking that requires high expectations for all. The goal of teaching and learning has to shift from rote learning and content memorization to problem solving and creative thinking. Just telling students how to do something is not enough; we need to *be* the change and to model the behaviors we expect. Even though we are working in an evaluation mode of standardized tests and test scores tied to teacher performance, we can still hold the ideal of assessment and learning from our mistakes as a way to improve how students succeed in our classrooms. Our challenge is to raise the bar and empower our students and ourselves to do what it takes to succeed and to live a satisfying life. This book is my way of contributing to the transformation.

New to This Edition

- INTASC Standards that form the foundation of this practical manual have been updated to reflect the changes made in 2011 and are included in Chapter 1; in addition, specific standards are highlighted and integrated into each chapter, creating a current, relevant, and research-based guide to teaching.

- New Key Questions designed to inspire critical thinking, analysis, and self-assessment in new teachers are articulated at the beginning of each chapter and referred to throughout the text, ensuring comprehension and application of the conceptual framework behind teaching.

- PLAN pages now link and draw parallels between INTASC Standards and Key Questions, creating the foundation for learning for each chapter and helping readers focus on what to do to plan for teaching and learning.

- CONNECT pages have been updated and now contain the most to up-to-date research. Divided into three sections that create an organizational framework for each reader's further study, CONNECT pages present recommendations for books, websites, and personal connections that offer support for first-time teachers.

- Each Activity is now directly linked to a single Key Question that prefaces the chapter, allowing readers to identify the specific purpose and goal for each activity, and to focus on areas where more support may be necessary.

- REFLECT and SET GOALS sections on the final page of each chapter review each Key Question, allowing for self-assessment and comprehension testing, and offering additional, closing reflections to test knowledge and identify artifacts that belong in a teaching portfolio.

Organization

The three central parts of the book have stayed the same but are retitled and expanded to clarify their uses and reflective qualities. They are written to the student teacher, you, in the voice of a mentor guiding a novice through the stages of becoming a teacher.

Section 1—Beginning Your Journey into Teaching includes the activities and ideas needed to launch your student teaching experience successfully. The three chapters in this section have been reorganized to focus on the transition from college student to practicing teacher, learning about the context of your school and classroom, and understanding what it means to be supervised. Chapters 1 and 2 have been reorganized. Chapter 2 focuses on your entry into your school setting and learning about the context in which you will teach. Chapter 3 leads you through the entire supervision process with many opportunities to reflect on your own practice.

Section 2—Demonstrating Your Teaching Skills focuses on how you teach and helps you transfer what you have learned in courses into the context of a classroom. Chapters 4 through 8 survey topics you have learned in a format that will remind you of what you need to know and be able to do in the classroom with real students. In this edition, the discussion on assessment has been moved to precede instructional strategies and lesson planning to better reflect the current dialogue that assessment should drive practice. Classroom management is divided into two chapters but additional questions focus on the disposition and attitude of the teacher. Visible learning and classroom space find a place here, too. The focus of this book is not on teaching you these skills, but reminding you that now is the time to demonstrate that you are ready for your first classroom by showing that you can actually implement these skills!

Section 3—Completing the Practicum, the Job Search, and Your First Classroom This section completes your practicum journey and moves you in the direction of your first teaching position. These chapters provide checklists and suggestions for the job interview and your first classroom. The discussion on designing a portfolio, now precedes the information about completing the practicum, to allow you to apply the knowledge to creating and organizing your licensing portfolio. The suggestions for completing a hard copy or e-portfolio or website are more detailed in this edition.

Your transformation from college student to teacher will happen at some point during your practicum. You will feel it. Others will see it in you. That is when you will know that you are emerging as a professional teacher. Enjoy your journey into teaching.

Letter to Instructor

Dear University Administrator, Supervisor and/or Seminar Leader,

If you are reading this letter you are considering the use of this text as a guide for the practicum experience. As a former Director of Practicum Experiences and Licensure, I know how important it is for student teachers to have a common language that relates to the state and national teaching standards as well as to academic educational theories. This book was created after I wrote my first book, *Techniques and Strategies for Coaching Student Teachers*. As a result of being a former cooperating teacher who was always asking, "What am I supposed to be doing?" that book was born. This book is a companion to that book and also stands alone.

Strategies for Successful Student Teaching, Third Edition is my attempt to bring the disparate pieces of student teaching into a practical document that student teachers can use while they are in the process of student teaching. It is a place for them to write notes, check off skills they already know, review topics and apply them to the classroom, and add information they need to know that is not in this book. In some ways it is a reflective log, because it takes the student through the steps of the practicum from beginning to end. It is designed for all grade levels and all content areas because the focus is on the *process*.

It does not include everything the student has done in your program. It does not delve deeply into every topic, and it probably does not include all the key concepts from your program. It is designed so that you can add those pieces.

The beauty of the text is that it is designed to be used during student teaching. It can enhance and enrich seminar discussions or one-on-one meetings with the student teacher and their district cooperating teachers and/ or university supervisors. It will make those conversations richer and deeper.

This resource can also be required for student teachers to use on their own, between supervisor visits. It gives them a focus while they are in the school with the cooperating teacher, who is often asking "What am I supposed to be doing with you?"

Using the book as a conversational tool works. Selecting a page in a chapter and asking the student teacher to talk to the cooperating teacher about the idea presented there and how it works in the classroom or school is the purpose of this text. It is also a guide to reflection and conversations about practice . It serves as an agenda for rich and meaningful discussions that can forward these novice teachers' practice in authentic contexts.

I encourage you to review the table of contents and select the chapters or sections of the book that apply most to you. Each section of the book is written to stand alone, and you may consider customizing it.

Your students will transform from college students to teachers at some point during the practicum experience. That is when you will know that they are emerging as professionals. I hope you find some practical advice and inspiration in this guide that will help you in your goal to prepare future teachers for our nation's schools.

Sincerely,

Carol Pelletier Radford EdD
Center for University, School and Community Partnerships
University of Massachusetts Dartmouth

Letter to Student Teacher

Dear Future Teacher,

This guide serves as a practical comprehensive resource for you as you begin your full-time student teaching experience. Whether you are an undergraduate student or a graduate intern, you need a road map to guide you through the many details that will surface as you learn to teach. It doesn't matter if this is your first time in the classroom or if you have already completed a semester of experience, the text will remind you of what you need to know and need to be able to do. It will also provide you with lots of practical information about the job search!

You should not see many new ideas, because this resource serves as a summary of what you have learned throughout your teacher preparation program courses. This guidebook is designed to complement your knowledge and previous learning, not replace it or teach it. It is a capstone text to assist you in creating your teaching portfolio and meeting the standards required for a successful teaching experience. This resource designed to support you in your first year of teaching by listing the activities (Chapters 4 through 8) you will be expected to successfully execute in your first classroom.

Student teachers often ask, "Is this a workbook? Do I have to complete all these pages?" The answer is no! It is not a workbook adding more to your already busy day. No, you do not have to complete all the pages. This text is created as a tool for your personal reflection and to promote discussion with your cooperating teacher. Often cooperating teachers ask, "What are we supposed to be talking about?" and this guide can facilitate that discussion. It allows you to assess your progress on the pages you choose to complete alone, with your university supervisor or with your cooperating teacher.

Begin by reviewing the table of contents, skimming through the chapter topics, and selecting what YOU need right now to be successful in this experience. You know what you have learned in courses, but you do not know what you don't know. This book highlights the skills and knowledge that will make you successful as a teacher in a classroom. As you move through your experience, you can check the activities you need to spend more time thinking about or discussing with your cooperating teacher or university supervisor. Knowing what you are missing is one step, and actually APPLYING the skills in the classroom is another.

As comprehensive as this handbook is, there are probably topics that are not included here in depth that you may find you need. Discuss these gaps in your knowledge with your seminar leader, your district cooperating teacher, or your university supervisor to ensure you have the most current teaching skills required.

Strategies for Successful Student Teaching, Third Edition begins your journey into teaching in a comprehensive and practical way and moves you through to the creation of a job portfolio, the job search, and a checklist for accepting your first teaching position. To my knowledge, no resource book exists at this time that begins with the first steps of student teaching and follows through to the first teaching position. You will find *Strategies for Successful Student Teaching*, Third Edition is useful now, and it also will be a valuable resource for your professional library when you are a beginning teacher. Keep notes in the margins, jot ideas on the pages, write in the blanks, and copy the templates, fill in the bubble sheets, and set goals for yourself. Keep your learning notes with the book so you will have a journal of your successful (and not so successful) practices to refer to when you have your very first classroom.

Student teaching is most often rated as THE most important course in the teacher preparation program. I wrote this book as an overview/summary because

I believe student teachers need to see the information in one place from beginning to end. There is so much to implement and practice during this experience that the details of teaching can become overwhelming. The PLAN, CONNECT, ACT, and REFLECT and SET GOALS pages will focus your thinking and let you see the organization of the practicum and provide you with a structure for the entire experience. The reflection and goal setting pages at the end of each chapter will engage you and allow you to assess what you are learning and target your next steps as they relate to completing your program requirements.

Let this guide serve as your reflective companion: A silent teacher that provides a broad-brush summary of what you already know and are now implementing into the classroom with real students! Think of this text as a road map pointing out the "big ideas" of student teaching, as you travel through the weeks of your practicum. *Strategies for Successful Student Teaching*, Third Edition will make sure you don't miss the hot spots as you begin your journey into teaching.

Best wishes for a successful semester and a career in teaching. Your transformation from student teacher to teacher is on the horizon, and I hope you find this book both inspirational and practical for your journey.

Carol Pelletier Radford EdD
Center for University, School and Community Partnerships
University of Massachusetts Dartmouth

Acknowledgements

The *TEACH! SouthCoast* candidates who completed their student teaching experiences are the inspiration for this work.

Thanks to the reviewers of the second edition: Amy D. Broemmel, University of Tennessee; Mary Hitz, Oklahoma State University, Tulsa; Nancy Prosenjak, California State University, Northridge.

Special thanks to the Karen O'Connor, Executive Director, Center for School, University and Community Partnerships at the University of Massachusetts, Dartmouth for believing in me and encouraging me to share what I know with others.

Brief Contents

Contents

Chapter 2

Learning About the Context of Teaching: Where Do I Begin?   25

Chapter 3

Learning to Teach: How Do I Grow and Develop During This Experience?   49

Section 2

Demonstrating Your Teaching Skills   79

Chapter 4

Classroom Management: Creating a Positive Learning Environment   80

Chapter 5

Classroom Management: How Do Effective Teachers Promote Appropriate Behavior? 106

Chapter 6

Assessing, Documenting, and Communicating Student Progress: How Do I Know What to Do?   125

Chapter 7

Instructional Strategies for Diverse Learners: How Do I Teach to Varied Student Needs?   147

Chapter 8

Effective Planning Strategies to Promote Student Learning   171

Section 3

Completing the Practicum, the Job Search, and Your First Classroom Experience   197

Chapter 9

Designing a Portfolio: Where Do I Begin?   198

Chapter 10

Completing the Practicum: What Needs to Be Done?   216

Chapter 11

The Search for a Teaching Position: Where Do I Begin?   230

Chapter *12*

Your First Classroom!   248

Beginning Your Journey into Teaching

Beginning Your Journey into Teaching includes the activities and ideas needed to successfully launch your student teaching experience. The three chapters in this section are organized to focus on your transition from college student to practice teacher. You will be learning about the "context" of your school and classroom, and understanding what it means to be supervised and observed. Chapter 2 will concentrate more on your entry into your school setting and learning about the context in which you will teach. Chapter 3 steps you through the entire supervision process and will provide you with many opportunities to reflect on your own practice.

You may want to skim the Key Questions in each of the chapters to see if these are areas in which you need to grow and develop as you begin your journey into teaching. This section provides you opportunities to reflect on why you chose teaching, and also gives you practical topics to think about and discuss, such as your own professional boundaries and professional attire.

The context of your student teaching will certainly impact your experience. How you learn about where you will teach and who your students are is extremely important to beginning your experience in an informed way. Chapter 2 will provide you with activities that are practical and engaging. Doing the groundwork by creating your own survival packet will help you later in the semester. Instead of sitting in the back of a classroom room "watching," choose to *observe* in a systematic way using the forms in Chapter 2. Take notes on the forms provided, and if you really want to go deeper, reread what you have recorded and write a reflection about all of your observations.

Your personal and professional development is linked to your willingness to reflect on your teaching. Chapter 3 provides you with many options for reflecting and fully participating in your journey into teaching. Being supervised will allow you to gain a new perspective from someone who is observing you teach. In most cases you will have a district cooperating teacher and a university supervisor who visits you several times. Supervision models vary by program. Your goal in using this chapter is to select the ways in which you will grow through any of these activities. They are designed to be used more than once because learning to teach takes time and requires constant reflection.

The three chapters in this section provide a framework for your personal reflection, ways to look at your school setting, and the process in which you will learn and grow. Select the activities that are most meaningful for you with the help of your cooperating teaching and university supervisor.

chapter 1

Transition from College Student to Teacher: Am I Ready?

" Begin now to prepare yourself! Do not run out and buy a teacher's

plan book or a new pack of pencils for your future students. Instead,

take some time to think about what you are about to do and the

path you are on as you move from a pre-service teacher to an in-

service teacher. You are a lot farther than you think. Don't blink; it

will be over before you even know it.

Student Teacher

Beginning Your Journey into Teaching

Why did you decide to become a teacher? Did you always want to teach? Did you have an inspiring teacher during your years in school? Did you have teachers you didn't like and want to create a different experience for students than you had in school? Revisit your commitment and choice to this profession. Will teaching be your first career or are you changing careers after first trying something else? All these questions and your responses are important as you reflect on the events in your life that have led you to student teaching.

Teaching is more than a job. It is a way of life for those who choose it. Some even say it is a "calling" for special people. Others may not share these same feelings about teachers and the profession, and that is why teachers are often underpaid, overworked, undervalued, and criticized by the public, parents, and their own students. So why would anyone want to be a teacher?

Many teachers say it has been the small things that have kept them in teaching: seeing the smile on a student's face when he finally understands a concept, observing a young student reading a book for her first time, or challenging a student to strive for higher goals. There is also a built-in sense of renewal each year when one class moves on and a new group enters the classroom. Teachers have shared that although it is often sad to let their current students go, there is excitement in being able to challenge a new group.

Intrinsic rewards are not enough for many teachers today, as evidenced in their choice to leave the classroom after a few years because the realities of everyday life in the day-to-day context of the profession are difficult. Everyone says teaching is challenging, yet student teachers' idealism often outweighs the challenges of the profession and possibility of failure. Would you describe yourself as an idealist?

Preparing for student teaching is important. Are you preparing for a one-semester practicum or are you enrolled in a year-long experience? Take the time to inventory how well-prepared you are for entering the classroom, to reflect on your commitment to the profession, and to determine your personal reasons for becoming a teacher. If you are already in the classroom you must assess what you need to gain from this formal student teaching experience that will forward your teaching skills.

As a student teacher, you need to think about the following areas of preparation: (1) academic subject, (2) early field experience, (3) teaching strategies and methods, (4) emotional readiness, and (5) commitment to the profession. Are you prepared in all these ways? Do you know your

content and is that evidenced by your grades in your academic major? Have you visited schools during your methods courses? Do you know "how to teach?" and have a tool kit of methods to try in the classroom? Are you emotionally ready for this full time immersion course? Have you made a commitment to yourself that teaching is your career choice? Sometimes during student teaching this choice changes.
Use this experience to make your final decision to see if teaching is for you.

The activities and ideas in this chapter will assist in your transition from being a full-time college student to becoming a full-time teacher with your own classroom. Take the opportunity to assess what you have learned in your college classes, and notice where you may feel some gaps in your preparation. Remember the purpose of student teaching is to allow you to experience the rigors and the joys of a classroom. Make student teaching the top priority in your life right now. Put all your energy into your teaching, learn as much as you can, experience the school, work with your cooperating teacher, and enjoy the learning curve you will be on.

"Maintaining Your Balance": Guiding Principles for Becoming a Teacher

The most challenging aspect of student teaching is *maintaining your balance* in this whirlwind of new learning. In my work with both experienced teachers and novices I have learned that successful student teachers who maintain their balance are guided by these five principles.

- **Acknowledging who you are** and what you bring to this experience is your responsibility. Assessing your skills and sharing this information with your cooperating teachers and university supervisor allows you to bring your authentic self to this experience. This is not the time to pretend you have skills you do not have. It is the time to assess and learn how to teach so you will be ready for your first classroom. It is also the time to brag and let others know what you have been doing with your life. Do you speak another language? Have you traveled? Do you have a unique hobby that students would relate to? Everything about you is valuable and can be incorporated into your student teaching. This first chapter will provide you with a variety of reflective activities to prepare you for your visit to your assigned school.

- **Building trusting relationships** with everyone at the school is the key to your success. Confidentiality when needed, not repeating conversations from teachers' rooms, and using personal information about students to help them are some of the skills you need to learn how to fine tune in the context of a school. Chapters 2 and 3 will provide you with structures that

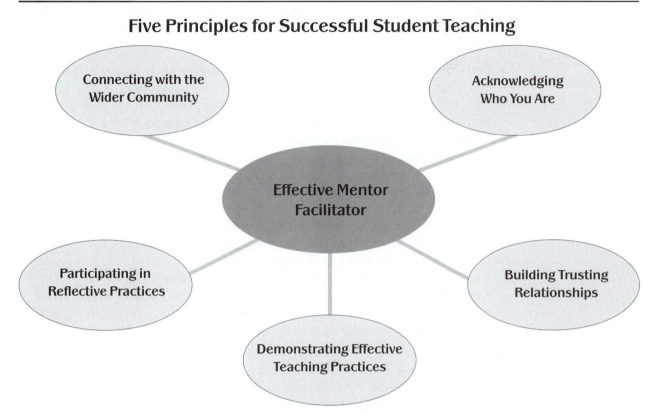

$Figure$ **1.1**   Maintaining Your Balance

Five Principles for Successful Student Teaching

Connecting with the Wider Community

Acknowledging Who You Are

Effective Mentor Facilitator

Participating in Reflective Practices

Building Trusting Relationships

Demonstrating Effective Teaching Practices

will guide you through a successful experience. Trusting yourself to make good decisions is important. Think before you speak or before you repeat anything you hear or observe. Your relationship with your cooperating teacher(s) is extremely important because you are a guest in this teacher's room. You may not agree with everything you see or hear. Establish professional boundaries with your students (see ACTivity 1.11 for specific professional boundaries exercises). Chapters 4 and 5 will give you practical ways to create positive relationships your students.

- **Demonstrating effective teaching practices** in the classroom is not as easy as it looks in print. You have been learning theories, teaching skills, and learning strategies as well as lots of ideas related to teaching in your courses. You may have already visited schools and tried some teaching and observing. Actually implementing these practices in a classroom all day long with students you are getting to know can be a challenge if you do not approach it with a caring disposition. Relating what you need to know while using state or national standards makes your work a bit more complicated. The professional teaching standards are discussed in the PLANing section of this chapter. You will be gathering evidence throughout your practicum to demonstrate that you do know what to do and that you are ready for your first classroom. Each chapter in this text will highlight the national standard you should be focusing on and will offer direction for what data you should be collecting for your teaching or interview portfolios. Chapters 4 through 8 will provide you with suggestions you may want to try during this experience.

- **Participating in reflective practices** will include your personal reflections and your supervision conversations. Will you be a student teacher who seeks out opportunities for professional growth to enhance your knowledge and skills, or one who does just enough to meet the minimum requirements? Will you be receptive to suggestions from your university supervisor and cooperating teacher, or will you be defensive and unresponsive? Will you be personally inspired to reflect on your lessons after you teach them to improve them? Will you be able to modify lessons while you are in the act of teaching? Developing your own teaching portfolio for this program and creating a job interview portfolio will help you summarize your learning and effective practices through reflection. Use the REFLECT pages at the end of each chapter to guide you. All of these practices contribute to your growth and development and readiness for your own classroom. This entire book is a reflective practice that can be useful for self-assessment and to set goals that will enhance your learning.

- **Connecting with the wider education community** may simply mean reading a book listed on the CONNECT pages or clicking on a website that you may use in your classroom. Are you curious about what is happening in other classrooms, other schools, and in the state and national agendas? Can you see beyond your own classroom to the state and national agendas of the professional organizations that relate to your field? Are you willing to stay after school and share ideas with teachers and fellow student teachers, or do you have other responsibilities that take you away from the school? How you choose to participate in your own learning will depend on the choices you make when enriching opportunities are presented.

Use these five principles as touch stones to maintain your balance during your student teaching experience.

This book is organized around the following strategies: PLAN, CONNECT, ACT, REFLECT, and SET GOALS. This structure will provide focus as you move through the experience. The format adds another way to maintain your balance because you will know what topics to expect in each section of every chapter. Reflection and self-assessment are important skills but you also need to put your ideas into ACTion. SET GOALS is paired with REFLECT at the end of each chapter, to keep you moving toward the successful completion of your student teaching experience. The word practicum will be used interchangeable with student teaching throughout this guide.

Strategies for Success	*Using the Book...*
🖎 PLAN	PLAN pages offer a strategy that keeps you focused on questions and professional standards for teaching. Plan time to read and discuss chapter topics to be knowledgeable and to familiarize yourself with all the material.
🖎 CONNECT	This strategy suggests you connect with people, books, and online resources that relate to the chapter topic.
🖎 ACT	An important strategy for success is action! Activities are listed that have been successful with other student teachers. Select the activities that will forward your learning.
🖎 REFLECT and SET GOALS	Review the key questions and assess your understanding of the concepts. Set goals for what is next for you, and decide what could be a useful addition to your teaching portfolio.

What's Your PLAN for Learning?

Directions for Getting the Most out of This Section The PLAN section is designed to give you the "big ideas" for this chapter in the form of key questions. PLAN to meet regularly with your cooperating teacher so you can review the topics in this book. PLAN your time wisely so you can think about, talk about, write about, and learn about teaching. Document your work in this text if you choose to do so.

Read the key questions and assess your understanding and competence: Are you really a beginner or do you bring some experience to student teaching?

Key Questions

1. **What are my beliefs and experiences related to teaching and learning?** The *Beliefs* activities on the ACT pages will provide you with two ways to review what you believe.

2. **How do I know I am prepared to teach?** The *Readiness* activities on the ACT pages will provide you with a variety of ways to document your abilities so far.

3. **How has the university prepared me?** The two *Preparation* activities will allow you to review your program of studies work.

4. **What will be expected of me?** Many student teachers are unaware of all the many expectations required for a successful experience. The *Expectations* activities included in the text provide you with valuable information so you will know what to expect during your practicum and as a full-time teacher.

An important part of planning a successful experience requires you to create a support team. Successful student teachers who *maintain their balance* using the principles shared in this chapter proactively seek out people to support them. There may be a time when the boss at your off campus job has to reschedule your shift at work so you can attend a school play or perhaps your roommates have to have the dorm party on another floor so you can complete your lesson plans. Communicate with the people in your life and share with them that you are participating in the capstone experience of your college career. Ask for their help and support during this important time. Who are the people in your life right now that will support you? After you have created your support team, think about the person(s) who could impede your progress. How will you handle this?

PLAN to Discuss Professional Standards

National standards guide new teacher preparation in the United States. The Interstate Assessment and Support Consortium *(InTASC) Model Core Teaching Standards: A Resource for State Dialogue* (2011) provides you with a set of standards that outline common principles for teaching and learning. These standards are offered to you as a way to focus your attention on these key elements of practice. The "bottom line" is all about student learning. Are your students learning? How do you know? Print out the 23-page document from the InTASC website (**ccsso.org**) and review it with your supervisor. It will provide you with professional standards for all teachers in this country, not only those for beginning teachers as was presented in former InTASC documents.

This chapter lists all ten standards for your review. As you progress, the text will focus on those standards that are most relevant to the discussion in a particular chapter. Also use the REFLECT pages at the end of each chapter to deepen your thinking and discussion as they relate to these professional standards. Plan to read and understand the InTASC standards during this practicum experience. Compare them to your own state and university standards.

inTASC Standards

InTASC Model Core Teaching Standards are organized into four key ideas:

The Learner and Learning

Standard #1: *Learner Development.* The teacher understands how learners grow and develop, recognizing the patterns of learning and development vary individually and implements developmentally appropriate and challenging new experiences.

Standard #2: *Learning Differences.* The teacher uses understanding of individual differences and diverse cultures and communities to ensure inclusive learning environments that enable each learner to meet high standards.

Standard #3: *Learning Environments.* The teacher works with others to create environments that support individual and collaborative learning, and that encourage positive social interaction, active engagement in learning, and self motivation.

Content

Standard #4: *Content Knowledge.* The teacher understands the central concepts, tools of inquiry, and structures of discipline(s) he or she teaches and creates learning experiences that make these aspects of the discipline accessible and meaningful for learners to assure mastery of the content.

Standard #5: *Application of Content.* The teacher understands how to connect concepts and use differing perspectives to engage learners in critical thinking, creativity, and collaborative problem solving related to authentic local and global issues.

Instructional Practice

Standard #6: *Assessment.* The teacher understands and uses multiple methods of assessment to engage learners in their own growth, to monitor learner progress.

Standard #7: *Planning for Instruction.* The teacher plans instruction that supports every student in meeting rigorous learning goals by drawing upon knowledge of content areas, curriculum, cross-disciplinary skills, and pedagogy, as well as knowledge of learners and the community context.

Standard #8: *Instructional Strategies.* The teacher understands and uses a variety of instructional strategies to encourage learners to develop deep understanding of content areas.

Professional Responsibility

Standard #9: *Professional Learning and Ethical Practice.* The teacher engages in ongoing professional learning and uses evidence to continually evaluate his/her practice.

Standard #10: *Leadership and Collaboration.* The teacher seeks appropriate leadership roles and opportunities to take responsibility for student learning, to collaborate with learners, families, and colleagues, and other school professionals, and community members to ensure learner growth, and to advance the profession.

Source: The Interstate New Teacher Assessment and Support Consortium (InTASC) standards were developed by the Council of Chief State School Officers and member states. Copies may be downloaded from the Council's website at **ccsso.org.**
Council of Chief State School Officers and Interstate Teacher Assessment and Support Consortium. (2011, April). *InTASC Model Core Teaching Standards: A Resource for State Dialogue.* Washington, DC: Author, 2011.

CONNECT

CONNECT is a resource page with ideas and suggestions to support you during student teaching. Select and complete any CONNECT items that will enhance your experience in the classroom.

CONNECT with people

- Your college practicum (student teaching) office: Have you applied to be supervised in addition to registering for the field courses required?

- Favorite teachers, parents, guardians, or significant adults in your life:

    How have they influenced you? Are they teachers?

- Student teachers: Talk to some friends who have completed their student teaching practicum. Ask what they learned about themselves as beginning teachers, and ask for any advice they have to offer you.

CONNECT with readings and resources

- College handbook, practicum handbook, and syllabus requirements; Review mission, policies, procedures, requirements, and deadlines.

- Books and authors to explore on the Internet or at your local library:

    Improving Schools from Within, by Roland Barth (Jossey-Bass)

    Stories of the Courage to Teach, by Sam Intrator and Parker Palmer (Jossey-Bass)

    This I Believe: The Personal Philosophies of Remarkable Men and Women, edited by Jay Allison and Dan Gediman in association with NPR (Holt paperbacks)

CONNECT technology to teaching

- Explore and discover websites to visit and use in your classroom. Try these:

    Education Week (**edweek.org**)

    National Education Association (**neatoday.org**) offers a wide variety of information about schools and teaching

    American Federation of Teachers **aft.org** provides information about educators

ACT

ACT pages are designed to offer you options for learning about teaching practices. These activities may require you to self-assess, have a conversation, interview someone, or simply read the page and make notes. The menu here includes activities that student teachers with whom I have worked say have been most helpful to them. The activities listed here relate to the central key questions provided at the beginning of the chapter. Select the activities that apply to you and complete them on your own or in your seminar.

Directions: Skim the activities listed here and in the following pages and select the ones that will prepare you for a successful student teaching experience. ACT now!

Key Question Topic	Activity	Page	Check
Beliefs	1. Why Did I Choose Teaching?		
Beliefs	2. What Do I Believe About Teaching and Learning?		
Readiness	3. What Do I Bring to the Experience?		
Readiness	4. Am I ready?		
Readiness	5. Advice from Former Student Teachers		
Preparation	6. Linking Theory and Practice		
Preparation	7. Guidelines for Teacher Preparation		
Expectations	8. Professional Ethics During Student Teaching		
Expectations	9. How Does the Law Relate to Me?		
Expectations	10. Professionalism		
Expectations	11. Professional Boundaries		
Success	12. Seven Steps to Success		

ACTivity 1.1 Why Did I Choose Teaching?

Key Question: What are my beliefs and experiences related to teaching and learning?

Directions: Use a hard-copy journal or create an online journal or blog to capture your thoughts. Be prepared to discuss your answers in a seminar and/or share them with your cooperating teacher.

THE PAST

Describe your first memories of thinking about becoming a teacher. How old were you?

_____

_____

List any names of people who affected your decision to become a teacher.

_____

_____

Who were some of your favorite teachers and why do you still remember them?

_____

_____

Ask your cooperating teacher and university supervisor the same questions. Compare your answers and discover their motives for teaching.

_____

_____

THE PRESENT

How do you feel right now about beginning your student teaching and becoming a teacher? Now interview your cooperating teacher and ask him or her the same questions. Compare and share what you learn about each other. You may also want to do this with your university supervisor.

_____

_____

YOUR FUTURE as a teacher!

Where do you see yourself in five years? Interview your university supervisor and cooperating teacher about their journey into teaching.

_____

_____

ACTivity 1.2 What Do I Believe About Teaching and Learning?

Key Question: What are my beliefs and experiences related to teaching and learning?

Directions: As you begin your student teaching, you have an opportunity to think about what you believe about teaching. What assumptions are you making as you begin this process? Take some time to think about the following questions and write your responses by hand in a journal or in an online journal. Compare your entry to your responses to questions in ACTivity 1.1.

To begin the process, write three words that come to mind as you describe yourself as a teacher. What are your natural or learned qualities that bring you to teaching? How would others describe you?

_____

_____

Next, list two feelings you are having as you think about entering your student teaching classroom. If you are already in the classroom, how do you feel about your role?

_____

_____

Now write one core belief you bring to this experience. I believe...

_____

_____

Reread your entry and respond to it on paper or on the computer. Add any other thoughts you have about the experience you are beginning. Have you waited a long time for this? Are you prepared?

_____

_____

Tip for Teaching Portfolio: This entry could be used to document your journey.

ACTivity 1.3 What Do I Bring to the Experience?

Key Question: How do I know I am prepared to teach?

Directions: Create an information sheet that you can share with your cooperating teacher and university supervisor. Use the following prompts to help you provide as much useful information as possible that will demonstrate your readiness to teach. In ACTivity 1.1, you may also want to share why you chose teaching and your motivation for being in this practicum.

Consider using the following information in your profile:

1. Your full name and mailing address

2. The best way to reach you: phone or email address

3. Your major and minor at the university

4. The teaching license you are seeking, such as field of certification and the grade level you are required to teach in to meet state and university requirements

5. Your skills, hobbies, areas of expertise or interests (e.g., foreign language or travel, musical ability, drama, dance, sports, coaching)

6. Your technology skills, such as phone use (texting), computer, iPod and/or MP3, digital camera, webcam, video camera, scanner, thumb drive, website creation, wiki participation, googling, online research, Mac and/or PC use, and so forth. How would you rate yourself as a technology user? Beginner, intermediate, advanced?

7. Your computer program skills, such as your competence with software like Excel, Word, slide-shows, PowerPoint, Publisher, video editing, and so forth. How would you rate your computer skills? Beginner, intermediate, advanced?

8. Your previous experiences in a classroom; this may be pre-practicum related or work related.

9. Attach a transcript (highlight content and methods courses) and a resume (if you have one).

TIP for Teaching Portflio: The responses to these question are the basis of a resume for your portfolio.

ACTivity 1.4 Am I Ready?

Key Question: How do I know I am prepared to teach?

Directions: Assess your teaching skills as you begin your practicum. Rate each question in two ways. First, do you know the information from books and classes you have taken? Put a corresponding number on the first line. Second, do you have experience with this topic in the field (related work experience or pre-practicum)? Put that number on the second line.

Rate your Experience 1–3:

1 = Little understanding/experience
2 = Some understanding/experience
3 = Extensive understanding/experience

	Content	Practice
1. Student learners (at the level I will be teaching)	____	____
2. Differentiating instruction for learners at this level	____	____
3. Creating learning environments for this level	____	____
4. Content knowledge for this grade level	____	____
5. Methods for teaching content knowledge at this level	____	____
6. Assessing how students learn	____	____
7. Lesson and unit planning	____	____
8. Variety of learning strategies	____	____
9. Professional ethics	____	____
10. Collaboration and leadership	____	____

Share this self-assessment with your university supervisor and cooperating teacher so they can assist you in learning how to become an effective teacher.

ACTivity 1.5 Advice from Former Student Teachers

Key Question: How do I know I am prepared to teach?

At the end of the practicum, student teachers commonly share that they were surprised to learn that teaching took so much time. They had thought they were prepared, but when they arrived in the classroom, the fast pace and the spontaneous change in daily practices often threw them off.

Directions: Read the challenges that follow and see how they might relate to you. Interview student teachers in your teacher preparation program who have successfully completed their practicum. This can be done by phone or email. Ask your cooperating teacher or university supervisor to provide names of several former student teachers if you don't know any yourself.

Here are some common challenges student teachers often mention, and some suggestions they offer, gained from their experiences.:

Time to do it all. Being in the assigned school all day was different from attending college classes and a schedule that offered breaks to do homework. Time—there just didn't seem to be enough of it!

Talking with another adult regularly in a supervisory relationship is stressful. Being observed is really stressful. Meeting with the cooperating teachers and supervisors, attending seminar meetings, and correcting papers is exhausting.

Being tired! Some student teachers found it difficult to adjust from a college schedule to a student teaching schedule. It may be necessary to ask your roommates to be mindful of your new schedule.

Teaching duties were a surprise to some student teachers. They didn't anticipate how much extra work teachers did in addition to actually teaching students. Student teachers who accept full responsibility should be doing these additional duties too. That means you will have to step up and participate in duty schedules.

Parent communication is a new area for most student teachers. Arrange with your cooperating teacher for you to sit in on as many parent–teacher meetings as possible. Make sure your schedule allows for these meetings: They will require additional time and energy in your already-busy calendar, but the experience will be instructional.

Attending staff meetings and professional-development workshops before, during, and after school also adds to a student teacher's day. Will you be able to attend? If you are looking to apply for a job at your student teaching school, it is good advice to be visible at meetings and workshops. The administration and others who have input into hiring will notice those student teachers who tend to leave the building earlier than appropriate at the end of the school day.

First-year teachers recognized the following issues and wished they had paid more attention to them during student teaching. Read through this list and make note of the topics; take the opportunity to learn from former student teachers' experiences. During your practicum, learn

1. How to navigate the culture of a school: Where to get supplies and get questions answered.

2. What the principal really expects of a new teacher and how the evaluation process works for new teachers.

3. How to connect with parents more effectively in all situations, and not just for misbehavior reports.

4. How to stay current on education reform and state and national issues that impact the classroom, and recognize the role the teacher unions play in these discussions.

ACTivity 1.6 Linking Theory and Practice

Key Question: How has the university prepared me?

Directions: Collect and organize all the resources and ideas you have completed in your preparation to become a teacher. You have done a lot of work already. You just need to be able to access it and use it now. Use this list as a guide to organizing these resources, and check off that you have completed each suggestion to your satisfaction.

_____1. Gather books or magazines that could be useful. Put them together in a bookcase or crate and keep it easily accessible.

_____2. Collect kits, manipulatives, documents, displays, or resources you would like to incorporate into your teaching this semester or year. Bring them to school if there is space in the classroom and let the students use them when they finish their work.

_____3. Assemble lesson plans and units that you developed in courses you have taken. Review them and see how any of these lessons could fit your use in your current classroom.

_____4. Keep a record of online resources and websites for students, and your cooperating teacher, and you.

_____5. What else would be helpful for you to include here?

ACTivity 1.7 Guidelines for Teacher Preparation Program

Key Question: How has the university prepared me?

Directions: Check off these topics to be sure you are ready for student teaching.

UNIVERSITY GUIDELINES

_____ Have you met the requirements to enter student teaching? How do you know?

_____ Have you completed the appropriate paperwork to receive your teaching license? Who do you ask?

STATE GUIDELINES

_____ License: Do you know what the state requires for a teaching license?

_____ Curriculum Frameworks and Common Core Standards: Does your state have guidelines for curriculum that you should be familiar with before you enter the classroom? Use the Internet to find out, and ask your director of practicum experiences how you can learn about state initiatives.

_____ Principles of Effective Teaching: Are teachers assessed in a consistent way statewide? If your state has a state evaluation instrument for inservice teachers, you can review it by asking the teachers in your district when you begin student teaching. This gives you a context for understanding how inservice teachers are assessed.

_____ Other guidelines you need to know or be able to use?

ACTivity 1.8 **Professional Ethics During Student Teaching**

Key Question: What will be expected of me?

NEA PROFESSIONAL ETHICS

The NEA (National Education Association) Code of Ethics adopted by the 1975 Representative Assembly serves as a guide for all teachers. You will be expected to follow an ethical code for your behavior during your practicum.

The preamble states, "The educator, believing in the worth and dignity of each human being, recognizes the supreme importance of the pursuit of truth, devotion to excellence, and the nurture of democratic principles." The Code of Ethics includes two major principles: *Commitment to the Student* and *Commitment to the Profession.* Both are based on striving to reach the highest potential.

(NEA Representative Assembly 1975)

Directions: Visit the NEA website (**nea.org**) to read the entire Code.

1. What did you learn from reading the NEA Code of Ethics? Are there other codes from your university that you should be aware of?

   _____

   _____

2. List any ethical situations that come to mind as you begin student teaching.

   _____

   _____

3. Interview your cooperating teacher about his or her view of the ethics and profession of teaching. Ask the teacher what his or her perspective is on ethics in his or her classroom and in the school.

   _____

   _____

4. Discuss the ethics with your supervisor. Review the NEA Code of Ethics and talk about areas that may be confusing to you at this time.

   _____

   _____

ACTivity 1.9 How Does the Law Relate to Me?

Key Question: What will be expected of me?

THE LAW AND STUDENT TEACHING

You will need to know your legal rights, responsibilities, and liabilities as a student teacher and future teacher. Talk with your school-site cooperating teacher and principal to become knowledgeable about local and state laws that govern your student teaching experience. If there is an education law course offered at your college, you may want to meet with the professor to obtain current information. Specifics are also available on the Internet and in the books located in the CONNECT section of this chapter.

Directions: Review the laws for the following, and understand how they relate to teaching:

_____ Discipline (corporal punishment in your state)

_____ Negligence (parents, guardians, or in classroom)

_____ Child abuse (emotional, physical, sexual, and how to report)

_____ Handicapped Children and IDEA Individuals with Disabilities Act (Public Laws 94–142 and 101–476)

_____ Individualized education program (IEP) requirements

_____ Liability insurance (What is it? Do you need it?)

_____ Search and seizure (drugs, weapons, and obscene materials)

_____ Self-defense and excessive force (How are they defined?)

_____ Copyright laws (Internet, hard copy: What is fair use for teaching?)

_____ First aid and medications (Who is responsible for giving to students?)

_____ Academic freedom (censorship, banning books, religious issues)

_____ Personal life (what you do when you are not teaching)

ACTivity 1.10 Professionalism

Key Question: What is expected of me?

A very important aspect of becoming a professional is looking like one. Before you enter the school building, review the dress codes with your university faculty. Even if the teachers at the school dress casually, it is better for you, as a beginning teacher, to dress more formally. The quickest way to distinguish yourself as a teacher to the students is to "look" like a teacher. Remember, you will be observing for a few days or weeks and the students will be observing you too!

Acting like a teacher is also expected. If you look and act like a college student or like one of your pupils, the students will respond to you as a friend not a teacher. Using your cell phone to make or receive calls; texting; or surfing on your phone, laptop, or school computer when you are learning about your assigned school may be seen as disinterest. Turn off your cell phone when entering the school. Be aware that there may be rules about cell phones and other devices in the building.

Directions: Answer the following questions based on observation or by asking your cooperating teacher. Remember, you are not trying to do the minimum, you are learning how to teach so you can obtain a job and a good recommendation.

- What is the dress code for faculty or students at your school?

  _____

  _____

- Do teachers carry briefcases or backpacks? Why would that matter?

  _____

  _____

- If there is no formal dress code, what are the expectations for teachers' attire?

  _____

  _____

- What are the professional rules for cell phones and other devices?

  _____

  _____

ACTivity 1.11 Establishing Professional Boundaries

Key Question: What is expected of me?

As a beginning teacher, you will be tempted to become friends with your students. You will want them to like you and you will want to like them.

Be aware of professional boundaries with other teachers, who may your age or older. They may approach you for dates or after school meetings. Boundaries apply to them as well as your students. Creating professional boundaries for students and teachers is a must during student teaching!

Directions: Talk with your cooperating teacher about this topic. Review the following situations listed on this page and seek your cooperating teacher's perspective.

- If a student says: Can I talk to you privately and will you promise not to tell anyone what I am telling you? I trust you more than my teacher.

    . . . just say NO! *You have no idea what the student will say to you and if you are legally bound to tell authorities.*

- If a student says: Can you come to my house to help me study tonight? My parents won't be home and I need extra help. You are the only one who understands me.

    . . . just say NO! *You should not go to any student's home without their parents present. Suggest that the student stay after school with you in the library or a classroom that is supervised.*

- If a student says: Can you give me a ride home? My bike is broken (my car broke down, I missed the bus, etc.).

    . . . just say NO! *You should not give any student a ride in your car. Offer to assist the student in finding a way home.*

    Discuss what else is a NO! NO! during student teaching?

1. No personal calls or emails to students (do not give them your personal email or phone number).

2. No personal meetings outside of school with students.

3. No touching students, i.e., no physical contact.

4. No home visits without administrator approval.

5. No "friending" students on Myspace or Facebook. Don't post anything you wouldn't want the school superintendent to read. Note that there is no privacy on email. Limit computer use to academic use only, during school hours. Administrators have access to all computer use at a school. Limit cell phone and other devices that do not relate to working on your practicum assignments.

    Always go to your cooperating teacher with situations that are uncomfortable. Stay focused on your practice teaching!

ACTivity 1.12 Seven Steps to Success

Key Question: What is expected of me?

Student teachers often ask, "What can I do to be successful?" "How can I survive this experience?" Here are seven steps many student teachers have shared that will lead you to success:

Step 1. Stay organized! Clip all those loose pieces of paper, Post-it notes, and folders together in a crate or binder and label it "Student Teaching." Use this text to write notes, jot down ideas, and reflect on your teaching. Keep it with you to add notes daily.

Step 2. Make lists of things to do each day! There are so many small tasks and big ideas that are easily lost among the requirements for the practicum. Make your list at the end of the day for the next day.

Step 3. Take risks! The practicum is your opportunity to practice teaching. Don't play it safe. Try out the ideas your professors suggested in your methods classes. Find those lesson plans you developed, and actually implement them in the classroom. If they don't work, ask why, and modify them to meet the needs of your students.

Step 4. Identify your support system! You are entering a stressful and exciting time in your life. You will need support to achieve your goals; use your support team you identified earlier in this chapter to help you succeed.

Step 5. Get to know your students! The key to a successful experience is knowing who your students are and what motivates them to learn. Every successful teacher will tell you to learn their names, find out what they like, and create a relationship from day one.

Step 6. Acknowledge yourself! Be sure to note what you are doing right! Student teachers tend to focus on what they can't do and often see only what is wrong with their teaching. What is working is important to note. You *will* do some things well!

Step 7. Find your joy in teaching! Teaching is a complex and often difficult career, but many experienced teachers will state they wouldn't do anything else with their lives. How will you know what joy feels like in your teaching? Remember to Maintain Your Balance (figure 1.1. page 6) by using the Guiding Principles for Successful Student Teaching.

REFLECT and SET GOALS

Think about...

Directions: Review the four Key Questions for this chapter and respond to the four questions below in your hard copy or electronic journal.

Key Questions:

1. What are my beliefs and experiences related to teaching and learning? (ACTivities 1.1, 1.2)

2. How do I know I am prepared to teach? (ACTivities 1.3, 1.4, 1.5)

3. How has the university prepared me? (ACTivities 1.6, 1.7)

4. What will be expected of me? (ACTivities 1.8–1.12)

Reflect...

Reflect on the activities related to your beliefs, readiness, and preparation

What one belief is motivating me to a successful experience?

How do I know I am prepared to student teach?

SET GOALS: Possible Next Steps...

Purchase clothes that reflect that you are a teacher; make the best-possible first impression.

Create and Collect Portfolio Artifacts from Chapter Activities

If you are creating an e-portfolio, format your documents appropriately.

✓ Create a photo journal and/or slide show of who you are and what you bring to teaching.

✓ Update your resume with answers from the ACT pages.

✓ Rewrite your philosophy of teaching.

All of these artifacts can be used to meet final student teaching requirements and job interview presentation portfolios. Begin now!

2

Learning About the Context of Teaching: Where Do I Begin?

"Observe as many teachers and students as you can during your practicum. Many variables exist in the world of education. You will see students who are new, old, immature, mature, disruptive, silent, smart, struggling, stable, and unsure. You will see teachers who are new, old, secure, insecure, conforming, nonconforming, professional, unprofessional, skeptical, and nurturing. It is amazing to see teachers use many strategies with different classes and levels. Observing allows us to see how things work and more importantly why.

Student Teacher

Beginning the student teaching experience at the school site is exciting. Be mindful of what you are seeing and feeling as you begin the experience. The context for teaching is as important as the content you will be teaching. You will be noticed as you arrive to begin your practicum—your goal is to make a positive first impression. Learning about the context or culture of a place means you will allow yourself to research, observe, and present yourself to others as a professional. Observation without judgment takes practice. How will you observe this school? The district? The neighborhood? How will you compare this context to that of your own schooling?

The school culture has been established over many years of operation and relationship building among staff members. As a student teacher coming into a new setting, you will need to be observant of the social structures that exist around you. Who is new to the school (like you)? Who has been at the school for many years? Remember, you are a guest in a school that has been willing to welcome and host a "practicing" teacher. Even though it is advantageous to take on the role of teacher as often as possible, you are not an employee of the school. Establishing relationships with your cooperating teacher, as well as many other teachers and educational support staff, is vital to your success as a student teacher. Introducing yourself to the department chairperson, the secretaries, and other professional staff members—such as counselors, the school nurse, school psychologist, bilingual teachers, special education teachers, and custodians—is a necessary part of integrating into an existing school setting.

You need to research the school and district to learn about the students. Student teachers often want to jump into teaching without observing carefully first to learn about the culture of the classroom and the school. To avoid this mistake, think of yourself as a detective or an ethnographer collecting data in this phase of your practicum. Don't think of this as the boring part of teaching. It is a useful exercise to gather evidence about the current practices.

Observe carefully and listen to others as they talk about the school. Is this a positive place for teachers? What are the difficult issues? How do teachers interact with the principal? How does the school "feel" to you? These questions can be documented in your journal or can be part of the CONNECT conversations you might have throughout the semester.

In some cases, you may work with more than one cooperating teacher, especially if you are placed on a team or if you are part of a high school department. In this case, you should work with the department chair to identify the one teacher who will be signing your paperwork and who will serve as your cooperating teacher. Clearly, it is an advantage to be able to work with more than one teacher because you will be able to observe several teaching styles as you discover your own.

Your university supervisor may be familiar with your assigned school and may be able to assist you as you meet people. If your supervisor is not part of this school culture, ask your cooperating teacher to introduce you to other adults in the building. If you are looking for a career opportunity upon completion of student teaching, meeting other teachers who can recommend you is important.

If you are taking a university course or seminar along with student teaching, be sure to read the syllabus and stagger your assignments wherever possible. Courses are designed to support your work in the classroom and to promote inquiry into your teaching. Use them to enhance your experience and deepen your reflection about teaching and learning. It is important to stay on schedule with any readings and to start early in the semester with your assignments, because as you move toward full-time teaching you will be extremely busy every night preparing lessons.

Some student teachers minimize the importance of school context and learning to observe. Don't make that mistake. As you enter the classroom, take your time to observe and learn. The forms in this chapter can be duplicated and used multiple times. Observation is not for only the first two weeks, it is valuable for the entire experience. You can learn a lot by watching.

What's Your PLAN for Learning?

Directions for getting the most out of this section: The PLAN section is designed to give you the "big ideas" for this chapter in the form of Key Questions. PLAN to meet with your cooperating teacher regularly so you can review the ACTivities in the chapter and discuss how they could help you learn. Document your work in this text if you choose to do so, or copy the templates and put them in a binder for future review.

Read the Key Questions and assess your understanding. Are you already familiar with this school? Did you complete a pre-practicum here? Understanding the culture and setting of your practicum is critical to your success with the students. Do not underestimate the impact of your research in learning about the school, district, and community.

Key Questions:

1. **What do I need to know about the school, the district, and the community to help me succeed in my practicum?** The *Learning* activities on the ACT pages will provide you with efficient and practical ways to create a school profile, get to know the district, create a survival packet, and learn from students who are at the school.

2. **How will I introduce myself to the cooperating teacher, the students, and the parents?** The *Introducing* activities on the ACT pages will provide samples of ways to formally introduce yourself.

3. **How can I use observation and interview tools to capture teaching and learning experiences?** The observation and interview *Tools* on the ACT pages will provide ways to learn the context of your school setting quickly and easily.

$\mathcal{P}$LAN to Discuss Professional Standards

inTASC Standards

Professional Responsibility

Discuss this standard with your cooperating teacher and/or your university supervisor.

Standard #9: *Professional Learning and Ethical Practice* The teacher engages in ongoing professional learning and uses evidence to continually evaluate his/her practice, particularly the effects of his/her choices and actions on others (learners, families, other professionals, and the community), and adapts practice to meet the needs of each learner.

How does this professional standard relate to the *Key Questions* assigned for this chapter?

Standard #10: *Leadership and Collaboration.* The teacher seeks appropriate leadership roles and opportunities to take responsibility for student learning, to collaborate with learners, families, and colleagues, and other school professionals, and community members to ensure learner growth, and to advance the profession.

Source: The Interstate New Teacher Assessment and Support Consortium (InTASC) standards were developed by the Council of Chief State School Officers and member states. Copies may be downloaded from the Council's website at **ccsso.org.** Council of Chief State School Officers and Interstate Teacher Assessment and Support Consortium. (2011, April). *InTASC Model Core Teaching Standards: A Resource for State Dialogue.* Washington, DC: Author, 2011.

CONNECT

CONNECT is a resource page with ideas and suggestions to support you during student teaching. Select and complete any CONNECT items that will enhance your experience in the classroom.

CONNECT with People Through Personal Interviews

- Teachers: Find out why they chose this profession.
- Educational-support personnel: Find out the strengths of the school by talking to these individuals (nurse, custodian, secretary, and others).
- Students: Find out what they like and don't like about school.

CONNECT with Readings and Resources

- Collect and read all curriculum materials you will be teaching.
- Review school policies and procedures as written in the school handbook.
- Authors to explore are Gloria Ladson-Billings, Lorraine Monroe, Eleanor Duckworth, Vivian Paley, Beverly Tatum, and Roland Barth.
- Two books to investigate are *Teacher's Survival Guide,* by Warner and Bryan (Park Avenue) and *The Student Teacher's Handbook,* by Carol R. Schwebel, David C. Schwebel, Bernice L. Schwebel, and Susan L. Schwebel (Erlbaum).

CONNECT Technology to Teaching

- Explore and discover websites to visit and use in your classroom. Try these:

    Education World (educationworld.com)

    This page is good for survival:

    ideas (ed.gov/teachers/become/about/survivalguide/message.html).
- Bookmark new sites you discover!
- Ask and observe how teachers use technology in their classrooms at this school.

ACT

ACT pages are designed to offer you options for learning about teaching practices. The activities listed here relate to the central Key Questions provided at the beginning of the chapter. Select the activities that apply to you and complete them on your own or in your seminar.

Directions: Skim the activities listed here and in the following pages, and select the ones that will prepare you for a successful student teaching experience.

Key Question Topic	Activity	Page	Check
Learning	2.1 Creating a School Profile		
Learning	2.2 Getting to Know the School District and the Community		
Learning	2.3 First Impressions: Meeting My Cooperating Teacher		
Learning	2.4 Creating a Survival Packet		
Learning	2.5 The Language of Schools		
Introducing	2.6 Sample Letter of Introduction to Students		
Introducing	2.7 Sample Letter of Introduction to Parents		
Observing Tool	2.8 Teacher Observation: The "Big Picture"		
Observing Tool	2.9 Teacher Observation: Visible Learning		
Observing Tool	2.10 Teacher Observation: Class Structure		
Observing Tool	2.11 Teacher Observation: Lesson Plan Objectives		
Observing Tool	2.12 Student Observation: Creating a Case Study		
Observing Tool	2.13 Student Observation: Whole Class Dynamics		
Observing Tool	2.14 Student Observation: Small Group Dynamics		
Interviewing Tool	2.15 Teacher Interview: Rationale for Teaching the Lesson		
Learning	2.16 Student Interviews		

ACTivity 2.1 Creating a School Profile

Key Question: What do I need to know about the school, the district, and the community to help me succeed in my practicum?

Directions: Approach this activity as a "scavenger hunt" that will help you learn about the school. Use the school's web page or any documents you have about the school to begin your search. Then expand your research to your cooperating teacher, other personnel, secretaries, the custodian, students, parents, and your supervisor. Clue: You might call the school and listen to the voice message to find some of these answers. If more than one student teacher is at the same school you can work in teams. How many questions can you answer? What score did you earn?

Full Name of School: 1 point

Why it is named this?: 2 points

Mission of school or special theme or focus: 2 points

Name of current principal or headmaster (clue: website may not be current!): 1 point

Names of assistant principals or headmasters: 2 points

School secretary(ies) How many are in front office and their names: 5 points

Name of head custodian: 5 points

Number of classroom teachers employed at the school: 3 points (3 more points if you include the grade levels or subjects they teach)

How many special-area teachers are assigned to the school (i.e.. math lab, music, etc.): 3 points

How many support personnel (i.e.. guidance counselors, bilingual teachers, special education teachers): 3 points

How to contact the school (phone, email, etc,): 3 points

Is there a school library? 1 point

Is there a computer lab? 1 point

How can student teachers or teachers use the library or computer lab? 5 points

Is public transportation nearby? If yes, explain. 3 points

How many students attend this school? 3 points

What is the percentage of student diversity at the school? 5 points

How many different languages are spoken by students at the school? 5 points

Is there a parent organization? If yes, what is the name and the leader's name? 5 points

Bonus Points: Map of the school building with layout of classrooms, exits, and bathrooms: 5 points

Bonus Points: Write your initial impression of the school and why you feel that way based on evidence: 5 points

Bonus Points: Some other information that is important to know that is not on the scavenger hunt. 5 points

Total Points: _____ How many people did you have to ask to complete this scavenger hunt? Was it difficult to find information? Why or why not?

ACTivity 2.2 Getting to Know the School District and the Community

Key Question: What do I need to know about the school, the district, and the community to help me succeed in my practicum?

Directions: As a prospective teacher, learning about the school district and the community in which the school is located is important to understanding your students. Drive by the school and observe the area; you can also do some research to respond to the questions that follow.

Observe

1. What do you notice about the neighborhood near the school? Why is this important to note?

2. Are students walking to school or are they bused in from other parts of the city or county?

3. Can you walk the neighborhood or are you teaching in a rural area?

4. Is public transportation available or do parents drop students off?

5. What does the building look like: old? new? entrance? parking?

6. Write your impressions or take photos to document your observation. Compare this school setting to your own school experience. Is it similar or very different? How will that impact your success in your practicum?

Research District Leadership

1. What type of school is this: pubic? private? charter? other?

2. How is the school district organized? For example, how many schools are in the district? List high schools, middle schools, and elementary schools.

3. Who is the leader of the district (i.e., superintendent of schools)? How are decisions made to fund the school (i.e., school board? school committee?)

4. How does the professional community impact your school? Are there resources or people you should connect with during student teaching?

Research Community Resources

1. Are there resources for students and teachers in this district and community?

2. Is there a public library in the town?

3. Is there an art museum?

4. Is there a resource center or recycle center?

ACTivity 2.3 First Impressions: Meeting My Cooperating Teacher

Key Question: How will I introduce myself to the cooperating teacher, the students, and the parents?

Directions: After receiving your student teaching placement assignment from your college, make an appointment to meet your cooperating teacher. Note: If you have already met your teacher for a previous interview to receive this placement, just complete the parts of the agenda that apply to you now.

Sample Agenda

1. Share your student teacher profile and resume and list the courses you have taken. (See Activities 1.1, 1.2, and 1.3 from the previous chapter.)

2. Interview your cooperating teacher using these sample questions:

    How many years have you been teaching? in this area? at this school?

    Why did you become a teacher? a cooperating teacher?

    What do you see as the strengths of this class/school/community?

    What will your expectations be for me?

    How can I assist you in making this a positive experience?

3. Ask your cooperating teacher to suggest a student(s) you could interview, and use the interview form in ACTivity 2.7.

4. Share the sample letters to students and parents and discuss how they can be modified and distributed so you can introduce yourself formally (see Activities 2.6 and 2.8).

5. Discuss the Survival Packet (ACTivity 2.4) and Language of Schools (ACTivity 2.5) and ask for suggestions as to completing them.

6. Ask for copies of books you will be using so you can read ahead.

7. Discuss the observation forms in this chapter, and ask your cooperating teacher if there are other teachers you could observe that can model teaching practices.

8. Confirm your start date, end date, school vacation days, and procedure for calling in sick.

9. Exchange phone numbers and establish appropriate call times.

10. Schedule time for the first meeting with your university supervisor to discuss the cooperating teacher's role during the practicum. Chapter 3 will provide details of supervision during student teaching.

ACTivity 2.4 Creating a Survival Packet

Key Question: What do I need to know about the school, the district, and the community to help me succeed in my practicum?

Directions: Knowledge is power. The more you know about the working policies of the school, the more quickly you will integrate yourself into the faculty and staff. Start collecting hard-copy or electronic documents and refer to them when you have questions. The following checklist will guide you. Check off items as you collect them.

Sample Survival Items

_____ School and student handbooks with mission statements and policies

_____ Curriculum guides and textbooks with teacher editions

_____ Daily schedules for all classes you will eventually teach

_____ Class lists and seating charts for students, and faculty list of teachers and other staff

_____ Fire-drill and building-evacuation procedures

_____ List of students with special needs or health issues (e.g., first aid and medications)

_____ Sample of report card and progress reports

_____ Map of school with room numbers for location of copy room, restrooms, faculty room, and library

_____ Policies for communicating with parents: any special forms required?

_____ Discipline policies for school and classroom: written and informal procedures

_____ Guidelines for referring students to principal: forms and expectations

_____ Supervisory duties during the school day: cafeteria? hall duty? study hall?

_____ Policies for reporting child abuse, neglect, and other legal issues: state laws

_____ Professional development opportunities during student teaching

_____ At-risk students: How they are supported?

_____ Other _____

ACTivity 2.5 The Language of Schools

Key Question: What do I need to know about the school, the district, and the community to help me succeed in my practicum?

Directions: One thing students quickly notice when they begin the practicum is that teachers talk in code! As you observe and get started, find the definitions to the following common school terms. Review your teacher-education courses or ask your cooperating teacher, principal, or university supervisor to share the definitions with you. Write any additional buzzwords below.

AFDC	Inservice education
AFT	Integrated curriculum
AYP	KWL
Assertive discipline	Least-restrictive environment
At-risk students	NBPTS
Authentic assessment	NEA
Behavior modification	Networking
Block schedule	Prep time
Bloom's taxonomy	Professional status
Classified personnel	RTTT
Compensatory education	SIOP
Core curriculum	Specials
Cumulative folder	Split class
Curriculum frameworks	Tenure
Evaluation (teacher)	Tracking
Heterogeneous	Whole language
Holistic scoring	
Homogeneous	
InTASC	
IEP	

Are there buzzwords you are hearing every day that are not on this list but are afraid to ask what they mean? Just ASK someone!

ACTivity 2.6 **Sample Letter of Introduction to Students**

Key Question: How will I introduce myself to the cooperating teacher, the students, and the parents?

Directions: Discuss this letter and the format with your cooperating teacher and university supervisor at the beginning of your practicum. This letter's style will vary depending on the age level of the students. Primary students could receive a large-text, "big-book" style of letter; you could send older students a letter in a more formal, traditional form.

Date: _____

Dear Students,

My name is _____ and I will be student teaching with Mrs.

Jones for the next ____ weeks. I am completing my senior year at University College with a double major

of history and education. I have taken several exciting courses in archeology, and I thought it would be

interesting to share the information I have learned with you.

I have traveled to several different parts of the United States, and I collect artifacts of Native

Americans, particularly Southwestern Indians. I hope to design several history lessons that relate to

this topic.

I decided to become a teacher because I like my subject area and enjoy sharing it with others. Although this is the first time I've taught at this grade level, I've taught museum programs for students and

summer YMCA extension courses already.

Mrs. Jones and I will be working together to make this a positive learning experience for all of you. I

look forward to meeting you next Monday.

Sincerely,

Student Teacher

ACTivity 2.7 Sample Letter of Introduction to Parents

Key Question: How will I introduce myself to the cooperating teacher, the students, and the parents?

Directions: Discuss whether this letter is appropriate for your teaching situation. Use it as a guide.

Date: _____

Dear Parents,

Our class is very fortunate to have _____ (name

of student teacher) from Higher Education College join us as he begins his student teaching. The Anytown

Public schools have always been involved in the preparation of teachers, and this is another opportunity

for our school and classroom to experience the enthusiasm of a beginning professional teacher.

     Having a student teacher participate in our classroom allows your students to experience a variety

of teaching methods. It also provides our classroom with two teachers so that more individual attention

may be given to each student. Many of the lessons will be cotaught with me. Please be assured that I will

be working cooperatively with _____ and that all that activities and lessons

will be supervised by me. If you have any questions, do not hesitate to call me. _____

_____ will be attending our school Open House next week. Please join me in welcom-

ing him to our staff for the fall term.

Sincerely,

Cooperating Teacher

_____ (name of student teacher)

ACTivity 2.8 Teacher Observation: The "Big Picture"

Key Question: How will I introduce myself to the cooperating teacher, the students, and the parents?

Directions: Observe your cooperating teacher and see if you can document the big picture of what is going on in the classroom. Teaching is complex work and you will have to do all of these things when you begin, so take careful notes in a binder or in an online journal. You may also want to attach a drawing of the classroom layout. Note: If there are two teachers, paraprofessionals or other adults in this class, make note of the roles and responsibilities.

Things to Look for When Observing a Teacher

How the Teacher Manages the Classroom

> Physical organization of classroom
>
> Pacing of lesson
>
> Beginning and ending of lesson
>
> Monitoring of students
>
> Traffic flow of classroom
>
> Routines and procedures used
>
> Structure of lesson

Which Instructional Strategies Are Used During the Lesson

> Instructional practices used: lecture? cooperative? combination?
>
> Teaching materials and audiovisual
>
> Technology use incorporated into lesson

How the Classroom Environment Is Organized and Executed

> Teacher's "style": How would you describe it?
>
> Interactions with students
>
> Engagement of students with diverse needs
>
> Positive reinforcement
>
> Disruptions: How are they handled?

How the Lesson Was Planned as Part of a Larger Curriculum

> The lesson plan: Was there one?
>
> The plan as part of a unit: How does this fit into the bigger picture?
>
> Curriculum objectives for learning: Are they clear?

How the Lesson Was Assessed for Learning

> Formal assessment
>
> Informal assessment

ACTivity 2.9 Teacher Observation: Visible Learning

Key Question: How can I use observation and interview tools to capture teaching and learning experiences?

Teacher's Name: _____ **Subject:** _____ **Time:** _____

Directions: On another day, observe the same teacher and just look for the following evidence of learning that is listed here. Refer back to your own notes to remind you of what you saw on the first observation. Take photos (with permission) of visible-learning artifacts to discuss with your cooperating teacher or university professor. Optional: Create a PowerPoint presentation using good examples of what you would use in your own classroom.

_____

_____

_____

What is the evidence you see of students being part of this learning community? (e.g. names of students, wall of fame, student helpers, etc.)

_____

_____

_____

Look for visual examples of students in the process of learning: Are there student papers or photos posted on the walls of the classroom showing students involved in learning activities? Are models or other manipulatives visible in this room?

_____

_____

_____

How do students work as teams in this room? (e.g., are names of teams posted, cooperative rules listed, etc.?)

_____

_____

_____

What other visible evidence is there of students working cooperatively in this room?

Note: You may want to add some of these questions to student interviews in ACTivity 2.7.

_____

_____

_____

ACTivity 2.10 Teacher Observation: Class Structure

Key Question: How can I use observation and interview tools to capture teaching and learning experiences?

Teacher's Name: _____ **Subject:** _____ **Time:** _____

Directions: On another day, observe this same teacher or select a new teacher and note the following strategies this teacher uses. Keep a journal of strategies and notice what is successful with students so you can replicate these techniques when you are teaching. Complete this activity at least three times, and compare and contrast different teachers' strategies. Which are most successful?

1. **Classroom management/routines:** How is the classroom organized? *Sketch a classroom setup and attach it to this observation.* Do any special features of classroom management or teacher routines stand out for you, such as passing out papers or taking attendance? What special materials are in the classroom: computers? student areas? mailboxes? posters?

2. **Class start:** How does the class begin: "housekeeping" activities? calendar? What else? How long does this take?

3. **Lesson purpose/objective:** Exactly how does the lesson begin? What is the transition between starting routines and the content of the lesson? How are directions and overall objectives and goals of lesson shared with students?

4. **Effectiveness of lesson for diverse learners:** What was the most effective part of the lesson in your opinion? Were there any special materials used? Was technology used? audiovisuals? props? How did these assist diverse learners?

5. **Behavior management:** How did the teacher handle any disruptive students? How about students who were not listening?

6. **Students' reaction to the lesson:** What did you observe generally? Were all students listening? learning? What evidence do you have for this impression? If you asked a student what the purpose of this lesson was, what would he or she say?

7. **Modifications of the lesson:** If you were asked to teach this same lesson, would you add or delete anything? Would you use other materials? How would these changes enhance student learning?

8. **Closure of a lesson/class period:** How does the lesson end? Does the class period end when the lesson ends? If not, what happens between the lesson ending and the period ending?

What is your overall impression of the lesson?

ACTivity 2.11 Teacher Observation: Lesson Plan Objectives

Key Question: How can I use observation and interview tools to capture teaching and learning experiences?

Directions: Observe your cooperating teacher or any teacher in the department or school. Complete this lesson-plan template by writing the parts of the lesson as you see or hear them. Can you document what this teacher is actually teaching without seeing the lesson plan?

Discuss what you have observed with this teacher, if you are comfortable doing that, and compare how close you come to his or her objective.

Teacher: _____ Subject: _____ Date: _____

Teaching Objectives

1. _____

_____

_____

2. _____

_____

_____

3. _____

_____

_____

(continued on next page)

(continued from previous page)

ACTivity 2.11 Teacher Observation: Lesson Plan Objectives (*continued*)

Key Vocabulary Taught

1. _____   4. _____

2. _____   5. _____

3. _____   6. _____

Key Questions for Class

1. _____

2. _____

3. _____

Materials/Resources/Technology

Procedure (beginning, middle, closing)

Assessment

Classroom Management Notes/Lesson Modification

Homework/Follow-Up/Enrichment

ACTivity 2.12 Student Observation: Creating a Case Study

Key Question: How can I use observation and interview tools to capture teaching and learning experiences?

Directions: Learning about students is essential to any effective teacher's practice. A good way to begin is with a case study of one student. Ask the cooperating teacher to suggest a student whom you can get to know for this assignment. Think about why this is an important exercise.

First Name of Student: _____ Grade/Subject: _____

Part 1: Observe, and record both what you see and your impressions.

1. What do you notice about this student (physical appearance, estimated age, cultural background, language, social interactions, skills and abilities, motivation, attitude, self-concept, etc.)?

2. How is the student responding to the teacher's lesson?

3. Is the student interacting with any other students? Describe.

4. What is the quality of the student's work? (Review it at the end of class.)

5. Name something positive the student did during the lesson.

6. What other things did you observe?

Part 2: Interview Follow-Up

1. How old are you?

2. Why have you been named XX?

3. Ask any questions you feel would help you understand this student. See ACTivity 2.7 in this chapter for sample questions.

Part 3: Student Records

Ask the cooperating teacher to share the file that goes with the student; read it and make some notes to enhance your case.

Part 4: Cooperating Teacher's Information

Share what you have learned, and listen to your cooperating teacher's information about this student. Ask where she learned this information.

ACTivity 2.13 Student Observation: Whole–Class Dynamics

Key Question: How can I use observation and interview tools to capture teaching and learning experiences?

Directions: For this observation, just focus on the students, not the teacher. Document your answers in your e-journal or make hard-copy notes that you can refer back to at a later time.

Class Period: _____   Time of Day: _____

Grade Level/Subject Observed: _____   Date: _____

1. Sketch the classroom and how students are seated. How does class seating impact the lesson being taught? How does it impact the students' behavior?

2. How would you describe the group dynamics of the students in this class? How do they relate to each other? How do they relate to the teacher?

3. Can you notice any individual learning difference among students? What makes you say this? How might this impact the group dynamic in this class?

4. Are there cliques in this class? Who are the leaders, academic or social? Are the leaders used by the teacher in a positive way?

5. Is there a need for any student to receive attention from the teacher or peers?

6. Are any students disengaged from classroom dynamics (for example, those who are bored, hostile, doing another task, sleeping, etc.?)

7. What is the teacher's expectation for learning and behavior in this class? How do you know? How does the student respond to the teacher?

Optional: Observe a group of children or youth hanging around a location outside of school, for example, at the mall, basketball court, ice cream stand, or other likely spot. Try to find at least two groups in different locations so you can compare elements of each. What are the social interactions you see? How do they talk to each other? What do they look like outside of school (dress, makeup, behavior?) How does this observation compare to what you saw in the classroom?

ACTivity 2.14 Student Observation: Small Group Dynamics

Key Question: How can I use observation and interview tools to capture teaching and learning experiences?

Directions: Document how a teacher organizes groups to do a project or an assignment, and note what happens when the class works in groups. Document your answers in your e-journal or make hard-copy notes that you can refer back to at a later time.

Class Period: _____ Time of Day: _____

Grade Level/Subject Observed: _____ Date: _____

Background Information

How were the groups chosen and why? Where are they located in the room? Do students need to move to get into groups? How is this done? How were instructions for group work given?

What Happens While Groups Are Working?

How does the teacher assist all the groups? Which group does the teacher assist first? Is there any reason for this? How does the teacher move around the room? What is the teacher doing when he or she is not working with a group? How does the teacher monitor the groups to ensure on-task behavior?

What Happens Within a Group?

You may want to walk around and observe the differences in how each group is, or is not, completing the task assigned.

Notice for each group: Who is the leader? Why? Are all members of the group participating? How does participation vary? Is the group effectively completing the assigned task? How will the group be assessed for successful completion of the task? Was this group successful in your opinion?

ACTivity 2.15 Teacher Interview: Rationale for Teaching the Lesson

Key Question: How can I use observation and interview tools to capture teaching and learning experiences?

Directions: Students often ask, "Why are we learning this?" and teachers say, "Because we have to—it is in the curriculum for the test." Can you go beyond that rationale to explain to students why they are learning the content of a particular lesson? Respond to the questions in your hard-copy or online journal.

1. **Purpose of the lesson**

   Why is the teacher teaching this lesson? Do the students know why?

   _____

   _____

2. **Goals and expected learning objectives**

   What is the teacher expecting to achieve in this class period? Key questions? Key vocabulary? Do the students know this is the objective?

   _____

   _____

3. **State curriculum frameworks/school curriculum focus areas**

   How does the teacher's lesson plan relate to curriculum standards? Do the students know? Are the standards posted or were they verbally stated?

   _____

   _____

4. **Procedure/activities for the lesson**

   How does the teacher organize his or her time to meet the objectives? What did the teacher plan for the students who finished early? Do the students know what to do?

   _____

   _____

5. **Assessments/evaluation of student learning**

   What did the teacher use informally or formally to measure whether students learned? What modifications were made for diverse learners? Do students know they can ask for help?

   _____

   _____

ACTivity 2.16 Student Interviews

Key Question: What do I need to know about the school, the district, and the community to help me succeed in my practicum?

The more you learn from the students, the more successful you will be in understanding their needs. Ask the cooperating teacher for names of students to interview for this activity, and also invite student to participates. Tell them who you are and why you are asking them these questions. Teachers are often surprised by the responses. What might you discover that will help you be an effective teacher?

Directions: Copy this template and use it as a guide to interviewing students in your classroom or school. Feel free to add your own questions. Modify the questions that follow for the grade level you are teaching, and interview at least three students so you can compare responses.

What is your favorite subject in school? Why? What is your least favorite?

Who is your favorite teacher? Why?

How do you learn best in school? What can a teacher do to help you learn?

Where were you born? What languages do you speak? Have you traveled?

What would you want me to know about you that would help me teach you better?

Do you have a favorite hobby? sport? instrument? club at school?

What do you do in your free time?

What do you use the computer for?

Do you have a phone? Tell me how you use it.

What is your opinion about homework and how could a teacher make it work for you?

What advice do you have for someone like me who is a beginning teacher at your school?

REFLECT and SET GOALS

Think about...

Directions: Review the three Key Questions for this chapter and note which activities you completed once or more than once. Can you answer these questions with confidence now?

Key Questions:

1. What do I need to know about the school, the district, and the community to help me succeed in my practicum? (ACTivities 2.1– 2.5, 2.7)

2. How will I introduce myself to my cooperating teacher, the students, and the parents? (ACTivities, 2.7, 2.16)

3. How can I use observation and INTERVIEW tools to capture teaching and learning experiences? (ACTivities 2.8–2.14)

Reflect...

Reflect on the student interviews and observations (ACTivities 2.7, 2.14, 2.15, 2.16)

Think back to when you were a student of this same age. What did you look like? (Find a photo of yourself in school.) What did you feel like at that age? Which type of student were you in the class you are observing? Respond to this prompt. I felt _____ in this grade because _____ and my teacher could have helped if she/he _____.

SET GOALS: Possible Next Steps...

Create and Collect Portfolio Artifacts from Chapter Activities

✓ Summarize what you learned from observing and interviewing students and teachers.

✓ Prepare a school profile for the context page in your portfolio.

chapter 3

Learning to Teach:
How Do I Grow and Develop
During This Experience?

"The most important part of the supervision relationship is communication. Remember that relationships with either your supervisor or cooperating teacher involve give and take. Don't be afraid to share your ideas too.

Student Teacher

You will be the subject of the supervision process during your student teaching experience. Through meetings, visits to the school, observations of your teaching, and a review of your requirements, the university supervisor and district cooperating teacher will supervise your growth and development as a beginning teacher.

Supervision will be both formative and summative. This means that as you are developing and learning, you will be coached and supported in mastering the competencies of teaching. You will not be expected to be an accomplished teacher the first week you enter a classroom. But you will be expected to learn, observe, model effective practice, think about what you would do differently, write, reflect, plan, and respond to coaching from both your cooperating teacher and university supervisor. The *formative* supervision period prepares you for more formal evaluation. Formative supervision provides "practice" time—where you should try new ideas and strategies, and assess your comfort level in teaching. Along with your own self-reflection, formative supervision will help you focus on the teaching competencies which need further development. By paying attention to your own strengths and weaknesses, you will be better prepared to meet all the required teaching competencies.

Practice is to formative supervision as *test* is to summative supervision. A summative meeting with your university supervisor usually involves an observation that has been selected to measure competencies as well as a summary of your progress in all requirements to date. The final grade for your practicum is the summative evaluation based on your supervision from the whole semester. Your teaching portfolio is also a summative demonstration of your knowledge, your skills, and your disposition for teaching.

Your college supervisor wears two distinct hats—one as "coach," during the formative phase, and then that of "evaluator," at the end of the practicum. Typically, the supervisor will work with your cooperating teacher to collect information about your daily work in the field; she will read and respond to your weekly journal entries, provide support for you throughout the practicum, and recommend a final summative grade or pass/fail evaluation that will be part of your university transcript. However, these requirements vary from university to university. Keep in mind the summative reports, whether at the midterm or final, are a summary of your progress to date and will also include *all* other requirements, such as lesson plans, completed journals, attendance in seminar classes, and your student-teaching binder. This means supervision is cumulative—much more than just a midterm or final observation of a lesson.

Your practicum supervision is completed in a student teaching "triad" in which you play a key role in self-assessing your progress and setting skill development goals. The cooperating teacher serves as a "practice coach," who works side by side with you to provide you with on-the-spot feedback. Your university supervisor is a "visiting coach," who provides support and feedback during your formative stages, and is a final evaluator who observes your development from an outside perspective and checks on all other college requirements.

In addition to school-site visits to talk with you and to observe you teach in the classroom, your supervisor may meet with you privately or in a small group to discuss common issues of student teaching. She may also use email to communicate with you and/or to respond to your journal or arrange times when you can discuss issues privately with her. Find out which support system is available to you during this supervised experience. Consider each visit, conversation, and response to your journal as a guide to assist you in your development as a teacher.

What's Your PLAN for Learning?

Directions for getting the most out of this section: The PLAN section is designed to give you the "big ideas" for this chapter in the form of Key Questions. Schedule time to skim the chapter to see which pages make most sense for you to complete. PLAN to meet regularly with your cooperating teacher so you can review the ACTivities in this chapter and discuss how they could help you learn. PLAN your time wisely so you can think about, talk about, write about, and learn about teaching. Document your work in this text if you choose to do so, or copy the templates and put them in a binder to use.

Read the Key Questions and assess your understanding of them. Do you already know some of the answers—or is this unfamiliar territory for you?

Key Questions:

1. **How will the triad support me?** The *Triad* activities on the ACT pages in this chapter will provide you with general guidelines for student teaching. Check your own university requirements for specifics.

2. **How will supervision help me learn how to teach?** How will I learn to teach using supervision tools? Supervision requires your university supervisor and cooperating teacher to provide you with feedback about your teaching performance and disposition for teaching. The *Supervision* activities on the ACT pages will provide you with guidelines for getting the most out of the supervision experience.

3. **What is reflection and how will I use it to forward my teaching?** Reflection is usually happening in action while you are teaching, and it can often get lost if it is not practiced consistently. The *Reflection* activities on the ACT pages will

provide you with several options for documenting your reflections so you can measure your own success throughout the practicum as a member of the triad.

4. **How will I document my learning using evidence?** Use the *Document* activities to give you ideas for demonstrating your practice. Your university program may also have specific requirements.

5. **How will I be evaluated?** At the end of the practicum experience you will be assessed to see if you met the standards for becoming a teacher. Use the *Evaluation* activities on the ACT pages to review how you could be evaluated.

$\mathcal{P}$LAN to Discuss Professional Standards

inTASC Standards

Professional Responsibility

Discuss these standards with your cooperating teacher and/or your university supervisor.

Standard #9: *Professional Learning and Ethical Practice.* The teacher engages in ongoing professional learning and uses evidence to continually evaluate his/her practice, particularly the effects of his/her choices and actions on others (learners, families, other professionals, and the community), and adapts practice to meet the needs of each learner.

Standard #10: *Leadership and Collaboration.* The teacher seeks appropriate leadership roles and opportunities to take responsibility for student learning, to collaborate with learners, families, and colleagues, and other school professionals, and community members to ensure learner growth, and to advance the profession.

How do these professional standards relate to the Key Questions assigned for this chapter?

Source: The Interstate New Teacher Assessment and Support Consortium (InTASC) standards were developed by the Council of Chief State School Officers and member states. Copies may be downloaded from the Council's website at **ccsso.org.**
Council of Chief State School Officers and Interstate Teacher Assessment and Support Consortium. (2011, April). *InTASC Model Core Teaching Standards: A Resource for State Dialogue.* Washington, DC: Author, 2011.

CONNECT

CONNECT is a resource with ideas and suggestions to support you during student teaching. Select and complete any CONNECT items that will enhance your experience in the classroom. Networking and learning from people and resources will add to your experience and to your chances of being hired.

CONNECT with People

- Experienced teachers: Interview your cooperating teacher about his experiences of being observed by the principal or department chair. Ask how he has used this feedback to become a better teacher.

- Administrators: Ask the principal or department chair which procedures she uses to supervise teachers in her building or department. How does this relate to your own supervision this semester?

CONNECT with Readings and Resources

- DVDs for beginning teachers are Harry K. Wong for beginning teachers (Wong)

- Books and authors to explore on the Internet or at your local library include *The Road to Teaching: A Guide to Teacher Training, Student Teaching, and Finding a Job*, by Eric Hougan; and *Stories of Student Teaching: A Case Approach to the Student Teaching Experience*, by Debra Eckerman Pitton (Merrill-Prentice Hall)

CONNECT Technology to Teaching

- Check out these websites:

    The New York Times Learning Network (**nytimes.com/learning/**) *Teacher* magazine (**edweek.org/tm/**)

    (**teachnet.com**)

    (**teachingheart.net**)

ACT

ACT pages are designed to offer you options for learning about teaching practices. The activities listed here relate to the Key Questions provided at the beginning of the chapter. Select the activities that apply to you and complete them on your own or in your seminar.

Directions: Skim the activities listed here and in the following pages and select the ones that will prepare you for a successful student teaching experience. Ask your cooperating teacher to complete some of the pages with you or prior to a meeting with you.

Key Question Topic	ACTivity	Page	Check
Triad	3.1. My Expectations for Student Teaching		
Triad	3.2. Triad Roles and Responsibilities		
Triad	3.3. Sample Agenda for a Triad Meeting		
Supervision	3.4. Being Observed		
Supervision	3.5. Receiving Feedback		
Supervision	3.6. Written Feedback from Cooperating Teacher		
Supervision	3.7. Observable Behaviors		
Supervision	3.8. Microteaching and Coteaching		
Reflection	3.9. Self-Assessment of a Lesson		
Reflection	3.10. Bubble Reflection: Student Teacher		
Reflection	3.11. Bubble Reflection: Cooperating Teacher		
Reflection	3.12. Bubble Reflection: University Supervisor		
Reflection	3.13. Reflective Journal Guidelines		
Reflection	3.14. Problems to Possibilities: Collaborative Problem Solving		
Documentation	3.15. Documenting Your Practice Using Audio		
Documentation	3.16. Documenting Your Practice Using Video		
Documentation	3.17. Participatory Action Research		
Documentation	3.18. Your Teaching Portfolio		
Evaluation	3.19. Standards for Success		
Evaluation	3.20. Using a Performance Rubric to Measure Progress		

ACTivity 3.1 My Expectations for Student Teaching

Key Question: How will the triad support me?

Directions: You are a member of the student teaching triad and should participate fully in this experience. List your questions or assumptions for support and ask your cooperating teacher and supervisor to confirm your answers in the triad meeting (see the sample agenda in ACTivity 3.3). Write your answers to the questions in your hard-copy or online journal.

What do I expect of my cooperating teacher?

Am I expecting daily meetings?

Am I assuming the cooperating teacher will stay in the room with me until I am ready to be alone?

Am I expecting someone to show me how to teach through the modeling of lessons?

Am I expecting to stay after school to talk about the day?

Am I expecting to use all the teacher's materials or make my own?

What does my cooperating teacher expect from me and why did she agree to accept me as a student teacher? This is always a good question to ask! Did your teacher agree because she will be leaving class to work on another project at the school and will need help in the room, or because she wanted to mentor a new teacher? Find out the motivation for her saying yes!

What do you assume the university supervisor will be doing to support you during this experience? Review general roles and responsibilities in ACTivity 3.2 and compare them to your assumptions; then confirm all of this with your real cooperating teacher and university supervisor. Your triad will make the rules, and you need to know what they are as you begin to avoid confusion and disappointment!

ACTivity 3.2 Triad Roles and Responsibilities

Key Question: How will the triad support me?

Directions: Highlight any of the following responsibilities that the three of you agree to do; include your own ideas in the list. Read the section defining "full participation," and add other skills that would demonstrate that you are attaining that level of involvement.

COLLEGE SUPERVISOR'S ROLE

"Visiting coach," checking in periodically to see how you are doing and to assess your development as a teacher

Responsible for providing overview of all requirements

Responsible for giving feedback that promotes your development

Responsible for preparing you for certification/teacher licensure

COOPERATING TEACHER'S DAILY ROLE AND RESPONSIBILITIES

"Daily coach," working side by side with you

Responsible for welcoming you into the classroom

Responsible for working collaboratively with your college supervisor

Responsible for offering suggestions and models for teaching

Responsible for modeling professional behavior

STUDENT TEACHER'S ROLE

"Prospective teacher in practice"

Responsible for completing all college requirements including reflection and portfolio

Responsible for attendance at school every day and making up any sick days

Responsible for completing all certification/licensing requirements

Responsible for accepting constructive feedback and implementing ideas suggested

Responsible for professionalism and confidentiality

Your most important role as a teacher in practice is to *participate fully in this experience.*

FULL PARTICIPATION

What does that mean? Simply showing up at the school every day does is not evidence that you are participating fully. Participation requires that you be present in the experience: You cannot be thinking about other issues, reading, checking messages, or being distracted in side conversation. Student teaching is a full-immersion experience into the life of a school and classroom. It is a collaborative learning process. To be successful must interact with adults and students. Teaching is a complex social activity. If you are participating fully you are *listening, volunteering,* and *sharing*.

Listening: Full listening requires you to take in what is going on around you without making judgments. As you begin your practicum, you will start forming your impressions of the school, the classroom, the district, and staff in the school as they perform their roles. Be open to what is going on, and use the observation and interview forms in this chapter to learn what others do and think. Full listening to your cooperating teacher means maintaining eye contact and offering continual cues that demonstrate you are listening. Listening to the supervisor may mean you have to hear suggestions about your teaching. How you receive and interpret feedback is an important skill of listening.

You also need to listen to yourself. What are you thinking and feeling during the experience? Embrace your ideas about the ways you would teach. These ideas may be different from what you are seeing in your cooperating teacher's classroom. Listening does not mean agreeing. Use the REFLECT pages at the end of each chapter to record your thoughts so you can refer to them when you have your own classroom. Listening to the students with an open heart to embrace their perspective will guide you to understanding what motivates them to learn.

Volunteering: Offering to assist the cooperating teacher before being asked is your primary method of volunteering. Notice what needs to be done and make suggestions for helping in the classroom. Ask yourself, "How can I be helpful here without overstepping my role as a student teacher?" If you are shy, you will need to challenge yourself to speak up. But remember, you won't get extra points for overdoing it. Find the delicate balance.

Sharing: Asking questions, sharing your perspective, challenging the status quo in a professional way, and communicating your ideas will demonstrate your full participation.

Your actions and disposition reflect your participation and, ultimately, your success in student teaching.

ACTivity 3.3 Sample Agenda for Triad Meeting

Key Question: How will the triad support me?

Directions: Find out when the initial meeting will be held with your cooperating teacher and university supervisor. This kick-off meeting will set the tone for the entire experience. Be sure to review your expectations from ACTivity 3.1 and bring any additional questions to this meeting.

SAMPLE AGENDA: WHAT YOU CAN EXPECT

1. Introductions and a review of the roles and responsibilities (see ACTivity 3.2)

2. From the cooperating teacher: expectations for the student teacher (including school policies and procedures), such as dress codes, class times, substitute-teaching policies, and why he accepted a student teacher)

3. From the university supervisor: documentation of experience, including forms, paperwork, dates for observations, school visits, licensing requirements, substitute-teaching policies and so forth

4. From the student teacher: questions (refer to the expectations you listed in ACTivity 3.1)

5. Setting the semester or year calendar for observations and/or school visits

6. Other topics as required: (Bubble sheets in this chapter may be used to stimulate discussion. Each person in the triad completes three bubbles on their sheet and shares with the group.)

How will you contribute to the agenda? What questions do you have that should be discussed at this time?

ACTivity 3.4 Being Observed

Key Question: How will supervision help me learn how to teach?

Directions: Read the page and discuss the observation process and how it will be implemented during the practicum.

Both your cooperating teacher and your university supervisor will observe you during your practicum. The observation process is designed to give you feedback specific to your teaching. To formalize the process of observing, a clinical model is often used by university supervisors. This model includes a preconference, observing a lesson, and a postconference.

Clearly, instructional practice is an important part of your preparation, and many aspects of your practice can be observed in the lessons you plan and teach. Please note, however, that all competencies are not seen in the clinical observation, and that is why conversations with your cooperating teacher and other forms of reflection are so vital to developing all your teaching competencies. Carrying out a well-planned lesson is important, but not if it is achieved at the expense of professionalism, communication, and knowledge of subject matter.

You may want to invite your cooperating teacher to use this observation model any time she would like to formally review a lesson you are teaching. This allows her to view your teaching in a more organized way, and also prepares you for your supervisor's visit.

The cooperating teacher and university supervisor may observe together; this will provide you with "double vision" and more feedback. The postconference would then be a triad, and you would receive different perspectives and data from each person.

PRECONFERENCE

A preconference is held prior to your actual teaching of a lesson. This may be just a few minutes before you start the lesson; you meet with your supervisor or cooperating teacher to share your plan for the lesson. A preconference does not have to take a long time, but it should not be skipped. It sets the stage for your lesson and gives the observer insights into your intended goals.

Sample Agenda for a Preconference

1. Share the purpose of the lesson along with a detailed plan for assessing student progress.

2. Review how you will engage students in learning activities.

3. Ask your supervisor or cooperating teacher for any last-minute advice.

4. Discuss how your lesson will be observed and how data will be collected.

5. Schedule time for a postconference.

(continued on next page)

(continued from previous page)

OBSERVING THE LESSON

Your supervisor will select a technique for observing your teaching. Samples of possible observation methods and options are listed at the end of this activity. The purpose of the observation is to agree on what you would like to see observed. The teaching competencies will serve as a guide for the supervisor, so you can expect the observation to focus on behaviors that relate to these.

Options for Collecting Data

- Scripting: The observer writes everything that is said or done.

- Selective verbatim: The observer "selects" a focus and comments only about that.

- Movement: The observer draws the movement of the student teacher around the room and notes the time the teacher spends in different locations.

- Pacing: The observer records the time taken for each part of the lesson.

Other ways to collect data are available from the university supervisor.

Sample Agenda for a Postconference

1. Discuss how your expectations for the lesson compare to the reality.

2. Review summary feedback (see ACTivity 3.6) and the data your supervisor collected.

3. Set goals to meet those competencies that observation feedback shows to need more attention.

How will you prepare for being observed?

How will you reflect on your lesson?

How will you receive feedback?

ACTivity 3.5 Receiving Feedback

Key Question: How will supervision help me learn how to teach?

Directions: Read this page and write responses to the questions in your hard-copy or e-journal so you can refer to them later.

Receiving and accepting feedback is an important aspect of participating in a supervisory model. During student teaching there will be times when your "coaches" will either offer you suggestions or provide objective data for you to reflect on. Being open to this information will provide you with increased opportunity to grow and develop as a teacher. Accepting feedback is not always easy. Reflect on how you typically respond to critiques or feedback; then think through any difficult feedback sessions and allow yourself to see the personal growth that may have resulted. When can you recall receiving feedback recently? Did you take it personally? Why do you think you recall this incident? What kind of feedback was it?

HOW DO YOU LIKE TO RECEIVE FEEDBACK?

Do you prefer your feedback in writing so you can think about it? Do you like to receive verbal comments at the end of the day? How would you describe your feedback "style"? Perhaps your feedback preference can be accommodated. Are your supervisors' responses in writing to your journals effective or would you prefer to talk on the phone about what you wrote? Do you thrive on group discussions or prefer a one-on-one conversation? Perhaps you don't know your preferences at this point and will discover them as you experience the practicum. Remember to speak up and ask for feedback if you feel you need more.

Suggestions for Receiving Verbal Feedback

- Listen very carefully.
- Take notes.
- Ask questions to clarify what was said.
- Repeat back what the speaker said to get verification of what you heard.
- Clarify the feedback again, if needed.
- Turn the feedback into a goal that relates to a teaching behavior.

Try Not to Take Feedback Personally! Feedback is provided to help you learn how to teach. Ask your supervisor and cooperating teacher how you will receive feedback about your ongoing development.

ACTivity 3.6 Written Feedback from Cooperating Teacher

Key Question: How will supervision help me learn how to teach?

Directions: Make several copies of this form and ask your cooperating teacher to use it to provide you with written feedback. Be sure to give the observer a copy of your lesson plan prior to the observation. This is used as a summary page and can be shared at a postconference. Save all the feedback you receive and review it again at the end of the practicum to track your development.

Date: _____   Subject/Grade: _____

Time of Day: _____

Title of Lesson:

_____

1. How well was the lesson plan written?

   _____

2. Was it clear and easy to follow? Add suggestions.

   _____

3. How did the purpose/objectives relate to student learning?

   _____

4. How well did the student teacher carry out the lesson plan's objectives? Rate 1–5 points

   _____

5. Describe one positive aspect of the lesson that demonstrates the student teacher's skills as a beginning teacher.

   _____

6. Describe the level of student engagement during the lesson: beginning of the class, middle of the class, end of the class.

   _____

7. Provide a compliment related to a teaching standard demonstrated.

   _____

8. Provide recommendations (suggestions for future lessons).

   _____

9. What did the student teacher want to focus on in the preconference? How was data collected to respond to this request? The data collected would be attached to this summary report.
   (See options for data collection at the end of ACTivity 3.4.)

   _____

10. Set goals for the next lesson. (See ACTivity 3.7 for suggestions.)

   _____

ACTivity 3.7 Observable Behaviors

Key Question: How will supervision help me learn how to teach?

Directions: Review the inTASC principles in Chapter 1 as well as your own teacher-preparation standards. This is what you will need to know and be able to do at the end of the practicum to ensure that you are ready for your own classroom. In the chart that follows, review the specific observable behaviors and documented evidence that provide examples of expected performance. Discuss observable behaviors and evidence with your supervisor.

inTASC Standards

Instructional Practice

Discuss this standard with your cooperating teacher and/or your university supervisor.

Standard #6: *Assessment* The teacher understands and uses multiple methods of assessment to engage learners in their own growth, to monitor learner progress, and to guide the teacher's and learner's decision making.

inTASC	Observable Behavior	Documented Evidence
Standard #6(a)	The teacher balanced formative and summative assessment in the lesson at the beginning and end of class	Copies of the activity and quiz were provided.
Standard #6(d)	The teacher engages learners in understanding and identifying...	Questions were listed on the board during the lesson.
Standard #6(e)	The teacher engages learners in multiple ways...	Groups had different reading levels of the same content.
Standard #6(i)	The teacher seeks appropriate ways to use technology...	Students used document viewer to share examples of their work with the class.

This sample table uses the inTASC Standards with the Performances, Essential Knowledge, and Critical Dispositions. Download Model Core Teaching Standards 2011 (ccsso.org) to see all the indicators of effective teaching.

ACTivity 3.8 Microteaching and Coteaching

Key Question: How will supervision help me learn how to teach?

Directions: Review the options listed here and invite your cooperating teacher to support you in learning how to teach by using one or both of these methods.

Microteaching is a structured observation where the cooperating teacher uses her instruction of a class to model her practice in a transparent way. The roles are reversed from a typical observation protocol where the supervisor or cooperating teacher leads the meetings and you become the leader.

Step 1. Preconference with the cooperating teacher. Ask what she will be demonstrating and why she chose this lesson. Review the lesson plan and materials before the observation. Ask how she would like you to collect data for her.

Step 2. Observe the cooperating teacher and collect data that will be discussed at postconference. Write down questions you have as the lesson progresses.

Step 3. Postconference with the cooperating teacher. Share the data and ask your questions! The cooperating teacher will discuss her transparent teaching with you so you can see what she is doing and why.

Coteaching is an opportunity to learn from the cooperating teacher while you are actively participating in the classroom. Divide a lesson plan, which the teacher is planning to teach, into three or four parts:

(1) beginning (directions and motivation),

(2) mini-lecture (teaching),

(3) activity (student engagement),

(4) closing (summarizer/assessment).

Select ONE part to try to coteach with the cooperating teacher. Add another part, and then another, until you are solo teaching!

ACTivity 3.9 Self-Assessment of a Lesson

Key Question: What is reflection and how will I use it to forward my teaching?

Directions: Every time you coteach or solo teach, respond to these questions. You may prefer to type the questions and save them on your computer so you will not have to manually write your answers in your journal. A summary of the responses over time may be used as an artifact for your portfolio. Compare your self-assessment with the written feedback form you receive from your cooperating teacher.

Date: _____   Title of Lesson: _____

_____

Class: _____

What did the students learn from this lesson?

How do I know?

How do I know the students were actively engaged in the lesson?

How closely did I follow my lesson plan?

Did I have to modify during the lesson? Why?

What do I think was the most effective part of the lesson?

Were the materials/visuals/aids appropriate? Why? Why not?

How would I modify this lesson if I taught it again?

What should I anticipate as I plan future lessons?

What do I see as my teaching strengths in this lesson?

A goal I would like to have my cooperating teacher/supervisor assist me in reaching is

_____

_____

_____

_____

_____

ACJivity 3.10 Bubble Reflection: Student Teacher

Key Question: What is reflection and how will I use it to forward my teaching?

Directions: This "bubble sheet" gives you a chance to jot down thoughts that "bubble up" during the course of the week and can serve as reminders for issues you would like to discuss in more depth with your cooperating teacher or university supervisor. You may choose to complete as many thoughts as you wish each week, and use them as the basis for a longer journal entry.

ACTivity 3.11 Bubble Reflection: Cooperating Teacher

Key Question: What is reflection and how will I use it to forward my teaching?

Directions: Invite your cooperating teacher to jot down his or her thoughts in several of the bubbles. Do this process weekly for continuous feedback and maximum results.

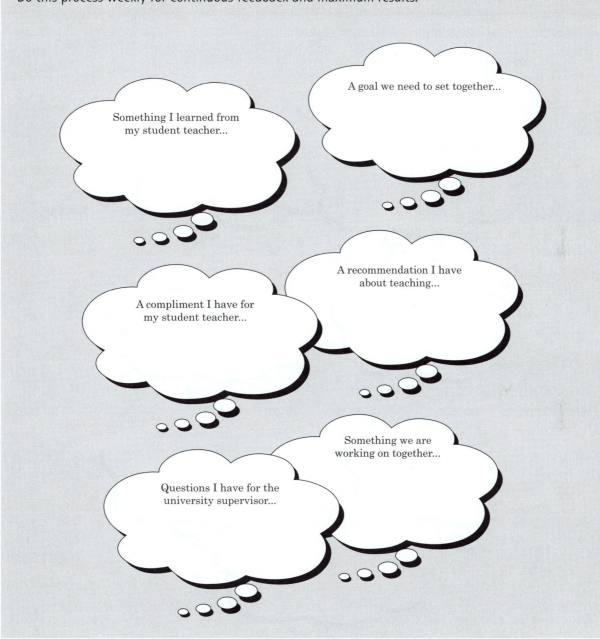

ACTivity 3.12 Bubble Reflection: University Supervisor

Key Question: What is reflection and how will I use it to forward my teaching?

Directions: Your supervisor may also want to complete a bubble sheet each time he visits during the semester or whenever he feels he has a constructive thought about you and your teaching. Each of you completing a form at the same meeting will lend structure to your communication and provide you with specific feedback to help you as you learn to teach.

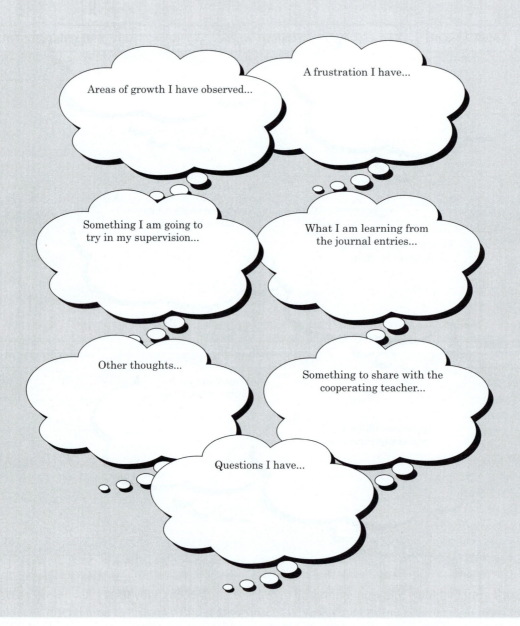

ACTivity 3.13 Reflective Journal Guidelines

Key Question: What is reflection and how will I use it to forward my teaching?

Directions: One way to reflect on your practice is to maintain a journal. You can do a "free write" at the end of each day, or think and write about your practice a couple of times a week. Whatever you decide to do, stay focused on your personal journey into teaching and how YOU can be a more effective teacher.

Suggestions for Maintaining Your Journal

✓ Write at least two or three times a week to be able to better document what is happening and your interpretation of what is happening. You may prefer hard copy to an e-journal, or you may use both. Hard-copy journals can be carried easily and do not require that you type during class time.

✓ Don't use the journal just as a diary or a log of what happened during the day. Instead, use it as a place to jot down questions you have, assumptions you are making, dilemmas you are facing, or any situation that needs further reflection.

✓ Some university programs require that journal entries be shared with the university supervisor. Be sure to check your spelling and grammar before submitting it for review. Supervisors often respond and give you more questions and ideas to think about. Remember, this is not about answers! It is about developing good questions!

✓ Use your journal to collect data on the students you are observing; these thoughts can then be used to fine tune your teaching to enhance their learning. You may notice something that works during the day—and you don't want to lose that thought! Use your journal to keep copies of observations and other activities you have completed together in one place.

✓ Reread your journal entries regularly to see how your thinking is changing over time. A thorough read of all your journals can be summarized into a final reflection artifact for your portfolio.

✓ A dialogue journal is an effective way to communicate with your supervisor, cooperating teacher, or another student teacher who is completing the practicum. One person starts the dialogue and you write back and forth throughout the practicum.

ACTivity 3.14 Problems to Possibilities: Collaborative Problem Solving

Key Question: What is reflection and how will I use it to forward my teaching?

Directions: One skill gained while learning to teach is learning how to solve problems. This process works best in a small group because many ideas are generated. In this ACTivity, each person will complete a problem-solving form individually, and then the group will work collaboratively to solve the problems.

Follow the directions for each section.

List three things related to teaching and learning that are working for you right now in the practicum; share these with the members of the group.

1. _____

_____

2. _____

_____

3. _____

_____

Acknowledge to yourself and to each other what is working for you before you list what isn't working.

Think about what is challenging for you right now. Many common problems arise during student teaching. There can be issues with managing the classroom and discipline, feeling stress to perform as an experienced teacher when you are just a beginner, feeling pressure to complete all requirements, having concerns and self-doubts about a successful experience, taking risks in teaching and lesson planning, working with a teacher who has a different teaching philosophy, managing your time to complete all tasks, communicating your needs to your supervisor and cooperating teacher, dealing with students who display inappropriate behavior when the cooperating teacher leaves the room, and being observed while teaching.

List three problems or issues you are struggling with this semester.

1. _____

_____

2. _____

_____

3. _____

_____

Select one of the problems listed to share with the group. Each person in the group will have an opportunity to share one problem.

Brainstorm as many possible solutions with your cooperating teacher, supervisor, partner, or small support group. Remember to think in terms of *observable* teaching behaviors.

After you have listed all the ways you have come up with to solve your problem, highlight the two ideas you would like to try immediately. If they do not work, select other options from the list. Repeat this process with each person in the group. Continue until all of your listed problems are solved!

Your Problem	Possibilities to Explore
	1.
	2.
	3.
	4.
	5.
	6.

Note: Following this procedure at various times during the practicum will reveal different types of problems. Save these sheets to document the range of teaching problems you are solving as your skills develop through the practicum.

ACTivity 3.15 Documenting Your Practice Using Audio

Key Question: How will I document my learning using evidence?

Directions: Audiorecording your voice will provide you with evidence that allows you to hear what you sound like in the classroom. Using a cell phone or other device, record 5 minutes of your voice as you are teaching. The first 5 minutes of the class or the last 5 minutes will let you hear how effectively you open and close a lesson.

GUIDELINES FOR DOCUMENTING YOURSELF

Before Recording: List two or three things you would like to listen for in the recording and write them down. Examples might be, What is my tone of voice? Do I call on girls and boys equally? How do I respond to student questions? How do I give directions?

_____

_____

_____

_____

After Recording: Listen to the recording for two or three of the things you wanted to focus on. Ask yourself, "If I were a student in this class, would I be engaged in learning?" Why or why not?

_____

_____

_____

_____

What did you notice that surprised you about your voice or tone? A copy of this recording could easily be uploaded to an e-portfolio. Be sure to include your reflection reaction to the recording.

_____

_____

_____

_____

ACTivity 3.16 Documenting Your Practice Using Video

Key Question: How will I document my learning using evidence?

Directions: Have someone use a camera, phone, or other device to record you in action. Videorecording is also a way to learn about and observe your students. (It is best practice to complete an audiorecording before you move on to videorecording.) Let this videorecording be for your eyes only; use it to gain valuable information about your teaching.

Note: Be sure to have signed permissions from students if you plan to include them in your recording.

RECORDING OPTIONS

1. Record yourself teaching a lesson. You can record the entire lesson or just the part you are trying to improve, such as your opening of class or your closing.

2. Record your students. You can learn a lot about your teaching and you can still hear your voice but you can see the students' reactions to your teaching. (Be sure to get signed permissions.)

3. Record yourself giving a tour of your classroom. Select a few areas of the room where visible learning is obvious and "tell the camera" why it is included in your classroom.

4. Record yourself in a conversation with your supervisor and/or cooperating teacher, and reflect on what you said and how you handled yourself.

5. Record yourself and view all or part of it with either your cooperating teacher and/or supervisor. Sit side by side and let them ask you questions and provide you with feedback.

What did you notice in the recording? How does it document what you are doing in the classroom? Upload all or part of the recording to your e-portfolio to document your teaching. Record yourself throughout the practicum to document your growing confidence over time.

_____

_____

_____

_____

AC*Tivity* 3.17 Participatory Action Research

Key Question: How will I document my learning using evidence?

Directions: Ask yourself, "What teaching behaviors will I implement and access in my own practice?" Documenting what you are actually doing to impact student behavior and motivation is a powerful insight for a novice teacher. Follow the steps in this activity to create a mini-study that documents one part of your teaching practice. The results can be used in your portfolio.

First Select a topic related to improved student learning that you would like to focus on, such as improving attendance at your school, promoting self-esteem in students, creating learning environments that acknowledge learners, developing respectful relationships with students, improving student engagement, improving student performance on teacher-made tests, and so forth. What is of interest to YOU?

Then Frame the topic as a question. YOU are the focus of the question as a participant. Your teaching behavior is being measured to see how you can impact student performance or self-esteem. You might ask, How do I create a motivating science classroom? How do students respond when I reward them for attendance? What happens when I do hands-on math activities regularly? What benefits emerge when I promote a math-talk-only classroom? How do students respond when I introduce project-based learning?

Start the study: Select a time frame of 2–4 weeks to implement your strategies to measure their effectiveness.

Document what is happening: Use a journal to capture your observations of your students. These field notes will be important to your findings. Interview students to find out their reactions to what you are doing. Create a survey or short assessment to learn what is working and what is not working.

Analyze and present your findings: Review your data and analyze it for patterns and themes. What did you learn from this mini-study? How did it document what you are doing and its impact on students? Create a short PowerPoint presentation or summary paper for your portfolio. Be sure to share your findings with your university supervisor and cooperating teacher.

ACTivity 3.18 Your Teaching Portfolio

Key Question: How will I document my learning using evidence?

Most student teaching programs require a student-teaching portfolio at the end of the practicum. This documentation serves as evidence of completion of the program as well as demonstrates progress over time. A student-teaching portfolio is a competency portfolio to demonstrate that course standards have been met, and differs from a presentation portfolio, which highlights the applicant's strengths for a potential employer (Chapter 10).

Directions: Decide which type of portfolio you would like to create to document your teaching practice. Will you create a hard copy to present in person? Will you create an e-portfolio or website to show your work? Or will you create a combination of the two? The following tips from former student teachers will give you some ideas.

Tips from Former Student Teachers: Collect–Select–Reflect

1. **Get started early!** Don't wait until the end of the student teaching semester to organize materials for your portfolio. ACT now!

2. **Review the university standards:** Be sure you clearly understand what needs to be assessed at the end of your practicum and label each document that relates to the standards so you can easily organize your work by the standard met.

3. **COLLECT artifacts throughout the semester or year:** Collect everything you think might be useful—samples of students' work illustrating their achievement, documentation indicating the ways you modified lessons, sample lesson plans, discipline strategies, and so on. Any activities from this text can serve as artifacts. Use a crate or file box and drop materials into folders clearly labeled with each standard requirement. Scan documents or create a folder on your computer's desktop for easy collection of relevant evidence, if you prefer. Or do both!

4. **Document classroom organization:** Draw diagrams and take photos of different ways in which you organized (or your teacher organized) the classroom. Write a rationale explaining the space organization in the room. This will document your learning environment and visible learning strategies.

5. **SELECT** the artifacts at the end of the practicum that clearly demonstrate your achievement in teaching.

6. **REFLECT** on what you selected and write a very short statement that explains why this artifact demonstrates the standard. Place the reflection near the artifact to tell the story.

7. **Add** photos, samples of student work, observations from cooperating teachers, any pages from this text, and so forth, to demonstrate your learning and skills.

Be sure to present your portfolio to your cooperating teacher and supervisor!

ACTivity 3.19 Standards for Success

Key Question: How will I be evaluated?

1. Talk with your supervisor to review which national and state guidelines will shape your program. You need to know how you will be evaluated at the start to avoid surprises at the end of the practicum!

2. State competencies vary but most agree that teachers need to have a command of subject-matter knowledge. This is often demonstrated in a content test or on your transcript through the content courses you have taken. Highlight them for easy review.

3. You also need to be able to (these standards may vary slightly)

   a. Plan curriculum and instruction.

   b. Deliver effective instruction.

   c. Manage classroom climate and operations.

   d. Assess student learning.

   e. Promote equity.

   f. Meet professional responsibilities.

4. Most teacher education programs include the following:

   a. Textbook and field-related readings

   b. The practicum with consistent attendance and procedures for making up days lost to illness or weather, and coming early and staying later to prepare all lessons.

   c. Journal reflections

   d. Attendance at on-campus events

   e. Course or seminar taken with student teaching

   f. Student-teaching binder or portfolio (e-portfolio option)

   g. Professional dress and boundaries at the school site

   h. Evidence of self-motivation—student teacher asks questions, volunteers to help, initiates ideas, and shares ideas with others

   i. Exhibits confidentiality related to children's records, subject of meetings with parents, and so on

   j. Professional communication with parents, students, and other teachers

   Note: You will be asked to rate yourself at the end of the practicum in all of these areas.

ACTivity 3.20 Using a Performance Rubric to Measure Progress

Key Question: How will I be evaluated?

Directions: Create a performance rubric with your supervisor and cooperating teacher that matches your teacher-preparation program standards. Be sure you are clear about what the documented evidence is that demonstrates your level of skill.

Sample Rubric

Note: The teacher understands how students differ in their approaches to learning and creates instructional opportunities that are adapted to diverse learners.

Examples of Documented Evidence	Unsatisfactory	Beginning	Emerging	Applying
	Have tried a number of times unsuccessfully 1	Just getting started 2	Have tried a few times with some success 3	Demonstrates Competence and Confidence 4
Uses a variety of teaching strategies				
Uses Bloom's taxonomy in designing lessons				
Manages small groups with varied instructional tasks				
Gives directions so all students understand what to do				
Provides differentiated instruction for learners				

REFLECT and SET GOALS

Think about...

Directions: Review the five Key Questions for this chapter and respond to the questions that follow.

Key Questions:

1. How will the triad support me? (ACTivities 3.1, 3.2, 3.3)

2. How will supervision help me learn how to teach? (ACTivities 3.4–3.8)

3. What is reflection and how will I use it to forward my teaching? (ACTivities 3.9–3.14)

4. How will I document my learning using evidence? (ACTivities 3.15–3.18)

5. How will I be evaluated? (ACTivities 3.19, 3.20)

Reflect...

How is the structure of supervision going to help me succeed?

Which reflection activity will be a stretch for me, and why?

SET GOALS: Possible Next Steps...

Create and Collect Portfolio Artifacts from Chapter Activities

If you are creating an e-portfolio, format your documents appropriately.

✓ Create a system for collecting artifacts . ACT now!

✓ Decide which type of portfolio will meet your needs.

✓ Select those ACTivities to complete that will provide you with the evidence to meet your requirements.

All of these artifacts can be used to meet final student teaching requirements and to help you compile your job interview presentation portfolios.

Demonstrating Your Teaching Skills

Demonstrating Your Teaching Skills focuses on your teaching skills and on your ability to translate, into the classroom, all you have learned in your college methods courses. Chapters 4 to 8 provide a survey of topics you have already learned; these are formatted in a way that will remind you of what you need to know and should be able to do in the classroom with real students!

Classroom management is a high priority for student teachers and Chapters 4 and 5 will give you an overview of what it takes to manage a classroom effectively. Try the activities on your own and then work with your cooperating teacher to discuss your ideas. Remember that you may not be able to apply what you learn in this chapter immediately during your student teaching practicum. So, even if you are not able to use all this information now, read it and reflect on how you will apply it in your future classroom. This is the time to create your plans, note your procedures, and declare your vision for creating a positive learning community. You do not have to imitate your cooperating teacher. Use this time to learn what will work for *you* in your classroom. Visible learning and classroom space are ways in which you create and support a learning environment. Skim the activities to see which ones will be most useful to you.

Chapters 6 to 8 provide you with an overview of assessment, instruction, and planning strategies. There is no single or best way to deliver this information to you. Assessment is listed first in this third edition because of the current focus on evidence and student-learning outcomes in education. Your understanding of assessment will drive your instruction as well as your lesson and unit designs. Skim the Key Questions in these chapters to remind yourself of what you need to know and be able to do, once you are standing in front of your own class.

Remember, the focus of this section is not to introduce or teach you these topics and skills. It is to reinforce what you already know from your courses and to remind you that now is the time to demonstrate that you are ready for your first classroom by showing that you can actually implement these skills!

4

Classroom Management: Creating a Positive Learning Environment

"Learn not to take yourself so seriously. Take the experience seriously, but learn to laugh at yourself and your mistakes. Enter the classroom with a sense of humor and humility. If it weren't for mistakes, we wouldn't learn. There are lots of ups and downs in the practicum. This is your opportunity to make risk-free mistakes. So, take risks!

Student Teacher

A teacher is only as good as the learning environment she can create for the students. How many times have you been in a classroom where you knew the teacher was brilliant, but she just couldn't seem to engage the learners or create an interesting lesson? We have all been in that situation. Creating a positive classroom environment and being able to design curriculum using effective lesson plans is the foundation for student learning.

Setting up a classroom and establishing routines are key components of classroom management. If your cooperating teacher does not have a permanent classroom, discuss how she adapts to this situation. Your cooperating teacher has already made decisions about how her classroom will be organized. Continue to observe the ways in which she has established procedures and how she follows up with her students. If you are student teaching in the fall, you will be able to observe how your cooperating teacher actually introduces and maintains the routines in her classroom. Try to visit the school before the fall session begins and assist the cooperating teacher in organizing her space. Ask her why she puts things in certain places and why she has created this organization. Is she trying anything new this year? Which procedures or systems is she retaining from previous years? Remember, you are a guest in this classroom and you will be following the routines and procedures this teacher has already established. You may observe things you do not agree with or that you would do differently in a classroom of your own. Try to learn and understand why the teacher has made the decisions she has. Use these differences in perspective as opportunities for your own journal writing and reflection.

Classroom management is often associated with classroom discipline or class control. It is more appropriate to associate it with gaining and maintaining student attention throughout the lesson or creating a respectful environment. Years ago, an effective teacher may have been one who kept his class orderly and maintained complete classroom control. Today, you of course want a sense of order and routine, and a student teacher's goal is to engage the learners and to have them understand the materials, concepts, or ideas being presented.

What are the cooperating teacher's expectations for learning? Instead of telling students what they *should not* do, are there systems that instead model what students *should* do? Does the teacher use positive statements when setting rules? "Don't interrupt other students" could be stated as, "Wait your turn to speak." Or, "Don't come to class without your materials" could be rephrased as, "Be prepared!"

The design of effective classroom management strategies and their incorporation into daily planning are the best techniques for preventing disruption and discipline problems. An effective teacher recognizes the fact that, regardless of what he does, there will be times when a difficult student or situation will need to be addressed. This issue will be discussed in a later chapter.

Your disposition and attitude as a teacher are critical factors in designing a well-organized classroom that is conducive to learning. Students respect teachers who respect them. Respect is demonstrated in your actions and body language. Do you smile? Do you greet students pleasantly at the door? Are you organized? Do you like to talk with students one on one? Do you move around the room? Would you consider yourself a positive force in the classroom? Do you respect differences and promote fairness for all? These are all things you are going to learn how to do in student teaching and it will be one of the most challenging skills you will learn.

Successful management minimizes discipline problems and leads to more effective teaching and learning. Use the CONNECT resource page for suggestions to learn more about effective classroom management. CONNECT provides specific recommendations for reading, topics to discuss with other experienced teachers, and sources on the Internet that will help you connect to successful strategies. Observe as many teachers' classrooms as possible and ask them how they organize and maintain routines in their classrooms. A respectful environment that is organized and maintained will allow more time for teaching and learning.

The ACTivities listed in this chapter may not always be modeled by your cooperating teacher during your practicum. You are still responsible for learning them so you can use them in your first classroom. Read the Key Questions and see how you can demonstrate these skills now. Refer back to this chapter when you are in your first classroom.

What's Your PLAN for Learning?

Directions for getting the most out of this section: The PLAN section is designed to give you the "big ideas" for the chapter and provides Key Questions to help you understand how to create a positive learning environment. REFLECT on what you already know and then focus on how you can learn the other skills you will need. Schedule time to talk to your cooperating teacher and go back to the observation formats in Chapter 2. For this chapter, use these formats to observe teachers' classroom-management strategies. Focus on what they do that "works," and maintain a journal or list of those successful techniques that you can use in your first classroom. Instead of being "directed" and told what to do by your cooperating teacher and supervisor, be "self-directed" and experience new ideas and skills through your observation of their practice so you will learn what you need to know and be able to do as a beginning teacher.

Key Questions

1. **What are the attitudes, dispositions, and beliefs of effective teachers?** The *Disposition* ACTivities will provide you with reflective ways to think about your core beliefs and how they can help you connect with students.

2. **How do effective teachers manage their classrooms using space, routines, rewards, and time management?** The *Space, Routines, Rewards,* and *Time* management ACTivities will provide you with concrete suggestions for demonstrating your skills during student teaching or in your first classroom.

3. **How do I create an environment that promotes learning and positive social interaction for all students?** The *Students* ACTivities in this chapter will guide you through some processes to assist you in student teaching and in organizing your first classroom.

$\mathcal{P}$LAN to Discuss Professional Standards

inTASC Standards

The Learner and Learning

Discuss this standard with your cooperating teacher and/or university supervisor.

Standard #3: *Learning Environments* The teacher works with others to create environments that support individual and collaborative learning, and that encourage positive social interaction, active engagement in learning, and self motivation.

How does this professional standard relate to the Key Questions in this chapter?

Source: The Interstate New Teacher Assessment and Support Consortium (InTASC) standards were developed by the Council of Chief State School Officers and member states. Copies may be downloaded from the Council's website at **ccsso.org.** Council of Chief State School Officers and Interstate Teacher Assessment and Support Consortium. (2011, April). *InTASC Model Core Teaching Standards: A Resource for State Dialogue.* Washington, DC: Author, 2011.

CONNECT

CONNECT is a resource page with ideas and suggestions to support you during student teaching. Select and complete any CONNECT items that will enhance your experience in the classroom.

CONNECT with People

- Teachers at your grade level: Talk with as many teachers as you can and visit their classrooms. Observe how they organize their materials and display their students' work.

CONNECT with Readings and Resources

- Teacher-education course materials: Review all materials you have been given throughout your courses. Put a note on each to relate it to a theme or topic you could use during student teaching or in your first classroom. Flag any with learning-environment information.

- Suggested books and authors to explore on the Internet or at your local library:

  How to Say the Right thing Every Time: Communicating Well with Students, Staff, Parents, and the Public, by Robert Ramsey (Corwin Press)

  Common-Sense Classroom Management for Middle and High School Teachers, by Jill A. Lindberg, Dianne Evans Kelley, and April M. Swick (Corwin Press)

  Elementary Classroom Management, by Evertson (Allyn & Bacon)

  The Dreamkeepers: Successful Teachers of African American Children, by Gloria Ladson-Billings (Jossey Bass)

  The First Days of School, by Harry Wong (Harry Wong Publications)

  Conscious Classroom Management: Unlocking the Secrets of Great Teaching, by Rick Smith (Conscious Teaching Publications)

  101 Ways to Develop Student Self-Esteem and Responsibility, by Jack Canfield and Frank Siccone (Allyn & Bacon)

  150 Ways to Increase Intrinsic Motivation in the Classroom, by James P. Raffini (Allyn & Bacon)

  Timesavers for Teachers, Book 1: Interactive Classroom Forms and Essential Tools, by Stevan Krajinjan (Jossey-Bass)

  Conquering Info Clutter: Timesaving Technology Solutions for Teachers, by Meghan Ormiston (Corwin Press)

CONNECT Technology to Teaching

- Check out these websites for more information about management:

  consciousteaching.com

  teachervision.com

  teachers.net./classroom_management

ACT

The activities listed here relate to the Key Questions provided at the beginning of the chapter. Use them as a guide for discussions with your cooperating teacher and university supervisor, or read them on your own. The goal here is to demonstrate your skills in the classroom. All of these ideas will be useful to you in your first classroom if you cannot practice them now.

Directions: Skim the activities listed here and on the following pages, and select and complete the ones that will forward your learning now.

Key Question Topic	ACTivity	Page	Check
Disposition	4.1 Respect for All Learners		
Disposition	4.2 Classrooms for Social Justice		
Disposition	4.3 Culturally Sensitive Teachers		
Space	4.4 What Does a Classroom Look Like?		
Space	4.5 Visible Learning and Silent Teachers		
Space	4.6 How Space Impacts Learners		
Routines	4.7 What Are Routines ?		
Routines	4.8 Routines and Learning Time		
Rewards	4.9 Why Use Rewards?		
Time	4.10 Time Management Works		
Students	4.11 Creating a Community of Learners		
Students	4.12 Using a Sociogram		
Students	4.13 Contracts and Agreements		
Students	4.14 Welcoming a New Student		
Students	4.15 Students as Leaders		

ACTivity 4.1 Respect for All Learners

Key Question: What are the attitudes, dispositions, and beliefs of effective teachers?

Directions: Reflect on you own classroom experiences as a student recall what made the learning experience positive and/or negative. How did the teacher's attitude impact the classroom learning environment? How did the teachers you remember demonstrate respect for all learners?

Teachers who establish routines, set up a well-organized classroom space, and create logical consequences are shaping an environment in which students know what is expected. With a structure and purpose in place, teachers can use class time to engage students in learning activities and to foster mutual respect among the members of the class. According to Sara Lawrence-Lightfoot, noted professor at Harvard's Graduate School of Education, "Respect is the most powerful dimension in defining successful relationships in schools" (2002).

WHAT DOES RESPECT ACTUALLY LOOK LIKE IN THE CLASSROOM?

The teacher will

Ask students what they think, and allow them to share their opinions. The teacher will LISTEN and provide opportunities for student input. For example, the classroom might have a suggestion box or a parking lot poster on the wall.

Post rules in a positive tone instead of a negative tone. The teacher might say, "Listen to others when they are talking," instead of, "Don't talk when others are speaking."

Know every student's name and how to pronounce it correctly. The teacher might post names and photos in the classroom; she will use the students' name s when calling on them.

The students will

Help one another and use each other's names

Work together cooperatively

As you observe during your student teaching, gather evidence of what respect looks like in your classrooms. What techniques and structures will you use in your first classroom to promote respect?

Optional: Reflect on the statement, "All children can learn," and discuss it with someone else to get their point of view on this statement. How does your response to this prompt influence your actions as they relate to respect?

ACJivity 4.2 Classrooms for Social Justice

Key Question: What are the attitudes, dispositions, and beliefs of effective teachers?

Directions: As you observe and learn how to teach, take note of how the classroom environment is created. What underlying beliefs of the school or of the cooperating teacher are apparent in the classroom, and how are they visible? What dispositions will you bring to your first classroom?

One way to encourage respect is to promote and practice equity in the learning environment. Do all of the students have equal access to the same curriculum and learning experiences, or are they grouped in ways that allow only certain students access to higher levels of learning? If not, ask yourself and others why this is so.

- Sonia Nieto is committed to asking culturally relevant questions so that all students will have access to the same resources. Search Nieto to see her questions.

- John Dewy talked about democratic classrooms as places where all students can do their part to contribute to the greater good. A classroom where students from diverse cultures are welcomed along with students with special needs is a place for all learners. A democratic classroom can be actualized when a teacher holds the disposition of acceptance and tolerance and creates a learning space to demonstrate those values. Search Dewy to read his philosophy.

- Paulo Freire suggests teachers can be in the role of "oppressors," controlling and manipulating students to do what they want them to do. Although that may sound appealing to you sometimes, it is not effective in the long run. The goal of an effective teacher is to create a space for dialogue, examining choices, and making decisions for the betterment of the class as a whole. Your beliefs and the ways you present yourself to your students will let them know if you are trying to control them or if you respect them and are facilitating their learning. Search Freire to learn his ideas.

Optional: List examples of what your classroom for social justice will look like.

_____

_____

_____

_____

ACJivity 4.3 Culturally Sensitive Teachers

Key Question: What are the attitudes, dispositions, and beliefs of effective teachers?

Directions: Students in American schools are coming from all over the world. They bring many strengths and needs. How will you utilize the variety of cultures in your classroom?

If you are teaching in a school with many cultures, interview as many students as you can to discover their learning needs and strengths. How do teachers at this school talk with students of different cultures? Are they sensitive to cultural differences? It is now understood that in some cultures, maintaining eye contact may not be considered respectful. Remember, all cultures that are reflected in your classroom will contribute to the "teaching context" as well as to the learning environment you are trying to create. Find out about the cultures represented in your school by talking with students, teachers, counselors, and families.

You will demonstrate your skills and develop your understanding of cultural differences by

- Being interested in cultures different from your own and learning about them so you can communicate effectively with students and parents
  How will you show interest?

- Acknowledging students publically for being from another culture and sharing their strengths
  How could you do this?

- Helping the entire class see the value of having a variety of cultures represented in one room
  What would that look like?

- Honoring and respecting the parents of the students in your classroom
  How will you demonstrate your beliefs in your students?

- Believing the students can succeed, even when they come with language limitations.
  How would you demonstrate honor and respect?

ACTivity 4.4 What Does a Classroom Look Like?

Key Question: How do effective teachers manage their classrooms using space?

Directions: Sketch the classroom layout in your cooperating teacher's room. If you have more than one cooperating teacher, compare your sketches and see if you understand why each space is organized the way it is. Be sure the sketch includes the teacher's desk, your desk, the students' desks, file cabinet, bookcases, large-screen monitor, computers, supply cabinet, plants, learning centers, bulletin boards, and all other physical items.

INTERVIEW THE TEACHER(S) AND ASK:

Why is your desk in this location?

Why are the students' desks arranged in this way? Does their placement change over the course of the school year?

Can all students see the teacher? Do they need to?

Ask Yourself:

Are there any awkward places in the room that relate to physical layout? Could these layouts be changed? Are there any safety issues?

How will you lay out your first classroom space? (Save these notes for your first classroom design.)

SPACE AND GRADE LEVEL

The grade you teach will impact the use of physical space. Early childhood teachers may have rugs and cubbies for their students, whereas high school teachers may use a lecture format, thus requiring different usage of space. If you have the opportunity, compare and discuss the variations in the usage of classroom space among grade levels.

Consider the placement of teacher desks, student desks (or tables), bulletin boards, computer stations, learning centers, supplies, books and other physical items that are in the room.

Observe several teachers at your grade level to see the norm at your school. Notice what works and what doesn't work. How do you know space is working for a teacher in the creation of a positive learning environment?

ACTivity 4.5 Visible Learning and Silent Teachers

Key Question: How do effective teachers manage their classrooms using space?

Directions: Look at evidence of student learning in your cooperating teacher's classroom and in other teachers' rooms at your school. What can you actually identify in the room that demonstrates that students are part of this learning environment? Use these reflective questions throughout your practicum to guide your evidence gathering. Think about how you will use visible learning indicators to create a positive space in your first classroom.

1. How do the names of the students appear in this classroom? Are there photos?

2. Is there evidence of collaborative work or teams?

3. How do you know this is a teacher who shows respect to students and honors multiculturalism?

4. Are there any silent teachers? (Silent teachers are posters, word walls, and other learning tools that students can see on the classroom walls as they are working.)

5. Are students acknowledged for their excellent work in this space?

6. Is the personality of the teacher evident in the space?

Student teachers that have been exploring the use of space to motivate and engage their learners have found many of the following suggestions and techniques to work well for them. Some high school teachers who tested these strategies reported that they were surprised with the positive results. Visible learning and silent teachers on the walls in a classroom help signify the teacher's values for the students. How will you use space to motivate and engage the students in your first classroom? Try including some of these visual-learning tools in your class:

1. Effort charts using stickers and stars posted in a place that everyone can see. This works at all grade levels; even high school teachers are surprised to learn that their students love stickers!

2. Attendance charts to acknowledge who is showing up have been show to work in many classrooms. This visible poster tells students that their attendance is important.

3. A place in the room for photos of students posted along with their names and their interests creates a place recognizing that each student is unique. Some teachers allow the students to add to their mini bulletin board regularly. Students of all ages love this, including high school students.

4. Photos of students in the act of working on projects or working in teams. Displaying these activities prominently reminds students of what it looks like to be in the act of learning!

5. Post student-created team names on the walls to organize classes and groups. Use unique names instead of "low group" and "special class" levels to minimize learning differences and promote collaboration.

Teachers who have used these methods minimize behavior problems and maximize student community building. Positive learning environments encourage learning!

ACTivity 4.6 How Space Impacts Learners

Key Question: How do effective teachers manage their classrooms using space?

Directions: Write or think about what you felt like when you entered your assigned school and/or the co-operating teacher's classroom. Use all of your senses to capture what students could be feeling and seeing.

Teachers spend their entire day, and perhaps years of their career, in the same school or classroom. For some teachers this could mean 30 or more years. If your cooperating teacher has been teaching for many years she may have accumulated clutter and lots of materials. Some science classrooms take advantage of these resources in a positive way and students can explore many parts of the room, other classrooms just feel overwhelming because they are cluttered and disorganized.

Some school designers are noticing that *feng shui* (the Asian art of design that uses the physical arrangement of a space to promote positive energy) or other design principles (such as those by Kristina Lamour Sansone designeducator.com) are having an impact on classroom behavior. Can the shape or color of a hallway discourage bullying and encourage cooperation? Can increasing a classroom's natural light raise test scores? Can carpeting turn the class clown into a reading whiz? Who can know for sure—teachers who are exploring with all of the senses and thinking about their space as a "place for learning" instead of just a school classroom are seeing positive responses from their students.

One teacher said, "I have no proof that any of this is working, but I know that I am more aware of my space and am open to making the environment comfortable for my students. I know I learn best when I am comfortable, so this makes sense to me."

Think how the use of space impacts your own learning and consider how that may affect the way you will organize your first classroom. How will you use space in your first classroom?

_____

_____

_____

_____

_____

_____

_____

_____

_____

_____

ACTivity 4.7 What Are Routines?

Key Question: How do effective teachers manage their classrooms using routines?

Teachers need routines to survive. Routines are the glue that hold the entire lesson and school day together; without them, there is usually chaos. Routines are important for maintaining consistency and for moving through a teaching day in a manner that students can expect. Routines can save valuable time and energy that can then be used more productively for academics. Their structure can also be used to teach respect, to model expected behaviors, and to generally promote the positive attitude and environment you are seeking to create in the classroom.

Directions: Observe your cooperating teacher's classroom and identify routines that have been established or are being currently integrated into the teacher's day. Make a note of all the routines, and identify the ones you will bring to your first classroom.

As you observe or discuss routines with your cooperating teacher, think about the following:
1. What is the purpose of the routine?
2. Are the students familiar with this routine? How do you know?
3. How does your cooperating teacher reinforce a routine already established?
4. How does your cooperating teacher present a new routine to the class?
5. What other skill(s) are students learning while participating in this routine?
6. Are routines saving time that can be used for teaching?

CATEGORIES OF ROUTINES AND EXAMPLES

1. Examples of **opening routines**
   - Attendance and how to get work/assignments to students who are absent
   - Lunch count, if applicable
   - Collecting homework and recording it
2. Examples of **operating routines**
   - Walking to classes or passing in the halls
   - Leaving during class time
   - Fire drills
3. Examples of **teaching routines**
   - Expected behavior in the classroom
   - Class discussion procedures for listening to others
   - Noise level for group work
   - Students who forget books or materials
   - Activities for students who finish early
   - Who has responsibility for materials
4. Examples of **closing routines**
   - Collecting work
   - Leaving classroom
   - Cleaning up

List other routines you observed:

What have you learned about routines and their affect on the classroom learning environment?

ACTivity 4.8 Routines and Learning Time

Key question: How do effective teachers manage their classrooms using routines?

Directions: Establishing routines saves a teacher's time so there is more time to teach content. Analyze the routines that already exist in your cooperating teacher's classroom to see how much time is spent on routine tasks such as passing out papers. Sometimes student teachers don't even write down time for routines in their lesson plan and then don't have enough time for the core of the lesson because the requirements for setting up the lesson took so long!

Complete the time frames required for the routines listed in the following table and add some of your own. Record how much time you spend on each routine during one class period. (Calculate how much time you might spend daily, weekly, and monthly—just on collecting papers!) Are you completing routine tasks as efficiently as possible?

Routines	Lesson Time Spent	Daily Time Spent	Weekly Time Spent	Monthly Time Spent
Passing out papers				
Collecting papers				
Recording homework				
Taking attendance				
Textbook distribution				

Ask your cooperating teacher to assist you in determining how you spend time on routines and how this relates to good lesson planning and creating a positive learning environment for all students. How can your students help you with these routine tasks to minimize time away from learning?

Remember, the goal is not just to save time for its own sake but to take that salvaged time and turn it into valuable learning opportunities for students. Routines and procedures should allow for flexible time and unscheduled events. Fire drills, students coming in from other classes to share information, the principal dropping by to visit and talk with students, and so on, are all part of a typical school day. Don't get frustrated by interruptions and changes in routines. A teacher is never fully in control of time. Learn to go with the flow and live for the teachable moment. Establish routines and be prepared to change them if you need to.

ACTivity 4.9 Why Use Rewards?

Key Question: How do effective teachers manage their classrooms using rewards?

Rules, rewards, and consequences are usually a part of a teacher's management system. Because these elements will vary significantly by grade and age of the pupils, as a student teacher you must understand and weigh their success when used in your classroom.

Complete the chart for the grade level in which you are teaching. Teachers who include the establishment of fair rules and consequences as part of the respectful learning environment generally have fewer discipline issues and disruptions during teaching time. The key is fairness, as well as equal, respectful treatment for all students.

Ask your cooperating teacher how the rules, rewards, and consequences she uses in her class were established. Did students have any input in creating them? How long has the teacher used these systems? What other systems has he used in the past? Why did he change? Communicating and establishing the classroom rules, rewards, and consequences with the students *before* they break them is key to successful implementation.

Complete the chart for your grade level. How effectively do you think your rules, rewards, and consequences transfer to other grade levels?

	Early Childhood	Elementary	Middle School	High School
Rules What are they? Who created them? Are they visibly displayed?				

Rewards
What are they?
Material items?
Verbal praise?
No homework?
    When are
    rewards given?
Do they work?
Do they match the
    rules?				

Consequences
What are they?
How often are they
    used?
Do they fit the
    misbehavior?
Are they grade-level
    appropriate?				

Would you use any of your cooperating teacher's rewards in your own classroom? Why or why not?

Rewards can be offered to individual students or to the whole class. The key here is to have the students recognize the reward as something that is valuable to them and worth working for.

Directions: Ask your students what they would consider a reward and integrate it into your classroom-management system if appropriate. Compare their ideas to this list of typical list of incentives that are commonly mentioned by elementary and high school students:

Possible Rewards

Elementary	Secondary
Free time	Free time
Watch a video	Read a magazine
Do errands for the teacher	Work on a computer
Lead the line	See a film/video
Go to the reading center	Food
Pick out a book	Class trip
Play with the pet in class	Play sports during day
Listen to music in class	Listen to a CD in class
Stickers	Use the video camera
Pencils	Be coach's assistant
Ice cream	Make a T-shirt
A certificate	Teach a class
Pizza party	Free homework pass
Magic markers	Read online
Sit next to a friend for a day	Sit next to a friend

How will you use rewards in your first classroom?

_____

_____

_____

_____

ACTivity 4.10 Time Management Works

Key Question: How do effective teachers manage their classrooms using time management?

Classroom management includes time management. Using strategies to organize the many details of day-to-day operations is imperative to getting the job done. Your cooperating teacher may have some strategies that will work for you.

Directions: To use classroom time efficiently, you need to assess how well you manage your time, are able to get things done, and your ability to stay on task with the students.

GETTING THINGS DONE FOR STUDENT TEACHING

Are you a checklist person or can you remember it all in your head? Will you keep notes in a hard-copy journal or will you use your phone or computer? Decide now! Make a decision about how you will keep track of all you need to do during student teaching. Use one system and stick to it. Your cooperating teacher may or may not be a good role model for this because she may be so comfortable with what she does that she no longer needs to write anything down!

CREATING TIME IN THE CLASSROOM FOR LEARNING

Although creating routines for doing normal tasks is invaluable, it is essential to develop them within a workable time frame. The allotted time must allow for the fact that not all students will learn at the same pace. It must accommodate that not all students will adhere to the rules established and that this may impact the required time for learning. Lesson planning requires that you line out how you will use your time. Grouping students who understand the material may allow you to work with a group that needs more help.

When observing, notice how teachers maximize their teaching time. You will have to discover what works best for you because there is no single strategy that works for everyone or at all levels. A measure of success in how you manage time could be demonstrated by asking the following question and determining its answer: If someone walked by your classroom, how would they know it was well managed?

They would see

Students deeply engaged in their work and talking about the content

Students moving around the room putting papers away without a teacher's prompt

No wasted time transitioning from one activity to another because students know what to do next

The buzz in the room is students talking–not the teacher directing

How will you use these ideas in your first classroom?

ACTivity 4.11 Creating a Community of Learners

Key Question: How do I create an environment that promotes learning and positive social interaction for all students?

Directions: To build a learning *community* the teacher needs to know the students and help them get to know each other. You must learn about your students as soon as possible. A good start is to learn their names the first day of school. You can also create a class profile to visually map out who is in the room. Details for these techniques are listed here. Decide which ones work for you.

LEARNING YOUR STUDENTS' NAMES

To begin engaging students, a teacher must first learn their names. This strategy cannot be underestimated. It allows you to say, "Hi, Joe," or to ask Jane to "hand me that paper, please." Learning names can be challenging, so try repetition. Review a class list and a seating chart and practice every day. This can be a challenge if you have more than 50 students. However, it is well worth it to learn every name. Think of the times you have had a teacher or professor who didn't know your name and how that affected how you felt in that class. Posting photos of each student on the wall beside their names to recognize your "community of learners" will help you remember. Do what works for you. *Be sure to pronounce each name correctly!* Have a contest where students have to get up and say every student's name in the class. The goal is that all students learn their fellow students' names. Award prizes for the most correct!

CREATING A CLASSROOM PROFILE

With your cooperating teacher's assistance, create a profile of the students in your classroom. If you are teaching secondary or middle school, select one of your classes. Find the information about the students through observation, their class record, a written survey, interviews, a class questionnaire, and talking with the cooperating teacher. The more you know about the class, the easier it is to create and maintain a positive learning environment.

List the names of the students and compile the table by writing one or two descriptive words for each category. When complete, you will have a summary of the class you will be working with this semester. Feel free to replace these categories with those you would find more useful.

Student' Name	Gender	Race/ Culture	Age	First Language	Multiple Intelligences	Artistic Ability	Athletic Ability	Learning Style	Learning Needs

After you fill this out, look at the patterns on the table. How will you use this information to differentiate instruction? Chapter 7 will talk more about this.

How can the strengths you see in your table enhance your community of learners?

(continued on next page)

(continued from previous page)

COMMUNITY BUILDERS: TEACHER BEHAVIORS THAT PROMOTE COMMUNITY

Discuss the following approaches to team building with your cooperating teacher. Add a checkmark next to each method as you discuss it, and consider how they could work in your own classroom.

_____ 1. **Sharing time:**   Students come to school with a lot on their minds. If it is appropriate, allow for a short period of time every day to let students listen to one another. Use this as an opportunity to have students be good listeners and speakers. Plus, the conversation is real life!

_____ 2. **Partners:**   At all grade levels, students are absent or miss parts of a school day. Assigning partners encourages students to care about each other and to take responsibility for the academic material. In secondary school, a log may be more appropriate than partners. The log should list homework assignments and other information important to the class. Absent students read it the day they return and can talk to the log writer for additional instructions.

_____ 3. **Teams:**   Within the elementary classroom, create small learning teams for various activities or projects. Let the teams create names, slogans, and strategies for completing assignments. Rotate teams often so the individuals in the class as a whole have many opportunities to work with different students. You may want to create the teams yourself at first, to be sure all students are included and that team making doesn't become a popularity contest. One strategy for knowing your classroom and making teams is using the *sociogram* technique. (This will be discussed shortly.)

_____ 4. **Groups:**   Within the secondary classroom, create either cooperative or collaborative groups to encourage team building while achieving the goal of the lesson. Give each student an assigned role.

_____ 5. **Compliments:**   At the end of the day or a class period, have . Set aside time for students to talk and share in class, even if it is only 5 minutes at the beginning or end of class. They can practice their listening and speaking skills, and the topic could relate to a current event or issue that is on everyone's mind.

What other team building approaches will you use in your first classroom?

_____

_____

_____

_____

ACTivity 4.12 Using a Sociogram

Key Question: How do I create an environment that promotes learning and positive social interaction for all students?

One way to illustrate the dynamics in a classroom is to construct a sociogram. Do this activity with your cooperating teacher to gain insights into the work preferences of the students. You can use the information to design cooperative groups or teams. It will also let you know what the students think of each other and whether you need to step in to include some students who had been excluded.

Directions: Creating a sociogram is a good activity to share with your cooperating teacher; it provides an opportunity for you to compare and discuss your impressions of the students' answers.

Step 1. Ask students in the classroom to list three students, by first, second, and third choice, with whom they would prefer to work in the classroom. (Make a distinction between *work* partners and *social* partners outside of school.) Tell them you are collecting the list of names for future group projects and that you may use their preferences to try to create teams that contain at least one person on their list.

Step 2. Have the students write why they selected each student. This will give you some insight; themes may repeat themselves.

Step 3. Collect the data and make a grid with students' names across the top and down the left side. Graph paper works well, or you can create a table on the computer and fill in the choices. Place a 1, 2, or 3 under each student's name as indicated to show the choices indicated by each student.

Sample

	José	Michael	Julia	Laura	Kristen
José	—	1	3	2	—
Michael	3	—	1	2	—
Julia	3	2	—	1	—
Laura	3	2	1	—	—
Kristen	—	3	1	2	—

Step 4. Tally choices to indicate most-preferred working partners (commonly called *stars*) and least-selected working partners (referred to as *isolates*). Notice patterns and themes emerging about working partners and the students who were not selected. José was the third choice for three students. Kristen made her choices but no one in the class chose her at all. This means she is an isolate, and as the teacher, you need to find out why and how to integrate her into the community of learners. Review the data on the grid and write your initial impressions of how it describes the classroom relationships. Discuss and compare them to your cooperating teacher's impressions. What do you notice?

_____

_____

_____

_____

(continued on next page)

(continued from previous page)

Step 5. Use a square for males and a triangle for females and cut the shapes to represent each student in your class. Place these shapes on a poster board to illustrate how students made choices. This may also be done using a computer program. Draw arrows with the choice number pointed to the student. Using three different colors for 1, 2, and 3 works well. If you prefer to just map first choices, that is a good start. The visual display will illustrate stars and isolates. As the teacher, it is important to know what the students think of each other. This may change over the course of the year (or of the day, in some cases!) and it is can only be considered a measure of classroom culture and how the individual students perceive each other as working partners.

Note: THIS IS A CONFIDENTIAL PROCESS. DO NOT SHARE WITH STUDENTS.

Sample of First Choices

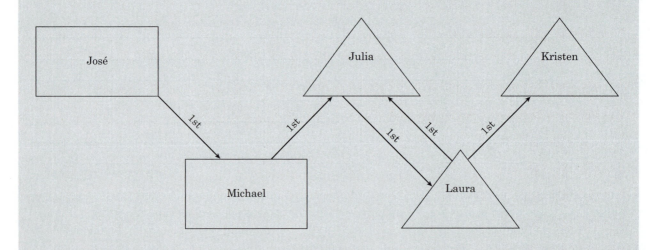

How will you use this process in your first classroom? Why will it be useful to you?

_____

_____

_____

_____

ACTivity 4.13 Contracts and Agreements

Key Question: How do I create an environment that promotes learning and positive social interaction for all students?

A short conference with students individually or in a small group can make a difference in the ways pupils respond in class. Instead of speaking directly out loud to a student in front of his peers, ask the student to see you after class.

Directions: Review these samples and see how they could work for you now or in the future. The contract can also be designed for groups by changing *I* to *we*.

Conference Report

Student's Name: _____ Date: _____

Reason for Conference: _____

_____

_____

_____

_____

Summary of Conference: _____

_____

_____

_____

_____

_____

Follow-up and Goal: _____

_____

_____

_____

_____

Signature of Teacher

_____

Signature of Student

_____

(continued on next page)

(continued from previous page)

Student Contract

Student's Name: _____

I state that I will (*Change a certain behavior.*) _____

_____

_____

_____

_____

_____

I will measure my success by (*How the behavior will be noted as being done.*)

_____

_____

_____

_____

_____

_____

For successful demonstration (*I will receive a reward; list reward. See page XX.*)

_____

_____

_____

_____

_____

_____

Signed (teacher):

_____

Date: _____

Signed (student):

_____

Date: _____

ACTivity 4.14 Welcoming a New Student

Key Question: How do I create an environment that promotes learning and positive social interaction for all students?

You may have experienced being a new student in school. Perhaps you know what it feels like to enter an established classroom after the school year has started and friends have already been made. If you have never been a new student, think about how a new student might feel. It doesn't matter how old the student is, whether he is in preschool or high school, there are always nervous feelings when a pupil enters a new environment in the middle of the year.

When students move after a school year has started, there are often transition issues. Sometimes the move is because of problems in the family, and other times there may be celebration of success (such as when a job promotion prompted the move). In either case, students have adjustments to make.

Directions: Find out if there are any students who are new to the classroom or the school and make them comfortable by doing any of the following.

- Introduce the student to the class and highlight some positive aspects you notice.

- Interview the student privately to find out why she moved, what curriculum she was using in the previous school, and so on. Ask the student what she likes about school, what she is most nervous about, and similar questions in this vein.

- Connect with the secretary in the school office or with your cooperating teacher to get any school records from the previous school.

- Connect the student to one or two students in your classroom (you might have designated "Welcome-to-Our-Class" students) who are trained to do this and who *want* to do this! They can give a tour of the school, eat lunch with the student, walk him around the high school, or play with him on the playground.

- Carefully integrate the student into groups and lessons, observing reading level and ability to complete tasks independently.

- Talk with the parents as soon as possible to learn more about the student.

- Present the new student with a "Welcome Wagon" gift (have these prepared for any new students who enter during the year). Include new pencils, paper, stickers, or high school notebooks—things related to the grade level that will get the student on board quickly. Consider asking town sponsors to pay for these Welcome Wagon gifts as a way to advertise the town.

ACTivity 4.15 Students as Leaders

Key Question: How do I create an environment that promotes learning and positive social interaction for all students?

Directions: Discuss ways in which your students can take on leadership roles in the classroom to ease your nonteaching responsibilities as a student teacher or future teacher. Use the following suggested duties as a guide to transition your community of learners into a community of leaders!

Your leadership strategies and duty assignments will vary depending on the age of the students.

1. Participants to distribute books and materials

2. Line leaders

3. Clean up materials leaders

4. Collecting homework

5. Attendance monitors and keeping papers for absent students

6. After-school tutors for students in need

7. Star-chart leaders (putting stickers on the chart for you)

8. Class readers

9. Problem solvers (when there is a student problem in the room, the student with the issue goes to the selected student before coming to you)

10. Chairs up at end of the day

Cultivating leadership is to encourage the students to take responsibility for their own classroom. You are ultimately the leader, but there is only so much time in a day, so let the students help you. The key to effective student leadership is to model the expectations! If you can learn these routines now, you will be ready to implement them in your first classroom.

$\mathcal{R}$EFLECT and SET GOALS

$\mathcal{T}$hink About...

Directions: Review the three Key Questions for this chapter and respond to the questions below.

Key Questions:

1. What are the attitudes, dispositions, and beliefs of effective teachers? (ACTivities 4.1, 4.2, 4.3)

2. How do effective teachers manage their classrooms using space, routines, rewards, and time management? (ACTivities, 4.4–4.10)

3. How do I create an environment that promotes learning and positive social interaction for all students? (ACTivities 4.11–4.15)

$\mathcal{R}$eflect...

How does the physical environment of the classroom enhance learning and student engagement?

How do routines minimize misbehavior and maximize time for learning?

$\mathcal{S}$ET GOALS: Possible Next Steps...

Create and Collect Portfolio Artifacts from Chapter Activities

If you are creating an e-portfolio, format your documents appropriately.

✓ Draw an ideal classroom and use it in your portfolio. Be sure to explain why you organize your room the way you do.

✓ Include a sociogram in your portfolio and explain why this process is helpful for a teacher.

✓ Include a paragraph in your portfolio that explains your beliefs about respecting all students.

These artifacts can be used to meet final student teaching requirements, help you compile your job interview presentation portfolios, and be useful as you prepare for your first classroom.

chapter 5

Classroom Management: How Do Effective Teachers Promote Appropriate Behavior?

"Try not to get discouraged. You are a new teacher, not a seasoned professional. Do your best with students who misbehave, and don't beat yourself up about any situation. There are some days when your students will be angels. On other days you will think they were sent to punish you for past wrongs. Always try your best and continue to learn.

Student Teacher

In theory, if a teacher organizes an effective classroom, designs lessons that meet the needs of the students, and presents information in engaging ways, she should not have problems with uncooperative students. In practice, however, all teachers encounter cases in which students break rules and must face the consequences. In the previous chapter, the notion of creating a positive learning environment was introduced as a skill set you need to practice as a student teacher and introduce later in your own classroom. This chapter builds on that knowledge and will remind you of the behavior-management models you have learned in your courses and readings.

As a student teacher you need to recognize that there are varying degrees of infractions that you may observe as you move into the role of teacher. A student sleeping in the back of the classroom is certainly not on task, but sleeping is a very different violation from hitting another student in class. Both situations require intervention and consequences, but the response from you as a teacher may be quite different. More-serious violent actions from students should always be reported to your cooperating teacher so the appropriate school policies can be followed. Discuss with your cooperating teacher how different kinds of rule breaking require different consequences.

In addition, repeated offenses by the same student may require a different response from you. A student who forgets her homework for the first time should not be disciplined in the same way as the student who has forgotten it several times. One definition from Webster's Dictionary of discipline is "to train or develop by instruction and exercise, especially in self-control." As the teacher, you can often use infractions of the rules as opportunities to teach students how to be responsible for their behavior. Leadership in the classroom, as introduced at the end of Chapter 4, is one way to encourage your students accept responsibility.

Classroom management and behavior management continue to be the two areas in which student teachers request more information and preparation. Often, student teachers express frustration in taking over a class from their cooperating teachers; they see that the teacher doesn't have any problems, yet the students misbehave when she takes over the class. One reason for this is that your cooperating teacher has a command of the class and the students "know" they can't get away with bad behavior. Experienced teachers know their students and can eliminate problems using "the look" or other subtle body language or movement to thwart a potential problem. Students will often "test" any new student teacher "taking over their class. In an effort to "be a friend" to the class, the student teacher loses control and the students misbehave. One lesson that student teachers must learn is that they can be *friendly* but *not a friend* to the students.

In all cases of discipline, the cooperating teacher needs to be consulted, especially if parents need to be called or notes need to be written and sent home concerning a student's misbehavior or lack of attention to schoolwork. This is your cooperating teacher's classroom, and all discipline-related communication to students or parents must be with this teacher's consent.

What's Your PLAN for Learning?

Directions for getting the most out of this chapter: The PLAN section gives you an opportunity to review the "big ideas" that relate to classroom management. What do you already know about classroom management? Compare what you know to this chapter's four Key Questions as you prepare yourself to demonstrate your skills with students.

Key Questions:

1. **How do behavior-management theories and research inform my practice?** The *Inform* activities on the ACT pages in this chapter will provide background information you most likely have already learned in methods courses. It is a good time to review them.

2. **How do effective teachers promote positive behavior?** The *Promote* pages on the ACT pages will provide you with practical ways to identify challenges to explore.

3. **How do effective teachers resolve classroom-management challenges?** Use the *Research* activities to collect data and solve your own problems.

4. **How do effective teachers get help for students in need?** The *Needs* activities on the ACT pages will provide you with three options for solving your own behavior related problems.

PLAN to Discuss Professional Standards

inTASC Standards

The Learner and Learning
Discuss these standards with your cooperating teacher and/or university supervisor.

Standard #1: *Learner Development* The teacher understands how learners grow and develop, recognizing the patterns of learning and development vary individually within and across the cognitive, linguistic, social, emotional, and physical areas, and designs and implements developmentally appropriate and challenging new experiences.

Standard #2: *Learning Differences* The teacher uses understanding of individual differences and diverse cultures and communities to ensure inclusive learning environments that enable each learner to meet high standards.

Standard #3: *Learning Environments* The teacher works with others to create environments that support individual and collaborative learning, and that encourage positive social interaction, active engagement in learning, and self motivation.

How will these standards relate to you when you are teaching in your own classroom?

Source: The Interstate New Teacher Assessment and Support Consortium (InTASC) standards were developed by the Council of Chief State School Officers and member states. Copies may be downloaded from the Council's website at **ccsso.org**.
Council of Chief State School Officers and Interstate Teacher Assessment and Support Consortium. (2011, April). *InTASC Model Core Teaching Standards: A Resource for State Dialogue.* Washington, DC: Author, 2011.

CONNECT

CONNECT is a resource page with ideas and suggestions to support you during student teaching. Select and complete any CONNECT items that will enhance your experience in the classroom.

CONNECT with People

- Guidance counselors, school nurse, school psychologist: Learn as much as you can about the support systems available to students.

CONNECT with Readings and Resources

- Suggested books and authors to explore on the Internet or at your local library:

The Essential 55: An Award-Winning Educator's Rules for Discovering the Successful Student in Every Child, by Ron Clark (Hyperion)

Discipline with Dignity: New Challenges, New Solutions, by Richard L. Curwin, Allen N. Mendler, and Brian D. Mendler (ASCD—Association for Supervision and Curriculum Development)

Solving Discipline Problems: Strategies for Classroom Teachers, by Charles H. Wolfgang and Carl D. Glickman (Prentice Hall)

The Three Faces of Discipline for the Elementary Teacher: Empowering the Teacher and Students, by Charles H. Wolfgang (Allyn & Bacon)

Fires in the Middle School Bathroom: Advice for Teachers from Middle Schoolers, by Kathleen Cushman and Laura Rogers (The New Press)

Fires in the Bathroom: Advice for Teachers from High School Students, by Kathleen Cushman and Laura Rogers (The New Press)

School Discipline and School Violence: The Teacher Variance, by Irwin A. Hyman, Franklin Township, and Aviva Dahbany (Allyn & Bacon)

A Guide to Positive Discipline: Helping Students Make Responsible Choices, by Barbara Keating, Mercedes Pickering, Bonnie Slack, and Judith White (Allyn & Bacon)

The Student Teacher's Guide: Intervention Strategies for the Most Common Behavior Problems Encountered by Student Teachers in Our Schools, by Stephen B. McCarney (Hawthorne)

The Ultimate Classroom Control Handbook: A Veteran Teacher's On-the-Spot Techniques for Solving Adolescent Student Misbehavior, by Dave Foley (Jist Works)

Positive Discipline A–Z, by Jane Nelsen (Random House)

CONNECT Technology to Teaching

- Seek out teacher chat sites: Talk to other student teachers or beginning teachers about your issues and try to create solutions to problems you are having with behavior management.

- You can handle them all (disciplinehelp.com)

- Tips for successful discipline: Google *Maintaining a Life* by Margaret Metzger and read Calling in the Cosmos.

ACT

ACT pages are designed to offer you options for learning about this topic. The activities listed here relate to the Key Questions provided at the beginning of the chapter. Select the activities that apply to you and complete them on your own or in your seminar.

Directions: Skim the activities listed on the following pages and select the ones that will prepare you for a successful student teaching experience.

Key Question Topic	ACTivity	Page	Check
Inform	5.1 Research That Matters		
Inform	5.2 Policies and Procedures at Your School		
Promote	5.3 Avoiding Common Classroom Problems		
Promote	5.4 Identifying Challenges for Teachers		
Research	5.5 Common Classroom Misbehaviors Observation Process		
Research	5.6 Collecting Data on Student Behavior		
Research	5.7 Interviewing Students		
Research	5.8 Problems to Possibilities for Management		
Needs	5.9 Stop and Think Before Disciplining		
Needs	5.10 Communicating with Parents		
Needs	5.11 When to Seek Additional Help		

ACTivity 5.1 Research That Matters

Key Question: How do behavior-management theories and research inform my practice?

Directions: This is the time to review all of the materials on classroom and behavior management that you have collected in your education courses. Skim and highlight the theme or topic of each article or chapter and note why it is important for you to know. Organize your information across classes in themes, for example, routines, behavior strategies, parent-communication ideas, and so forth. Create a file system for easy retrieval so you can access this information and use it in your first classroom.

You get to decide what to keep and what to toss, select the research that matters to you! If you don't have materials relating to each of these research topics in your files, you may want to research them on the Web and include them in your files. Be sure to bookmark any relevant findings.

You might want to review these behavior-management/discipline models:

- Kounin model—Where the teacher is "with it" and is able to manage a group effectively
- Neo-Skinnerian model—Behavior can be shaped by the desired outcome and consequences
- Ginott model of discipline—Situations must be addressed with clear messages
- Glasser model of rational choices—Good behavior comes from good choices
- Dreikurs model—The teacher confronts mistaken goals
- Canter model of assertive discipline—The teacher assertively takes charge of the classroom
- Fred Jones positive discipline model—The teacher emphasizes learner motivation and classroom behavior

The responsive classroom model was developed in the 1980s and has met with success in elementary schools. If you don't know this model, this is the time to find out about it. Go online to review its principles.

The suggested books on the CONNECT page will bring you to other research sources such as Everson, Emmer, and Worsham. These authors work at both elementary and secondary levels and can inform your practice.

Harry K. Wong offers a book and a series of videos that many student teachers have found very useful when designing their own management strategies.

Barbara Larrivee's book, *Authentic Classroom Management, Creating a Community of Learners*, will also provide you with proactive strategies to prevent teacher burnout. Its focus is on making good choices as a teacher. Larrivee includes a multicultural approach to behavior management in the classroom. Ask yourself if you and your cooperating teacher are applying consequences appropriately for different cultures and academic levels.

You are in someone else's classroom now and you may not find his or her approach working for you. Collect information now so that you will be prepared to organized your management system the way you choose.

ACTivity 5.2 Policies and Procedures at Your School

Key Question: How do behavior-management theories and research inform my practice?

Directions: Find out what all the discipline policies are for student behavior and review them with your cooperating teacher. Are the policies readily available to students and parents? Do they understand them? Are they available in the students'/parents' first language? Do you understand all of the policies and procedures? How does the policy impact the school's and classroom's climate?

1. Is it clear to you when it is appropriate to send a student out of the classroom to the principal's office?

   List three key points of the school's behavior procedures:

   _____

   _____

2. What is your cooperating teacher's behavior-management philosophy and policy? Ask him to share any specific rules and procedures with you. Do the students understand the rules and follow them? What happens when they don't? List any key ideas from your cooperating teacher's classroom behavior-management philosophy here:

   _____

   _____

3. What is your discipline and behavior philosophy? How does it compare to that of the school and classroom where you are currently student teaching?

   _____

   _____

4. Describe an incident that has occurred and show how it could be handled two different ways depending on the teacher's philosophy.

   Incident:

   _____

   _____

   _____

   One way to respond:

   _____

   _____

   _____

   Another way to respond:

   _____

   _____

ACJivity 5.3 Avoiding Common Classroom Problems

Key Question: How do effective teachers promote positive behavior?

Directions: Review these key areas that could lead to behavior problems in the classroom. Discuss them with your cooperating teacher and decide how you will use them in your own classroom next year.

- **Physical-space management:** Has the cooperating teacher structured the classroom in an orderly way to avoid potential problems? How is the traffic flow? Room setup?

- **Lesson planning:** Has the cooperating teacher designed lessons that meet the needs of all students so they don't get frustrated and angry? Are the lessons challenging but feasible? Does the teacher have accommodations for grouping that avoid discipline issues?

- **Discipline: Rules, rewards, and consequences** Are the rules clearly posted and understood? Do students "own" them or are they imposed on them? Is the cooperating teacher consistent? Are you consistent when you apply the consequences? Do you treat all students fairly?

KEEP TRACK OF WHAT IS WORKING!

When you start solo teaching and taking over from your cooperating teacher, the students will sometimes test you. It is so easy to stay focused on the lone misbehaving student who is gaining all the attention in your classroom. You certainly want everyone to behave and to listen to you. Don't forget, you are doing many things right! List the behaviors you are observing in your classroom that are positive, and list why you think they are working. What are you doing to maintain that positive behavior? Keep it up!

Classroom Behavior	What You Are Doing	Why Is It Working?
Class is passing in papers in an orderly way every day with their names on them!	Stopping class 3 minutes before the bell to allow time to pass in papers	Consistently ask students to check their names and pass in papers.

ACTivity 5.4 Identifying Challenges for Teachers

Key Question: How do effective teachers promote positive behavior?

Directions: Read these pages and discuss your behavior-management challenges as a student teacher. What are your cooperating teacher's challenges? How do they compare to yours? The key is to identify challenges and then to spin them into "positive" behaviors instead of resorting to punishment.

WHAT ARE SOME COMMON CHALLENGES FOR TEACHERS?

The day to day problems that teachers face vary in early childhood, elementary, middle school, and high school settings. Approaches to dealing with these day to day recurring problems also vary. How do you know the difference between a common misbehavior and one that is more serious? For example, A student found sleeping in the back of a classroom in a high school or early childhood setting may be seen as a common problem (for very different reasons!), but a student found sleeping in an elementary school classroom may be looked at more seriously as a sign of other issues.

Common Problem	Grade Level Where You Might See This Behavior	Is This a Problem in Your Setting? How Will You Respond When This Happens to Promote POSITVE behavior next time?
Not bringing materials to class (books, pencils, etc.)		
Not completing homework		
Bringing toys to class		
Showing up late for class		
Disruptive talk during lessons		
Throwing things (spit balls, planes, desk, etc.)		
Not showing up for detention assigned by teacher		
Sleeping in class		

Why is it important to be consistent with all students when you are dealing with common problems?

(continued on next page)

(continued from previous page)

WHAT TO DO WHEN . . .

Four categories for misbehaviors are listed in the chart that follows; some possible steps to take to deal with each are included. A key to understanding discipline issues is to observe whether the problem is with one student or if it reflects a behavior pattern for a number of students in the class. Ask your cooperating teacher to share other typical issues that take place in this school and possible ways to solve them for this age group. You must remain consistent with the school's procedure and offer fair solutions that PROMOTE positive behavior changes!

Common Problems	What You Need to Do
Chronic Work Avoidance Evidenced by being absent regularly, fooling around in class, not passing in assignments, tardiness, sleeping in class, etc.	• Make sure student is capable of work • Keep accurate records of what is missing • Talk with cooperating teacher • Let student know how assignments affect grade • Talk with parents • Other?
Habitual Rule Breaking Evidenced by calling out in class, not bringing pencil to class regularly, being talkative, forgetting other materials, skipping classes, etc.	• Use consequences established • Try behavior-modification systems • Talk with student privately • Discuss issue with cooperating teacher • Talk with parents • Other?
Hostile Verbal Outbursts Evidenced by angry loud yelling, chip-on-the-shoulder attitude, defiance when asked to complete assignments, etc.	• Determine whether the outburst is just momentary • Don't engage in a power struggle • Remove the student if anger persists • Talk with cooperating teacher • Talk with principal • Talk with guidance counselor • Talk with parents • Other?
Fighting, Destruction, Weapons, Alcohol Abuse, Drug Abuse, Sexual Harassment, Bullying Evidenced by hallway pushing, violence with peers, threats, glazed look in class, etc.	• Send a student for help • Disperse crowds that may gather to watch • Calmly talk; do not shout or scream • Report the incident immediately • Other?

ACTivity 5.5 Common Classroom Misbehaviors Observation Process

Key Question: How do effective teachers resolve classroom-management challenges?

Directions: Observe the classroom and school where you are student teaching.

List the three *most serious* unacceptable behaviors you observe. Note how they have been handled, and how you could avoid them in your future classroom. How can you spin them to promote positive behavior?

Unacceptable Behavior	How Handled	How to Avoid
1.		
2.		
3.		

List three *less serious offenses* How were they handled? How could you avoid them in your future classroom and promote more positive behavior from the student(s)?

Unacceptable Behavior	How Handled	How to Avoid
1.		
2.		
3.		

Discuss these issues with your cooperating teacher to determine how she would address them. Do not make any disciplining decisions without the consent of your cooperating teacher. You need to work as a team so the students see you both as teachers.

ACTivity 5.6 Collecting Data on Student Behavior

Key Question: How do effective teachers resolve classroom-management challenges?

Directions: Common misbehaviors are expected by teachers and are dealt with on a daily basis using appropriate responses for all students. From time to time, a teacher will have a student who does not respond and repeats the undesirable behavior. It is important to document student misbehaviors in these cases with dates and descriptions. These data can be important to share with parents and your cooperating teacher. Before you find yourself in a classroom situation where you need to respond to a student's misbehavior, be sure to read ACTivity 5.9, "Stop and Think Before Disciplining."

How will you respond to these situations?

Did the student threaten or hit another student or teacher? If so describe the incident.

Does this student have learning disabilities?

Is this the student's first problem of this type?

Other information that may assist you or others in seeing a pattern in this students' behavior so more help can be assigned if needed.

Keep a hard-copy document on your desk for easy reference and then transfer the information to a computer file when you have time.

Date	Time/Period	What the Student Did	How You Responded

What have you learned by doing this ACTivity?

_____

_____

_____

_____

How will this help you in your first classroom?

_____

_____

_____

_____

ACTivity 5.7 Interviewing Students

Key Question: How do effective teachers resolve classroom-management challenges?

Directions: Interview at least five students who are having common or serious behavior problems in the classroom to find out what is going on with them. Compare their responses and see if you can find patterns to their behavior motivation. You must understand the "causes" of the misbehavior to successfully address them. You need to know your students to understand their behavior. Talking to students will help you understand them. Refer to the CONNECT page in this chapter for resources to help you meet these challenges. Read the two *"Fires in the Bathroom"* books by Kathleen Cushman and Laura Rogers for interview question ideas beyond those listed here:

Possible Questions:

What is going on?

Why are you behaving this way? How can I help you?

CAUSES OF MISBEHAVIOR COULD BE THE STUDENT'S NEED FOR:

Do any of the students have the motivations listed here?

Attention: *I only belong when I have your attention.* We all have seen students who need to speak out and talk to grab the teacher's attention. These students want to be part of the group and need you to pay attention to them. Think of ways to connect with these students so they are not acting out in front of the class. Ask your cooperating teacher what she suggests.

Power: *I have no power and I need it to prove myself.* I must win at all costs or at least you have to lose. Some students will challenge you and try to prove that in front of the class because they feel just the opposite. Think about ways you could minimize these outbursts and recognize that this student has low self esteem.

Inadequacy: *I just give up. I can't do anything right, so why bother?* These students seem depressed and lost and just don't try. Some teachers call them lazy and this is just not true. They have emotional issues that prevent them from trying.

Revenge: *If you hurt me I will hurt you back to feel better.* Hurting a teacher can be in the form of embarrassing her in front of the class by talking back or making her life miserable by not following directions and verbally saying this. This kind of power over a young novice teacher can be really frustrating. Talking to the student one-on-one after class and getting to know the student helps this kind of student.

All of these situation are challenging and require a skillful teacher who "sees through" the students behavior to the reasons the student is behaving this way. The cooperating teacher can help you with these students.

AC Jivity 5.8 Problems to Possibilities for Management

Key Question: How do effective teachers resolve classroom-management challenges?

Directions: Select an issue related to classroom management and use this process to solve it. If there are other student teachers or novice teachers at your school, invite them to help you sort this out.

WHAT WILL YOU DO IF . . .

You have a class clown telling jokes during your classes?

You have a bully in your classroom who hits students every day?

You have a student who lies to you about doing her own work?

You have a student who displays passive–aggressive behavior?

As a student teacher, you will observe many problem situations in your classroom. To maintain an academic focus and a climate for learning, you also need to respond quickly to misbehavior. If you don't, the issue can escalate and take away from learning time.

Step 1. Select a problem. Select one behavioral problem or issue that you are really having difficulty with this semester.

_____

Step 2. Create questions. List three questions you have about this student's problem or life situation and try to get them answered.

Q1: _____

Answer: _____

_____

Q2: _____

Answer: _____

_____

Q3: _____

Answer: _____

Step 3. Learn about the student.

   a. Compile major points from student's school history. Find out as much as you can about the student. Write a mini case study that gives a fuller picture of who the student is and where she has been in school. Background information of this type is usually available in the student's file. Ask the cooperating teacher for permission to view the file.

   b. Observe the student in action. Ask yourself, "What is the purpose of this behavior from the student's point of view?"

Step 4. Determine possibilities. Given the behavior and the history of this student in school, determine several possible ways in which you could change this behavior pattern. Review behavior-modification techniques from your strategies classes.

(continued on next page)

(continued from previous page)

Consider the following three techniques that could be used to resolve a behavior-management issue. Which is best for this student?

Preventive discipline promotes positive behavior where students model good behavior, make eye contact, learn how to be respectful to each other.

Supportive discipline is a process in which you help the student gain control through agreed-upon signals to help the student channel his own behavior appropriately. You are not controlling the student you are helping the student control his own behavior though supportive cues.

Corrective discipline requires the teacher to correct the student immediately, following school policy guidelines. The purpose is to correct, not to punish. This correction is done calmly following a procedure, and not allowing emotions to interfere.

Possibility 1:

_____

Possibility 2:

_____

Possibility 3:

_____

Step 5. Compare Your Possibilities.

Working in a small group with other student teachers or with your cooperating teacher and supervisor, brainstorm behavior-management and discipline ideas. All student teachers in the group can list their particular problem on a piece of paper and hang it on the board. What do you notice about these problems? Write possible solutions on the board beneath the problem. Compare solutions to those you already thought about. Consider any new ideas!

New possibilities generated:

_____

_____

Step 6. Try a Possibility with Your Problem!

Record the results here:

_____

_____

Did it work? Do you need to modify it? Should you try another possibility?

_____

_____

ACTivity 5.9 Stop and Think Before Disciplining

Key Question: How do effective teachers get help for students in need?

WHO IS THE STUDENT?

Does this student have a prearranged plan when disruptive (e.g., sent to guidance, principal, or resource or learning-center classroom)?

Is this a first offense or is this repeated behavior?

Does this student have a special need that has not been addressed?

Are there other adults that need to be notified when this student is disruptive?

WHAT RULE DID THE STUDENT BREAK?

Is it a major offense (e.g., hitting someone or possessing a weapon)?

Is it a minor offense (e.g., chewing gum or wearing a hat)?

Is it related to academic work (e.g., not doing homework or cheating)?

Is it related to work habits (e.g., not listening in class)?

What did the student specifically do or say?

Is this misbehavior appropriate for the student's age?

WHERE DID THE MISBEHAVIOR TAKE PLACE?

In the classroom?

On the playground, in a hallway, in the cafeteria, en route to class?

Off school grounds but near school?

IS THIS BEHAVIOR A COMMON OCCURRENCE?

For this student?

For others in the school?

DO YOU HAVE PERSONAL FEELINGS ABOUT THIS STUDENT?

Have you interacted positively or negatively before this?

Do you know this student at all?

WHAT ARE YOUR LEGAL RIGHTS WHEN DEALING WITH DISRUPTIVE STUDENTS?

State and local guidelines for restraining students, searching lockers, etc.?

School policies related to alcohol, drugs, weapons?

Students with educational plans (IEPs)?

ACTivity 5.10 Communicating with Parents

Key Question: How do effective teachers get help for students in need?

Directions: Discuss the ways your cooperating teacher communicates with parents regarding their student's behavior. It is important to note here that positive communication processes are effective when a teacher is trying to shape behavior patterns and prevent misbehavior. Think about how you will incorporate both types of communication in your classroom.

WHEN YOU HAVE A PROBLEM WITH A STUDENT . . .

How does your cooperating teacher determine what misbehavior is serious enough to warrant a call home?

Are there rules about talking first with an administrator before calling a parent?

If the student is on an IEP or special education plan, are there other people who need to know when there is a problem?

Is a face-to-face meeting required?

What if the parent does not speak English?

WHEN YOU ARE REINFORCING GOOD BEHAVIOR . . . THE STUDENT IS MAKING PROGRESS . . .

Is a daily journal book sent home with the student for the parent to sign?

Are the parents/guardians called and given an encouraging report each week?

Does the teacher email the parent or guardian to update them on how well the student is doing?

Is there a face-to-face meeting with the student to share and celebrate what is working?

Communication is key to reinforcing expectations and positive behavior in the classroom. Don't forget to communicate the positive!

ACTivity 5.11 When to Seek Additional Help

Key Question: How do effective teachers get help for students in need?

Directions: There are some situations when the student requires services that you cannot provide. Discuss this with your cooperating teacher so you can tell the difference between a common classroom behavior that a teacher should be able to handle and a more serious issue.

HOW DO YOU KNOW WHEN YOU NEED MORE HELP?

- When you have exhausted your possibilities
- When the student exhibits serious problems beyond the scope of common issues
- When your cooperating teacher has determined the student needs additional help
- When parents have indicated a need for support
- Other

HOW DO YOU KNOW WHAT KIND OF HELP IS AVAILABLE FOR A STUDENT?

Talk to...

- Teachers of students with special needs
- Guidance department
- School psychologists/school social worker
- Principal
- Department chair
- School nurse or health department

WHAT SHOULD YOU DO?

- Maintain accurate records of all misbehaviors with dates of offenses
- Write a request for help with your cooperating teacher

HOW DO YOU KNOW YOU HAVE DONE YOUR BEST?

- You have tried a number of approaches with the student and documented them
- Your cooperating teacher has made the decision to refer the student

This information will provide guidelines so you can understand the options and procedures for successful behavior management and discipline, making you better prepared for your first classroom.

REFLECT and SET GOALS

Think about...

Directions: Review the four Key Questions for this chapter and respond to the questions that follow.

Key Questions:

1. How do behavior-management theories and research inform my practice? (ACTivities 5.1, 5.2)

2. How do effective teachers promote positive behaviors? (ACTivities, 5.3, 5.4)

3. How do effective teachers resolve classroom-management challenges? (ACTivities 5.5–5.8)

4. How do effective teachers get help for students in need? (ACTivities 5.9, 5.10, 5.11)

Reflect...

How does your behavior-management philosophy promote respect and positive behavior?

How are you demonstrating your skills in managing common classroom behaviors with routines from the previous chapter?

SET GOALS: Possible Next Steps...

Create and Collect Portfolio Artifacts from Chapter Activities

If you are creating an e-portfolio, format your documents appropriately.

✓ Use one of your Problems to Possibilities (ACTivity 5.8) as an artifact.

✓ Include your behavior management philosophy in your portfolio.

✓ Select one challenge and show how you successfully resolved it.

All of these artifacts can be used to meet final student teaching requirements and to help you compile your job interview presentation portfolios.

chapter

6

Assessing, Documenting, and Communicating Student Progress: How Do I Know What to Do?

"Contact your students' parents. Don't wait to communicate

bad news. In retrospect, I would have sent a postcard to each parent

explaining who I was, including my email and phone. Throughout

the practicum I would have sent postcards to parents indicating

their child's strong and weak areas. Parental support is needed for

student growth.

Student Teacher

Assessment is defined by Webster's dictionary as "to sit beside." *Evaluation*, on the other hand, is defined as "to examine and judge." Teachers find themselves in both roles as they informally may sit beside students and coach them to understand, or formally require students to take tests that are used toward their final grade.

The purpose of assessment and evaluation is to increase student learning and understanding of a subject or skill. Sometimes students can pass the test yet cannot explain the concept if they are asked to verbally share it. Does this mean the student has mastered the material or has just learned enough to pass a test that you have designed? If teaching for understanding and having students demonstrate what they have learned is a teacher's purpose, then assessing knowledge is critical. This means that lesson plans and teaching objectives need to match the assessment tools used throughout the teaching unit as well as at the unit's end. Practice and learning objectives must be aligned with final assessment. For example, if you allow students to use calculators for math activities during practice sessions, then calculators should be allowed for final assessment.

How do you know whether the student really understands what he has learned? You can assess understanding by observing students explain, interpret, apply, persuade, create, design, defend, critique, correct, summarize, translate, compare, and contrast the information in their own words. Using Bloom's taxonomy as a guide, you can create assessments, whether informal or formal, that specifically document what the students are doing to demonstrate their understanding of the material. Higher levels of thinking and understanding are represented by assessments that are more complex and authentic. For example, a test at Level 1 (knowledge) could simply be a rote memorization of a list of vocabulary words, but a Level-6 assessment would have to include more open-ended, complex thinking.

Teachers can use assessment tools, such as pretest forms, to gather prior information about what students already know about the subject to be presented. Instructors use these same tools to discover what students don't know or are still confused about. Assessment tools assist teachers in making curriculum decisions and creating lesson plans that take students to the next level of learning.

Traditional assessments and evaluations include tests and quizzes. Alternative assessments are nontraditional and offer a variety of approaches that allow students to demonstrate their understanding by showing what they know. These alternative assessments include student portfolios, open-ended questions, and performance. During your student teaching, you have an opportunity to try multiple assessment strategies to create a balanced approach to measuring what your students know and can do.

Your assessment tools should be clearly matched to standards you are striving for in your classroom. Make sure the activities you design in your lessons actually relate to what you want the students to learn! Sometimes when students do poorly on a test, the teacher discovers after the fact that she did not write a test that matched what she taught. This is why tests should be designed with the objectives and lesson plans to ensure the assessment matches what is taught.

There are a wide variety of assessment tools available to you as a student teacher. Do not limit yourself to traditional paper-and-pencil tests and quizzes. Review the many alternative approaches discussed in this chapter to allow your students a variety of options for measuring success. Keep in mind the diverse learning styles of your students.

The dilemma most teachers are facing today is that federal initiatives are connecting teacher performance to student success on standardized tests. The teachers in many classrooms are struggling with choices about how much time to spend on topics that are not going to be on mandated tests. Even though formative assessment is highly valued to promote student learning, summative standardized tests are adding pressure to schools and teachers to achieve results. Curriculum is being designed to match the test content, and lesson planning is focused on these standards. This is not to say that standards are bad for schools or teachers. But it becomes a challenge to balance the assessments in lesson-plan designs to ensure that all learning is not just based on standardized tests.

Finally, don't forget to tell your students how you will be assessing their progress *before* you begin the lesson. Also, create opportunities for your students be part of both peer and self-assessment whenever possible. Evaluating your students' progress is the most important part of teaching. It lets you know what to do next, where to modify your instruction, and what students need to know and be able to do.

This chapter serves as an overview and reminder of the strategies you have learned in your teaching-methods courses. If you need more information about assessment, use the CONNECT page in this chapter to assist you.

What's Your PLAN for Learning?

Directions for getting the most out of this section: The PLAN section provides you with the three Key Questions for this chapter. Review what you have already learned in your courses and compare that information to what is included in this chapter. Assessment is tied to teacher effectiveness, so be sure you understand how you will measure your students' growth over time.

Key Questions

1. **How do effective teachers assess and evaluate student progress?** The *Assess* activities on the ACT pages in this chapter will provide suggestions for either evaluation or assessment, including rubrics. Be sure to refer to other assessments you have learned in your methods courses, as well.

2. **How do effective teachers record and document student progress?** The *Record* activities on the ACT pages will provide you a sampling of practical ideas for keeping track of student progress. Refer to other record-keeping strategies you learned in your methods courses.

3. **How do effective teachers communicate progress to students and parents?** The *Communicate* activities on the ACT pages will suggest some ways you may consider communicating. Refer to other ideas your cooperating teacher uses and to suggestions from your methods courses.

$\mathcal{P}$LAN to Discuss Professional Standards

INTASC Standards

Instructional Practice

Discuss this standard with your cooperating teacher and/or your university supervisor.:

Standard #6: *Assessment* The teacher understands and uses multiple methods of assessment to engage learners in their own growth, to monitor learner progress, and to guide the teacher's and learner's decision making.

How does this standard relate to your practicum classroom? Does your cooperating teacher model this for you? How will you demonstrate these methods in your first classroom?

Source: The Interstate New Teacher Assessment and Support Consortium (InTASC) standards were developed by the Council of Chief State School Officers and member states. Copies may be downloaded from the Council's website at **ccsso.org.**
Council of Chief State School Officers and Interstate Teacher Assessment and Support Consortium. (2011, April). *InTASC Model Core Teaching Standards: A Resource for State Dialogue.* Washington, DC: Author, 2011.

CONNECT

CONNECT is a resource page with ideas and suggestions to support you during student teaching. Select and complete any CONNECT items that will enhance your experience in the classroom.

CONNECT with People

- Parents: Talk with parents of your students and ask how they see "progress" with their children. Set up a regularly scheduled "phone home" contact plan in which you call each student's home at least once a month.

- Teachers: Talk with teachers who worked with your students in previous grades, so you can measure progress over time.

CONNECT with Readings and Resources

- Books and authors to explore on the Internet or at your local library:

    Multiple Intelligences and Portfolios: A Window into the Learner's Mind, by Evangeline Harris Stefanakis (Heinemann)

    Assessment Is Instruction: Reading, Writing, Spelling, and Phonics for All Learners, by Susan Mandel Glazer (Christopher-Gordon)

    Assessment Alternatives for Diverse Classrooms, by Beverly P. Farr and Elise Trumbull (Christopher-Gordon)

    Communication for the Classroom Teacher, by Cheri J. Simonds and Pamela J. Cooper (Allyn & Bacon)

    Assessment and Instruction of Culturally and Linguistically Diverse Students: With or At-Risk of Learning Problems—From Research to Practice, by Virginia Gonzalez, Rita Brusca-Vega, and Thomas Yawkey (Allyn & Bacon)

CONNECT Technology to Teaching

Teacher software and much more:

    (teachervision.com)

    (amle.org/portals/0/.../Formative_Summative_Assessment.pdf)

For a course in classroom assessment try this (fcit.usf.edu/assessment)

ACT

Directions: ACT pages are designed to offer you options for implementing activities related to the Key Questions in this chapter. Explore these suggestions and refer to the strategies you've covered in your methods courses. This is not meant to be a complete list, but rather a sample of strategies that other student teachers have found successful. Go ahead and look at the ACTivities for the next two chapters ("Instructional Strategies for Diverse Learners" and "Effective Planning Strategies to Promote Student Learning") so you know how assessment fits with overall lesson and unit design.

Key Question Topic	ACTivity	Page	Check
Assess	6.1. Standards: How Are Students Evaluated?		
Assess	6.2. Classroom Assessment: A Developmental Continuum		
Assess	6.3. Linking Lesson Planning to Assessment and Evaluation		
Assess	6.4. Tapping into Students' Prior Knowledge		
Assess	6.5. How Do Teachers Measure Student Learning?		
Assess	6.6. What Should Students Know and Be Able to Do?		
Assess	6.7. Rubrics and Standards		
Assess	6.8. Assessments for Diverse Learners		
Assess	6.9. Group and Self-Assessments		
Record	6.10. Grade Books and Other Systems		
Record	6.11. Portfolio Assessment		
Communicate	6.12. Communicating with Students		
Communicate	6.13. Communicating with Parents and Guardians		

ACTivity 6.1 Standards: How Are Students Evaluated?

Key Question: How do effective teachers assess and evaluate student progress?

Directions: Review all high-stakes tests that the students in your class will be required to take this year. Some students in high school may be taking SATs for college or performance tests for admission into trade or art schools. Elementary students may be taking basic-skills tests and preschool students may be taking readiness-skills tests to show where they are developmentally.

All these tests relate to the environment for learning that you are attempting to create with your students in your cooperating teacher's classroom. A *high-stakes test* is defined as one that has a consequence for failure. For example, if a student fails the high school exit test, she will not graduate; or if she doesn't attain a certain score on the SAT, she won't be accepted or admitted to certain colleges.

DISTRICT, STATE, AND FEDERAL TESTING INITIATIVES

What is the purpose of the test? Why is it mandated?

Does the state have a statewide testing program?

How does your school meet NCLB requirements?

Are the students required to pass a high school exit exam? When is it given? What is the test?

Are there other state tests required? At which grade levels? Ask to review a copy of the tests if they are to be administered at your assigned class's grade level.

On what standards or frameworks are the tests based? How will this state test affect the curriculum you teach in your classroom?

Does the district require tests for certain grades to advance to the next grade level?

Make note of the test names:

_____

_____

_____

ACTivity 6.2 Classroom Assessment: A Developmental Continuum

Key question: How do effective teachers assess and evaluate student progress?

As a teacher you should be creating a balanced approach for measuring student progress using both formative and summative tools.

Formative Assessment Is Practice: Your Dress Rehearsal It is authentic, ongoing, sit beside, self-assessing, learn as we go, practice, group work, conversations, checklists, surveys, drill, practice tests.

Directions: When would you use formative assessments in teaching? Ask your cooperating teacher to explain how this works in the classroom and how these assessments are listed in lesson plans you will be writing. List your ideas here.

_____

_____

_____

_____

_____

_____

Summative Assessment Is Final: The Opening Night of the Play: It is the final test, grade given to an individual student, final evaluation, judgment given at the end of the unit or term, report card grade, SAT final product, paper test, project artwork, final performance, Spanish oral exam and the state-mandated standardized test.

Directions: When will you use summative evaluation? Have your cooperating teacher share these tests with you so you understand the difference between a formative assessment and a summative test. List summative tests you will be required to use this semester and those you anticipate using in your first classroom.

_____

_____

_____

_____

_____

_____

ACTivity 6.3 Linking Lesson Planning to Assessment and Evaluation

Key question: How do effective teachers assess and evaluate student progress?

Lesson planning and assessment are linked. Your lesson plan and your assessment or evaluation of the lesson should be written at the same time. This ensures that your students will be responding to the key questions and objectives you established. What do you want students to be able to do?

_____

_____

_____

_____

Directions: Review a lesson plan you recently created. Were your objectives clear? Do you know what you wanted the students to learn? What type of assessment did you create, or do you need to create, to accurately measure student achievement? Did your assessment approach match your lesson's activities?

_____

_____

_____

_____

How does your cooperating teacher create forms of assessment? How do the forms relate to the lesson plan and the lesson taught?

_____

_____

_____

_____

_____

How do you know when students have developed an understanding of a skill or topic?

_____

_____

_____

_____

_____

ACTivity 6.4 Tapping into Students' Prior Knowledge

Key question: How do effective teachers assess and evaluate student progress?

An important aspect of assessment is knowing where students are before you begin teaching. Students come to your classroom with varied backgrounds and experience levels related to the topic you may be presenting. Being able to assess this knowledge as part of your regular planning process is important when designing lessons to meet the needs of the diverse learners in your classroom.

Directions: Ask your cooperating teacher these questions and observe how other teachers tap into prior knowledge. How do you know what students can do from previous grades? Do you use KWL before you teach a unit?

Discuss the strategies on this page with your cooperating teacher.

- Have students answer these questions privately on paper before the lesson begins:

    What do you already know about this topic/skill?

    What do you think you know or have you heard about this topic/skill?

    What would you like to learn or know?

- Collect the papers, and at the end of the unit or lesson ask students what they learned and have them write it on the bottom of the sheet they had previously started.
- Give a pretest on the topic, testing for spelling words, math skills, and so on.
- Have students write a paragraph about what they know about the topic.

Tapping in can avoid reteaching students who may already *know* the information. It also assists you in designing lessons to meet the current needs of your students. Tapping in can also serve as a check-in toward the middle of the term and near its end, letting you know how closely the lesson objectives are being met.

ACJivity 6.5 How Do Teachers Measure Student Learning?

Key question: How do effective teachers assess and evaluate student progress?

Directions: Review the many ways you have to assess whether a student has learned the intended content. Discuss with your cooperating teacher or think about how you can incorporate these assessments into your daily planning and units of study. This will help you meet the needs of your diverse learners and assess their progress beyond a paper-and-pencil test.

PRODUCT OR PROCESS?

How will you assess student achievement? Will a product, such as those mentioned in the following table, let you know that the student achieved the objectives, or do you need to observe the student perform and demonstrate the skill or understanding of the topic?

Your assessment and evaluation depend on the lesson's objective. Be sure the achievement measure you require matches the objective you designed in your lesson plans.

Product (paper/pencil)	Product (visual)	Performance Process (with or without product)
Essay	Poster	Oral report
Book report	Banner	Speech
Biography	Model	Rap
Journal	Diagram	Dramatization
Letter	Display	Debate
Editorial	Videorecording or audiorecording	Song
Script	Portfolio	Poem
Test	Exhibit	Demonstration
Research report	Painting	Interview
Short answers	Photo	Skit
Position paper	Website	News report

Do your lessons always require the same type of assessment or evaluation? Are you providing alternative assessments for all learners?

_____

_____

_____

_____

_____

_____

(continued on next page)

(continued from previous page)

Assessments and evaluations should include a combination of

- **Traditional**

  Teacher-made or standardized tests that have only one correct answer

  Standardized norm- or criterion-referenced tests

  Knowledge and comprehension levels of Bloom's taxonomy

  Individual's prior knowledge of objectives through pretesting

- **Open-Ended**

  Guided questions

  Multistep problems

  Higher levels of Bloom's taxonomy

  Problem-solving approach to thinking

- **Performance**

  Hands-on projects and demonstration of skills and understanding

  More than one correct answer

  Portfolios

  Creative problem solving through the arts

- **Informal**

  Observation of students individually or in groups

How are the students in your classroom being informally evaluated or assessed?

_____

_____

_____

_____

_____

What are the assessment tools being used by your cooperating teacher?

_____

_____

_____

_____

_____

ACTivity 6.6 What Should Students Know and Be Able to Do?

Key question: How do effective teachers assess and evaluate student progress?

Directions: Interview your cooperating teacher about the classroom standards and expectations for all learners in the class. How does the teacher know when to move on in the curriculum?

Select a lesson that you plan to teach and complete this table.

What SOME Students Need to Know and Be Able to Do	How are these students selected? What is the knowledge they will "go beyond" in the classroom. How will they get the information? How will you know they achieved "beyond:?
What MOST Students Need to Know and Be Able to Do	Who are these students? How did you select the information they need to know?
What ALL Students Need to Know and Be Able to Do	Minimum standard: "Passing" for ALL students. How is this determined?

Use this information to design your lesson plans, select appropriate instructional strategies, and assess progress as you go. You need to know when to leave a topic and move on.

ACTivity 6.7 Rubrics and Standards

Key question: How do effective teachers assess and evaluate student progress?

Directions: Discuss all the rubrics being used in this classroom. Some may be standardized for the state tests and others may be created by classroom teachers. Rubrics are sometimes difficult to create yourself because you really need to be clear on your objectives and expectations for all learners. Practice creating rubrics that relate to standards that your students are expected to reach.

Sample rubric for a writing assignment

4	**Demonstrates high skill** Well organized and clear; few grammatical errors; appropriate for level; exceeds standards
3	**Clearly demonstrates skill** Loosely organized but contains main ideas; some errors; most writing appropriate; meets standards
2	**Demonstrates progress** Some attempt to include main ideas; many errors but some clarity; partial answer; meets some standards
1	**Requires intervention** Lack of organization; lack of clarity; full of errors; does not meet standards sufficiently

Create your own rubric for a lesson you will be teaching: list the standard

4	
3	
2	
1	

ACTivity 6.8 Assessments for Diverse Learners

Key question: How do effective teachers assess and evaluate student progress?

Authentic is defined as an alternative approach to observing student achievement. It allows the teacher to see whether the student can explain, demonstrate, and justify the skill or information in his own words, revealing understanding of the concepts, objectives, and key questions. Authentic assessments are useful with all students, but they are particularly helpful to use with students who have special needs, bilingual students, as well as gifted and talented students.

Directions: Find out who in your classroom needs another option for assessment. Survey the class; talk with parents and your cooperating teacher to reveal students who may require special assessments.

Do any of the students in your classroom have special needs—emotional or physical?

How will you assess their progress and achievement?

Are any of the students second-language learners? Are they bilingual? How will you plan accordingly to assess and evaluate their progress?

Diverse learners require diverse assessments and instructional strategies. In Chapter 7 you will see a variety of learning options. Then, Chapter 8 will offer you a variety of templates for your lesson plans. Reading all three of these chapters first and then going back to review them repeatedly will remind you of these skills.

Your goal during student teaching is not just to know what assessment is; it is to know how to use assessment tools appropriately with the students in your class.

ACTivity 6.9 Group and Self-Assessments

Key question: How do effective teachers assess and evaluate student progress?

Directions: Does your cooperating teacher use any student self-assessment tools? Does she ask students to assess their own learning? If so, how? Examples here illustrate ways individuals and groups can assess their own progress. Self-assessment encourages student leadership and promotes the creation of a community of learners.

Individual Self-Assessment

HARD OR EASY?

- Ask students whether they are finding the work hard or easy. Thumbs up or down.
- Make a graph to see how many students are finding things hard or easy over time

WHAT ARE YOU LEARNING?

- Take a minute at the end of each class as part of your closing to ask students to share two things they learned in class today.
- Collect and review work to see how you did as a teacher in presenting your objectives. This exercise can serve two purposes: (1) to see what they recall and (2) to let you know how to plan the next lesson.
- Exit tickets when students leave at the end of the class. One thing you learned and one question you have for me.

MORE TIME?

- Have students vote whether they think they need more time on the concept.
- Let students reply anonymously on paper or by putting their heads down and raising their hands.
- Write your own prediction of how the lesson went and what students will say, before reading their responses.

WORK HABITS

Create a worksheet with questions that require the students to rate aspects of learning from 1 to 5. For example:

- I worked hard in groups today
- I understand the concepts presented.

TEACHER ASSESSMENT

Create a survey to assess your skills as a teacher. Have the students rate you 1–4 on each question. Design the rubric so they know what 1–4 means. For example:

- My teacher presents information in a way I can understand.
- My teacher listens to my questions.
- There is time in class for me to practice the skill.

GROUP ASSESSMENT

Create a sheet for cooperating groups to assess their ability to work together and to learn the required information. Require group members to reach consensus in their rating of each item you create.

Suggested sample questions for a cooperative group assessment form:

1. How did you contribute to the group work today?

2. What did each member of the group do to contribute to your learning?

3. How would you grade your groups today? excellent/very good/fair/poor

4. What grade would you give yourself? excellent/very good/fair/poor

5. What did you like most about working in this group?

6. What would you do differently next time you are working in a group?

7. Is there anything else the teacher needs to know?

   Have you ever had a teacher who asked your opinion?

   How will you include student self assessment in your practicum and in your first classroom?

   Why is it important for a teacher to ask the students' opinions and to require them to self-assess as individuals and as a member of a group?

ACTivity 6.10 Grade Books and Other Record-Keeping Strategies

Key question: How do effective teachers record and document student progress?

Directions: Teachers use a variety of systems to keep track of student progress. A common way is to use a grade book. However, many teachers use different systems within their grade books. Ask your cooperating teacher to share his system with you. Interview other teachers to see how they document their students' progress.

Your cooperating teacher may be using an electronic grade book. Discuss the pros and cons of paper and computer systems.

SAMPLE GRADE BOOK

Use this format or create one of your own to record student progress. In addition to the date, write what the activity is that is being graded. Be mindful about multiple assessments when collecting grades.

Name	Grade Date	Grade Date	Grade Date	Grade Date	Grade Date	Grade Date

Use a highlighter to mark any missing assignments, or "holes," in your grade book to make scanning for missing grades easy. Use a different color highlighter to mark any below-average grade to help you scan for problem areas quickly.

OTHER STRATEGIES

In addition to using grade books, teachers may make anecdotal comments and use journals, index file boxes, or their own plan books to keep track. Other teachers use checklists or progress charts. Student portfolios are often used to maintain a file of student work over time. Document three other ways to record information and why a teacher might use these systems in addition to a grade book. How will you decide whether a record-keeping system is effective?

- When reviewing a strategy, ask: **Is it easy to use?** (Is it something I will use?)

- Ask: **Is it easy to read?** (Can I scan it quickly for information?)

- Ask: **Can I derive patterns from it?** (Over time, do I see student progress easily?)

ACTivity 6.11 Portfolio Assessment

Key question: How do effective teachers record and document student progress?

Directions: How is your cooperating teacher using portfolios? How is the portfolio assessed?

How does this assessment relate to state standards? How will you use portfolio assessment during your student teaching? How could portfolio assessment be useful in a parent–teacher conference?

Discuss the information on this page with your cooperating teacher.

A *portfolio* is a collection of student work that represents growth over time. A writing portfolio may include drafts as well as final copies of writing over a term or a school year. One important element of a portfolio is the student's reflection about why she selected a piece to be included in the portfolio or her explanation of what she learned by completing a certain task. If this process is omitted, then the portfolio merely serves as a "folder" of student work.

Some teachers require that certain documents must be included as part of the portfolio, whereas others allow students to select what goes inside. A combination of both is often helpful in determining student progress. A rubric for assessing the value of the portfolio is necessary if you want to measure how effectively students collected and reflected on the work inside.

Portfolios are often difficult to manage and oversee in a busy teacher's classroom. However, they do measure skills that traditional paper-and-pencil assessments cannot. They also require students to use their multiple-intelligence skills as well as higher order thinking. All students may not want to, or need to, develop a portfolio, but it is an excellent option in a differentiated instruction classroom.

How will you use portfolios?

ELECTRONIC PORTFOLIOS AND WEB PAGES

Most classrooms now have computers, and electronic portfolios are becoming popular vehicles for documenting student progress. Explore the possibility of using a website or an e-portfolio in your classroom!

How can you use e-portfolios in your teaching?

ACJivity 6.12 Communicating with Students

Key question: How do effective teachers communicate progress to students and parents?

Teachers use a variety of systems to communicate with their students and to keep them on track. The most common formats are the progress slip and the report card, which both go home to parents. Many teachers show these to students first, before the reports are sent home. Remember that progress may include growth in behavior as well as in academics. In addition to these traditional approaches, teachers are using other procedures to directly communicate with students.

Directions: Ask your cooperating teacher to share samples/ideas of any of the following communication systems she is familiar with or has used. Explore ways in which technology is utilized. Consider email, blogs, and websites.

_____1. **Student mailboxes/teacher mailbox** Teachers and students can leave notes for one another about assignments, papers due, make-up work, and so forth.

_____2. **Student conference** Teacher establishes a schedule and meets with individual students privately about progress. All students meet with teacher, not just failing students.

_____3. **Progress chart** A subject-related progress chart is given to each student, which visually documents the number of assignments completed, scores, projects, etc.

_____4. **Warnings** When in danger of failing, a student receives a "red" note.

_____5. **Compliments** Written or verbal acknowledgement of quality work. Phone or email

_____6. **Checklist** Placed inside daily or weekly folders, students can see what has been checked by you and approved for credit.

_____7. **Progress list** Secondary students may be instructed to maintain their own list of grades.

_____8. **Midterm progress reports** These list completed assignments and suggestions for improvement.

_____9. **Student-led parent conference** Students attend and share their progress with the parents. Everyone looks at the work together and discusses the work and goals for the student, with the student leading the discussion.

Which ideas have you selected to try? Why are you choosing them?

ACJivity 6.13 Communicating with Parents and Guardians

Key question: How do effective teachers communicate progress to students and parents?

Teachers communicate with parents for many reasons, including how their child interacts with other students, how the child's behavior is in class, and/or what the academic progress of the student is at the time of the conversation. Student teachers need to be aware of the variety of ways to communicate this information.

Directions: Review this list and discuss other options with your cooperating teacher. Select one or more strategies and try them during student teaching.

Some common procedures include:

_____1. **Telephoneconferences** (Suggestion: Send a note home telling parents at what time you will be calling.)
- To compliment students
- To give warnings

_____2. **Written**
- Informal notes to parents
- Formal progress slips from school office/midterm reports
- Formal progress slips/behavior checklists—teacher designed
- Daily homework sheets initialed by teacher and sent home

_____3. **Meetings**
- Informal
- Regarding a particular issue
- Formal: Can use on a regular basis for particular students, and include other teachers, principal, and/or guidance counselor
- Parent conference: Appointments for parents on a certain day with or without students

_____4. **Report cards**
- Delivered by students
- Picked up by parents

_____5. **Group meetings with parents**
- Open house evening with or without students
- Special event in your classroom

Ask your cooperating teacher how he communicates with parents. List additional ideas here.

_____

_____

_____

$\mathcal{R}$EFLECT and SET GOALS

$\mathcal{T}$hink about...

Directions: Review the three Key Questions for this chapter and respond to the following questions.

Key Questions:

1. How do effective teachers assess and evaluate student progress? (ACTivities 6.1–6.9)

2. How do effective teachers record and document student progress? (ACTivities, 6.10 and 6.11)

3. How do effective teachers communicate progress to students and parents? (ACTivities 6.12 and 6.13)

$\mathcal{R}$eflect...

How do a teacher's assessment choices relate to equity for all learners?

How do assessment choices help teachers with classroom and behavior management?

$\mathcal{S}$ET GOALS: Possible Next Steps...

Create and Collect Portfolio Artifacts from Chapter Activities

If you are creating an e-portfolio, format your documents appropriately.

✓ Select several sample assessments you created to demonstrate your skills.

✓ Select a way you have successfully communicated with students.

✓ Select one example of parent communication that works for you.

All of these artifacts can be used to meet final student teaching requirements and to help you compile your job interview presentation portfolios.

7

Instructional Strategies for Diverse Learners: How Do I Teach to Varied Student Needs?

"Take time to connect with your generation of future colleagues—

your classmates and other student teachers. Take the time to con-

nect with them personally and professionally. Share strategies and

ideas for teaching lessons to diverse learners. It will broaden your

perspective and prepare you for your own classroom. Don't take the

easy way out—try lots of new strategies!

Student Teacher

A successful teacher is one who can observe and recognize the varying needs in her classroom while creating meaningful learning opportunities for all her students. This chapter builds on the Key Questions introduced in previous chapters related to observation, classroom management, and assessment. Who are the students in the class? What do they think of each other? How do they interact? How does the cooperating teacher relate to the students? Who are you as a teacher? How will you fit in this classroom? What is your "comfortable" style of teaching? How do you reach out to students with various learning abilities? All these questions affect the way in which you present curriculum and how students respond to learning.

Diversity can be defined in many ways. Race, gender, ethnicity, religious beliefs, academic ability, personality, physical ability, habits, fears, and family support vary from student to student. What is the cultural makeup of this school? Who are the students? Do they have special education needs? How culturally diverse is your class? With cultural diversity comes multiple perspectives, global awareness, and a responsibility to discuss issues of world significance. Diversity brings the world into the classroom and students of varying cultures, ethnicities, and abilities should be recognized as valuable and integral components in the learning community. Cultural diversity also may bring other needs, such as students who don't speak English as their first language. Diversity defined in this broad way illustrates that *all* students are unique, and that teaching to varying needs in today's classroom is a complex task.

Your own teaching and learning styles relate to how you choose to present instructional strategies to your students. How much do you know about your teaching style? Do you know how you prefer to teach? What is your learning style? How will you become aware of the preferred learning styles of the students in your classroom? What is your cooperating teacher's style? Are you similar or different in your approaches? Discuss teaching and learning styles with your cooperating teacher and supervisor to gain more insight into your own style. These discussions will help reinforce the importance of matching your teaching style to your students' learning needs, as well as to the state and district standards.

Curriculum, instruction, and *assessment* are the building blocks for teaching. As you design curriculum and create daily plans and longer units, keep in mind how this content will connect your students to the world beyond the classroom.

Become familiar with the current information that shapes the thinking of the educational community. As a student teacher you will hear lots of buzz words and there will be many "hot topics" raised as teachers plan and discuss practice. Some of these discussions will include performance assessment, differentiated instruction, inclusion, multiple intelligences, block scheduling, rubrics, outcomes-based instruction, time and learning, brain-based learning, communities of learners, data-driven decisions, instructional technology, performance standards, and more. This chapter will highlight some of these topics. This is just the beginning of your learning curve! Don't be afraid to ask what a term means if you do not understand what is being discussed.

Components of Effective Teaching	Description
Curriculum The expected learning outcomes for the school, district, and state. The curriculum is made up of daily lessons and longer units of study.	**WHAT** you teach and **WHAT** is expected to be learned by students
Instruction How the curriculum is presented to students using a variety of instructional strategies. Teachers learn through professional development and add to their "repertoire" of strategies that enhance student learning of curriculum.	**HOW** you teach
Assessment How you measure what students know and can do as a result of the instruction. Informal and formal assessments as well as high-stakes evaluations in the district or state provide data for curriculum or instruction revision.	**HOW** you know that students have learned

Use the activities in this chapter to begin to practice some of the key areas that you need to know and be able to do as you develop as a teacher. You don't have to master all of these approaches and strategies at this time! This is just the beginning. Listen, learn, and build on the knowledge bases established in your curriculum-methods courses. Your knowledge of assessment, and the discussion and activities in the previous chapter, will inform the ways in which you integrate instructional strategies into your lesson plans. Various forms of lesson plans will be covered in Chapter 8.

What's Your PLAN for Learning?

Directions for Getting the Most out of This Section: The PLAN section allows you to outline the ways in which you will demonstrate the topics covered in this chapter's Key Questions section. What do you already know about these topics from courses you have taken? Compare and share with your cooperating teacher and begin implementing your ideas to demonstrate your skills in this area. Remember, this is a survey of topics, it is not an all-inclusive list. Be prepared to expand on it to meet your university requirements for teaching.

Planning requires you to take time for meetings with your cooperating teacher. This means you need to find time each week to review what is included in this chapter and to select what you would like to focus on. Your ability to plan will impact your learning.

Key Questions:

1. **How do effective teachers engage students?** The *Engage* activities on the ACT pages will provide you with guidelines for thinking about student engagement in several ways.

2. **How do effective teachers differentiate instruction?** The *Differentiate* activities on the ACT pages will illustrate a variety of ways in which teachers vary instruction. Combine these ideas with the assessment strategies in the previous chapter to get the full picture of instruction.

3. **How do effective teachers modify for students with special needs?** The *Modify* activities illustrate the ways in which you may need to change your instruction to meet the needs of some of your learners. Again, relate these activities to the assessment discussions in Chapter 6.

4. **How do effective teachers empower students to take responsibility for their own learning?** The *Empower* activities on the ACT pages suggest ways to let students take more responsibility for their learning choices. Use these as a guide for creating more ideas to meet your students' needs.

$\mathcal{P}$LAN to Discuss Professional Standards

inTASC STANDARDS

Instructional Practice

Discuss this standard with your cooperating teacher and/or your university supervisor.

Standard #8: *Instructional Strategies* The teacher understands and uses a variety of instructional strategies to encourage learners to develop deep understanding of content areas and their connections, and to build skills to apply knowledge in meaningful ways.

How are instructional strategies being used in your cooperating teacher's classroom? How will you use a variety of strategies in your first classroom?

Source: The Interstate New Teacher Assessment and Support Consortium (InTASC) standards were developed by the Council of Chief State School Officers and member states. Copies may be downloaded from the Council's website at **ccsso.org.**
Council of Chief State School Officers and Interstate Teacher Assessment and Support Consortium. (2011, April). *InTASC Model Core Teaching Standards: A Resource for State Dialogue.* Washington, DC: Author, 2011.

CONNECT

CONNECT is a resource page with ideas and suggestions to support you during student teaching. Select and complete any CONNECT items that will enhance your experience in the classroom.

CONNECT with People

- Speakers at school or at the university who specialize in diversity: Attend any events that give you an opportunity to listen and learn about diverse learners and diversity issues.

CONNECT with Readings and Resources

- Books and authors to explore on the Internet or at your local library:

    What Teachers Need to Know About Children at Risk, by Barry Frieman (McGraw-Hill)

    Classroom Instruction That Works with English Language Learners, by Jane Hill (McREL)

    An Introduction to Multicultural Education, by James A. Banks (Allyn & Bacon)

    The Digital Classroom: How Technology Is Changing the Way We Teach and Learn, by David T. Gordon (Harvard Education Letter)

    Teacher Talk: Multicultural Lesson Plans for the Elementary Classroom, by Deborah B. Eldridge (Allyn & Bacon)

    Open Minds to Equality: A Sourcebook of Learning Activities to Affirm Diversity and Promote Equity, by Nancy Schniedewind and Ellen Davidson (Allyn & Bacon)

    Other People's Children: Cultural Conflict in the Classroom, by Lisa D. Delpit (New Press)

CONNECT Technology to Teaching

- Surf the Internet to chat about or find great lessons for diverse learners of all levels. Check out these websites:

    (cpt.fsu.edu?eseold/in/sttrmain.html)(tolerance.org)

    RTI (Response to Intervention)

    (rti4success.org)(rtinetwork.org)(interventioncentral.org)

ACT

Directions: ACT pages are designed to offer you a sample of strategies you may want to implement in your student teaching classroom. This is not a complete list, but it contains a number of ideas that you may find useful. Refer to your courses to add other strategies to your demonstration of teaching.

Key Question Topic	Activity	Page	Check
Engage	7.1 Using Diversity to Enhance Instructional Practice		
Engage	7.2 Teaching and Learning Styles		
Differentiate	7.3 Giving Directions to Diverse Learners		
Differentiate	7.4 Using Brain-Based Strategies		
Differentiate	7.5 Differentiating Whole-Class Instruction: Lectures and Presentations		
Differentiate	7.6 Flexible and Cooperative Learning Groups		
Differentiate	7.7 Using Multiple Intelligences to Teach		
Differentiate	7.8 Using Bloom's Taxonomy to Vary Questioning Techniques		
Modify	7.9 Students with Special Needs		
Modify	7.10 Students with Special Needs: Individual Education Plans		
Modify	7.11 Students with Special Needs: Modifying Lessons		
Empower	7.12 Giving Students Choices		
Empower	7.13 Enrichment and Homework		
Empower	7.14 Using Technology and Audiovisual Aids to Teach		
Empower	7.15 Service Learning: Contributing to the Community		

ACTivity 7.1 Using Diversity to Enhance Instructional Practice

Key Question: How do effective teachers engage students?

Diversity means understanding that each individual is unique; it is imperative that all teachers recognize and respect individual differences. These differences can be based on race, ethnicity, gender, sexual orientation, socioeconomic status, age, physical abilities, religious beliefs, political beliefs, or other ideologies. Our goal as teachers is to model our understanding of each other—to move beyond simple tolerance and embrace and celebrate the rich dimensions of diversity contained within each individual. Diversity means understanding and appreciating interdependence of humanity, cultures, and the natural environment, as well as practicing mutual respect for qualities and experiences that are different from our own.

Directions: Teaching is about relationships. The more you understand diversity in your classroom, the easier it will be to create a community of learners where all can contribute. Refer back to what you have learned in Chapter 2 and review the reflective questions on this page to further your knowledge base. How can your instructional practices include diversity? Discuss your responses with your cooperating teacher or university professor.

When you look at your students, what do you see?

How many cultures are represented?

How many languages?

How can you use this student diversity to enhance your curriculum?

Could parents be guest speakers?

Could students demonstrate rituals and customs as part of authentic instruction strategies?

Could the class research and honor other cultures?

Could books representing the cultures be displayed in the classroom?

Students have many experiences to offer. By using the students to provide rich and varied approaches to teaching any lesson, you will have an opportunity to model the value of diversity. Instructional variety and alternatives keep the classroom exciting.

ACTivity 7.2 Teaching and Learning Styles

Key Question: How do effective teachers engage students?

Directions: Review the teaching-styles and learning-styles information presented here and discuss with your cooperating teacher. Think about how this relates to your lesson planning and your students' learning.

LEARNING STYLES

Students learn in many ways. Being able to recognize these differences will assist you in designing lessons and bringing the students together as a team. Diversity of learning styles makes the team more resourceful, yet students also need to be aware of the differences so they don't argue about their different approaches.

Check your own preferred learning styles and compare them with those of your cooperating teacher. Review current learning-style theories and translate theory into practice by observing students. Many of these theorists have short learning-style tests that are available for use. Refer to ACTivity 7.7 for multiple intelligences.

Ask the students how they think they learn best. Students know what they prefer and which methods work best for them. Think of ways to train students to build on their own learning strengths so they can adjust conditions to suit themselves. As a student teacher, you should assist your students in becoming more comfortable with several learning styles.

1. Review your students to see who are primarily

   _____ Auditory   _____ Visual

   _____ Hands-on   _____ Random

   _____ Sequential   _____ Inductive

   _____ Deductive

2. Interview several students in the classroom about their preferred learning style. Ask the students why they prefer this style. If they use a combination, list them.

   Student   **Preferred Style(s)**   **Reason**

   _____   _____   _____

   _____   _____   _____

   _____   _____   _____

   _____   _____   _____

   _____   _____   _____

   _____   _____   _____

   _____   _____   _____

TEACHING STYLES: WHICH DO I PREFER?

An awareness level of your teaching style and how it matches your students' learning styles is important as you begin to teach lessons. Students may demonstrate a variety of "intelligences" and teachers need to be aware of them.

DO YOU LIKE TO TALK AND EXPLAIN CONCEPTS TO STUDENTS VERBALLY?

Then you probably...

lecture for a major part of the class period.

talk to students.

Students who prefer auditory learning will respond.

DO YOU LIKE TO WRITE AND SEE CONCEPTS ON PAPER?

Then you probably...

use the board to list ideas.

write outlines for students.

create study guides.

ask students to take notes.

Students who prefer to see things in writing will respond.

DO YOU ENJOY USING VISUAL DISPLAYS?

Then you probably...

use the computer to demonstrate a concept.

bring in models and posters to show students.

use webbing and graphic organizers.

Students who prefer pictures and drawings will respond.

DO YOU LIKE TO TOUCH AND SEE THINGS HAPPEN?

Then you probably...

create experiments for your classroom.

design hands-on lessons with manipulatives.

bring things to show and tell about.

Students who want to touch and observe the activity will respond.

Students in your classroom will have a variety of learning and preferred styles. Once you discover their styles and multiple intelligences, you will need to be sure that you adapt and vary your teaching so that all students will respond.

How would you describe your preferred style?

How will you expand your preferred style to reach all learners in your classroom?

ACTivity 7.3 Giving Directions to Diverse Learners

Key Question: How do effective teachers engage students?

Directions: Observe your cooperating teacher as he gives directions to the class. How does he state the directions? Does he present them in a variety of ways to accommodate all types of learners? How will you present directions when you are teaching? Notice how *you* prefer to receive directions when you are learning something new. Ask your English-language learners how they need to receive directions. Pay attention to any students who are hearing or sight impaired.

How does your cooperating teacher give directions?

Verbal: Are they clear? How long does it take to give them? Did they have several steps?

Visual: Are they written on the board, shown overhead, or given to students?

What does his voice sound like when giving directions?

Volume: Can the directions be heard at the back of the room?

Pronunciation: Are the words pronounced correctly?

Articulation: How clearly are words expressed?

Speed: Are key points spoken slowly enough for all to understand?

Where is the teacher in the classroom when giving directions?

Position: Where did the teacher stand? Was he sitting?

Movement: Did the teacher move around to check on the students?

What else did you notice about the teacher when he gave directions?

Clarification: Did he allow opportunities for students to ask clarifying questions?

What else did you notice?

How can complicated directions create problems for students who may be learning challenged or do not speak English?

What can you do to avoid potential problems related to the diverse students you have in the classroom?

ACTivity 7.4 Using Brain-Based Strategies

Key Question: How do effective teachers engage students?

Teachers are continuing to learn and understand how the brain works and how they can use this information to more effectively present curriculum and utilize instructional strategies to best advantage.

Directions: Talk with your cooperating teacher(s), university supervisor, and peers to see what they know about brain research.

Ten Concepts to Keep in Mind as You Prepare Lessons for Diverse Learners

1. Humans only use a small part of their brain capacity.
2. Effective effort has more to do with success than does intelligence, as it is currently measured in schools.
3. Learners are constantly trying to construct meaning by looking for connections and patterns.
4. People learn best when they feel safe and reasonably sure that they will be successful.
5. People learn best when they can use the new information learned in a relevant way.
6. The search for meaning occurs through *patterning*.
7. Learners' emotions are critical to patterning.
8. Learning involves conscious and unconscious processing.
9. Learning involves focus and peripheral attention.
10. Complex learning is enhanced by challenge and inhibited by threat.

What do you already know about brain research?

How will you use what you know in your classroom?

Go to **beginwiththebrain.com** for more information to help you choose effective learning strategies for your diverse learners.

ACTivity 7.5 Differentiating Whole-Class Instruction: Lectures and Presentations

Key Question: How do effective teachers differentiate instruction?

The most common practices in whole-class instruction are described in the following table. The problem with whole-group strategies is that the students are often "passive" participants in the process. When using these strategies, check for understanding throughout the lesson.

Directions: Review the chart and think about when this type of instruction is appropriate. Discuss with your cooperating teacher how to integrate other instructional strategies with whole-class instruction.

Strategy	Purpose
Lecture	Introducing unit or lesson, sharing a personal experience, summarizing a lesson or unit, providing information that students could not learn any other way, describing a problem
Class discussion	Creating questions that relate to the lecture and posing them to class during or after lecture
Demonstration lesson	Visually presenting an experiment or model for class to show "how" something should look
Simulation	"Hooking" students during introduction of a new concept
Reading	Reading a passage, book, or poem to the class to have them respond to it, etc.

Observe your cooperating teacher using these methods and ask why she has selected a whole-group strategy. Many times, whole-class strategies are incorporated into a lesson for either the introduction or the closing of a lesson, with small groups or paired learning in between.

How will you know if students are learning in a large group? Even teaching in a large group may require you to "differentiate" instruction.

Differentiated instruction means the teacher will provide:

1. Materials and readings that represent several reading levels

2. Choices for students as to "how" they will complete a task

3. A variety of possible product/process options that would provide evidence of learning by the students

4. A balance between whole-class, pairs, small groups, and individual learning

The teacher needs to pay attention to:

1. Readiness levels of students

2. Learning styles of students

3. Interests of students

Talk with your cooperating teacher about the learners in your classroom and how you can use differentiated instruction for struggling or advanced learners.

What do you see as the challenges of using differentiated instruction in the classroom?

ACTivity 7.6 Flexible and Cooperative Learning Groups

Key Question: How do effective teachers differentiate instruction?

Flexible grouping is a strategy for creating groups based on students' academic needs. *Flexible* means that the student is not "tracked" into this group for the whole year, but rather she works in this group only until the skill is mastered. Groups change regularly, so that no student stays with the same tracked group or is labeled as being in a low, middle, or high group. New groups are formed as the class moves on to new skills or material. The teacher works with the group while other students work independently. The teacher rotates to all groups during the week and has an opportunity to work with all students in this smaller setting. This allows the teacher to check for understanding and to get closer to each student. Flexible-grouping strategies vary by grade level.

Cooperative learning is currently being used in a variety of formats in schools. Teachers have students work in pairs, triads, and small groups. Some teachers use the groups for project work; others use the pairs or groups to practice new skills with each other. The key to cooperative learning is that you have to "teach" the students how to work cooperatively *before* you can expect them to do it.

Directions: How does an effective cooperative group or pair look in your classroom?

If you or your cooperating teacher has never tried cooperative learning, start by pairing students some time during your practicum so you have practice with this skill.

For young students, try using

- **Partners as coaches** Let each student in the room select another student who will be his partner for support. When he is absent, this person can collect the papers for him through the day. When he doesn't understand a concept, he can go to this person for help.

- **Paired learners** Pair students with pupils who are alike in learning styles, need, or interests, and let them enjoy working together on a special activity.

- **High/low learners** Let students who have grasped a concept work with students who have not.

- **Paired share** In any class for two or more minutes, let the students turn to the person next to them and share something you have already set up.

- **Paired readers** Either by choice or design, let students read aloud to each other.

For older students, ask them to

- Turn to the person next to them and share the answer to the question on the board.

- Read a page and answer the questions together.

- Predict what will come next and present it to the class together.

- Compare their homework and correct any errors before passing it in.

What are some other ways students can work in pairs?

How is cooperative learning different from flexible grouping?

ACTivity 7.7 Using Multiple Intelligences to Teach

Key Question: How do effective teachers differentiate instruction?

Howard Gardner's research on multiple intelligences has added new approaches to working with diverse learners.

Directions: Review these and brainstorm activities with your cooperating teacher that would demonstrate ways your students could express their learning though their own "intelligences."

Intelligence	Possible Activities for Demonstrating Learning in the Classroom
Bodily–Kinesthetic Processing though touch, movement, drama	Learning centers, models, etc.
Intrapersonal Processing personally through reflection	Journals, goal setting, etc.
Interpersonal Processing by sharing	Cooperative groups, teaching another student, etc.
Verbal–Linguistic Processing through reading, writing, speaking, listening	Discussions, etc.
Musical–Rhythmic processing through rhythm, moods, melodies, sounds	Choral readings, lyrics, etc.
Logical–Mathematical Processing through numbers, patterns	Logic, story problems, etc.
Visual–Spatial Processing through images and visualizing	Charts, posters, video, etc.
Naturalist	Nature walks, knowing names of trees, seasons, weather, etc.
Existential	Philosophy, religion—big questions: "Who am I?" "Why am I here?" etc.

Let the students create activities with you!

ACTivity 7.8 Using Bloom's Taxonomy to Vary Questioning Techniques

Key Question: How do effective teachers differentiate instruction?

Directions: Bloom's taxonomy of thinking is listed from most complex to least complex in the following table. Create a variety of instructional activities at different levels for the diverse learners in your room. Use the same content. This will be a good exercise to save for your first classroom.

Level	Taxonomy	Example of Strategy
6	**Evaluation** Examine all parts of a concept to evaluate or assess the significance.	Read a passage and evaluate the author's message and present it.
5	**Synthesis** Combine a new concept with what you already know to construct new knowledge.	Use the information given with your own ideas to pose an argument.
4	**Analysis** Separate a new concept into its parts and understand the relationships.	Compare and contrast.
3	**Application** Solve a problem by applying the knowledge learned.	Use the words in sentences, and make a chart to show what you learned.
2	**Comprehension** Explain or restate ideas.	Summarize in your own words.
1	**Knowledge** Recognize and recall facts.	Memorize or recite.

Use the taxonomy to note the types of questions you are using in your lessons. Also note the types of questions your students are asking in class. Are they asking questions during your lessons? Why or why not? Copy this chart and collect some data related to your use of questions.

Questions YOU Use in a Given Lesson	How Many at Levels 4–6?	Questions YOUR STUDENTS Ask in a Lesson	How Many at Levels 4–6?
Examples		Examples	

(continued on next page)

(continued from previous page)

Strive to Use Higher Levels of the Taxonomy in Your Lessons!

Open-ended questions allow students to expand their thinking on a particular topic. These types of questions require more than a yes or no answer because they require the students to think about the issue in a more complex way. Such questions would relate to the higher levels of Bloom's taxonomy.

You may ask open-ended questions as part of your introduction to a teaching unit and explain that students will be learning about this topic in such a way that this question will be answered.

Use the basic questions Who, What, Where, When, How, and Why to develop open-ended questions to bring your students to higher levels of thinking.

EXAMPLES OF OPEN-ENDED QUESTIONS

_____

_____

_____

_____

_____

_____

_____

_____

_____

_____

_____

_____

_____

_____

Open-ended questions can act as motivators to grab the students' attention as well as being part of the assessment process at the end of the unit.

Review your textbooks and teacher's edition for examples of open-ended questions. Are questions categorized in your texts? Do those sources provide questions at the rote knowledge/comprehension level or at higher levels?

Use **KWL** as a strategy to find out what students **K**now about the topic, what they **W**ant to know, and what they **L**earned (at the end of the unit).

Don't forget to **ask the students** what their questions are before, during, and at the end of lessons and units. They can write them on index cards and leave them in a "Question Box" for you to answer at a later time. If you are repeatedly receiving the same questions, you may want to clarify one of your objectives. Formulating good questions is challenging and an important skill for students to learn!

What types of questions are students asking in the classes you observe or teach?

ACTivity 7.9 Students with Special Needs

Key Question: How do effective teachers modify for students with special needs?

Directions: Take some time to observe the behavior of the special needs students in your classroom. Based on what you see, can you identify what they need to be successful?

In addition to observing, also review their files and individualized education programs (IEPs). Use the forms from Chapter 2 to organize your thoughts and document your observations.

A daily observation for as little as 15 minutes can reveal significant information about a student's learning style and needs. Observe students in your classroom, on the playground, and in any other learning environment. This collected data will provide you with practical teacher-applicable research to inform your practice.

1. Shadow one of your students who has special needs for part of a school day. Ask yourself these questions:

   In your opinion, does the IEP match the student's needs?

   Does the student behave differently on the playground? in the cafeteria? outside the building? in the large group? passing in the hallway? in small groups? in pairs? in another classroom setting— such as art, music, physical education? during instructional time? playing sports?

   What surprised you about the student?

   What is the student doing well?

2. Interview the student after you have completed your shadow observations. Ask the student:

   "What do you like about school?" "What do you find difficult?" How could you, as her teacher, assist her in learning?

   Think about and discuss with your cooperating teacher or supervisor how the information you collected can assist you in meeting the needs of other students who have special needs in your classroom.

   How does this process of observing help you become a better teacher?

ACTivity 7.10 Students with Special Needs: Individual Education Plans

Key Question: How do effective teachers modify for students with special needs?

Directions: *Special education* and *inclusion* are popular terms used in schools today. How a teacher groups students with special needs within the classroom is important. Are the students part of the flexible- or cooperative-grouping procedures? Ask your cooperating teacher how the school and district support students with special needs.

How much adapting will you have to do in your lessons to accommodate and enrich the lives of students who are dealing with physical or emotional challenges?

_____

What do you already know about the students with special needs in your classroom?

_____

What questions do you have?

_____

Discuss with your cooperating teacher any students who have been identified as "at risk" in your classroom. Ask him to explain what the criteria are for determining the risk and to share the student's individualized education program with you.

List the students' names here if you need to review their IEPs. (Note that these plans may be confidential and that parents need to sign them.) Review the plans for any learning adaptations you will have to integrate into your teaching.

_____

Interview the special education director or teacher in your school. Here are some sample questions to ask:

    Does the state have a law or policy relating to students with special needs?

    How is *special needs* defined in your state?

    If the school is currently using "inclusion," how does it work?

    Are some students "pulled out" of classrooms for tutoring? How does this work?

    What is the role of the teacher within special education inclusion models?

    Do classroom teachers coteach with special education teachers?

Additional Notes:

_____

ACTivity 7.11 Students with Special Needs: Modifying Lessons

Key Question: How do effective teachers modify for students with special needs?

Directions: Read this page and discuss with your cooperating teacher. Then interview your cooperating teacher and ask:

> How do you know which activities you can leave incomplete and which have to be done?
>
> How do you pace a lesson so that all or most students complete the task?
>
> How do you create high expectations for learners who work more slowly?

Optional: Discuss with your cooperating teacher how lessons can be modified for gifted and talented students.

Students with academic special needs often have a range of abilities. The lessons you design to meet the curriculum objectives may need to be modified or adapted to be in compliance with students' IEPs or to meet students at their own skill levels. Students think and work at different speeds. Include English-language learners in your special needs group so they can get the help they need.

Be aware that some students who finish quickly may not have actually understood the concept being taught. Some who work more slowly may be thoughtful thinkers who see the complexity in every concept. Notice how the students in your classes complete their work. The fastest workers are not always the most accurate or most creative problem solvers. Don't get trapped into rewarding those who finish first. Always check for accuracy! Sometimes it doesn't matter whether the whole assignment is complete—you can check for understanding with what IS done and not use the incompleteness as a negative assessment of growth.

EXAMPLES OF MODIFICATION

- Giving a student more time to complete an assignment
- Assigning fewer questions or examples to be completed
- Allowing students to record verbal answers instead of writing them
- Working with a partner who would write the answers the student stated verbally
- Accepting printed work instead of cursive
- Using a computer to complete work

ACTivity 7.12 Giving Students Choices

Key Question: How do effective teachers empower students to take responsibility for their own learning?

Directions: Discuss the ways in which you can give students choices in the classroom. Students usually know how they learn best, and if you can offer them a variety of ways in which to show you that they know the material, they will feel more successful and will be more invested in the work. Ask your cooperating teacher how he uses choice in the classroom. If he doesn't allow for choice, discuss how it might be used in limited, appropriate ways to provide opportunities for students.

Here are some examples of ways choice can be incorporated into your classroom:

- Choosing a homework assignment from three that are acceptable
- Choosing a partner to work with on a project
- Choosing an independent reading book
- Choosing the type of test (multiple choice, essay, short answer)
- Creating a test by choosing all the items that would go on the test

List other ways to incorporate choice into your classroom that would promote student interest.

_____

_____

_____

_____

Students could use the following to solve a particular work problem:

- Use paper and pencil
- Use manipulatives
- Draw the answer
- Work alone
- Work with a partner
- Act out the answer

Can you think of ways in which you could provide your students with choice without disrupting curriculum and while still supporting the needs of diverse learners?

_____

_____

_____

_____

ACTivity 7.13 Enrichment and Homework

Key Question: How do effective teachers empower students to take responsibility for their own learning?

Directions: Read this page and discuss with your cooperating teacher. Include your ideas for enrichment and homework.

ENRICHMENT

Enrichment can be offered to students who have a deeper interest in the topic or who may complete in-class work early (and accurately). Special activities in a learning center, questions on the board, or enrichment sheets provide opportunities for more connection to a particular topic.

Ask your cooperating teacher how she provides enrichment activities for gifted and talented students, students who complete work early, or students who have a genuine interest in a topic being covered.

Ideas for enrichment:

_____

_____

_____

_____

Note: Enrichment should not just be a reward for those who complete their work early. Students who have varying paces may never have a chance to try more challenging activities offered. Create one day a month as an "enrichment" period and let students select a topic they truly enjoy learning about. These topics could become "clubs" where students meet regularly to learn more about what they like.

HOMEWORK

Observe and interview your cooperating teacher about homework policies. Do students have to hand in homework? Is it always required? Does it only relate to the text? Do students get to select homework activities? Is homework extra credit? Does your cooperating teacher correct homework? If not, how does it count toward the grade? Is there such a thing as "creative" homework?

What are your ideas about using homework as part of the curriculum?

_____

_____

_____

_____

What happens if students don't do their homework? For example, what if some students did not read the chapter you assigned, and the lesson you have designed is centered heavily on their having read it? What do then you do about the planned lesson?

ACTivity 7.14 Using Technology and Audiovisual Aids to Teach

Key Question: How do effective teachers empower students to take responsibility for their own learning?

Directions: Audiovisual materials and computers can be an integral component in creating a rich teaching and learning environment. They also provide other ways for varied-learning-style students to approach a learning activity. Ask your students to tell you about innovative ways to use technology! Empower your students to become teachers!

Review the list of materials and code them by your level of familiarity as you begin your practicum.

Key   C = Comfortable with using this resource

         N = Need to learn how to use this resource—perhaps students can help!

C or N	Types of Technology	Where I Might Integrate into My Teaching
	Overhead projector	
	Document viewer (ELMO)	
	Computer/computer lab	
	CD/CD-ROM	
	HD video camera	
	VCR and TV/DVD	
	Tape recorder with headsets	
	LCD Projector- Infocus	
	Video recorder	
	Digital camera	
	Cell phone apps	
	Interactive whiteboard	
	Computer programs	

What other technologies should be on the list? Ask your students to keep you updated! Challenge yourself to use a new kind of technology during each week of your practicum! Have the students work with you so they are learning the technology with you.

ACJivity 7.15 Service Learning: Contributing to the Community

Key Question: How do effective teachers empower students to take responsibility for their own learning?

Directions: Service learning is a way in which students in your classes can participate in the larger community. Ask your cooperating teacher whether the school or her classroom is currently participating in a service-learning project.

WAYS TO CONTRIBUTE

Sometimes high school students receive academic credit for their projects and actually work as interns in public jobs during the school day. Elementary students may visit nursing homes or shelters and read to the residents. Connecting your students through the existing curriculum is a better way to include service than simply "adding" on another activity for already busy students. Service learning engages students and makes the curriculum come alive for all learners. Service projects can also be offered as enrichment, extra credit, and homework for those students who are committed to making a difference.

Examples of Service-Learning Activities

History, middle/high	Interview and audiorecord World War II veterans and then have them come to the classroom as guest speakers.
	Provide a service to the local veterans' association as part of this activity.
Science, middle/high	Connect with a recycling center on a project that relates to the science unit on recycling.
Elementary	Write to the elderly and visit them on holidays; use as language arts.
Elementary, middle/high	Work at a shelter or soup kitchen and write about the experience.
Elementary	Invite local businesses into the classroom while learning about professions and select one that needs a special project completed.
Other ideas?	

How can you integrate service learning into your student teaching practicum?

_____

_____

_____

_____

Why is it important to have students make the connection between learning information and service learning?

$\mathcal{R}$EFLECT and SET GOALS

$\mathcal{T}$hink about...

Directions: Review the four Key Questions for this chapter and then respond to the three questions in the "To deepen your thinking" segment.

Key Questions:

1. How do effective teachers engage students? (ACTivities 7.1–7.2)

2. How do effective teachers differentiate instruction? (ACTivities, 7.3–7.8)

3. How do effective teachers modify for students with special needs? (ACTivities 7.9–7.11)

4. How do effective teachers empower students to take responsibility for their own learning? (ACTivities 7.12–7.15)

$\mathcal{R}$eflect...

Reflect on the activities related to your beliefs, readiness, and preparation.

How do your expectations for learners influence your instructional strategies choices?

Why can engaging students minimize behavior problems?

How does empowerment contribute to your community of learners?

$\mathcal{S}$ET GOALS: Possible Next Steps...

Create and Collect Portfolio Artifacts from Chapter Activities

If you are creating an e-portfolio, format your documents appropriately.

✓ Include your students' learning-styles assessment as an example.

✓ Create an enrichment activity to show you know how to do that.

✓ List the ways you know how to modify lessons for students with special needs.

All of these artifacts can be used to meet final student teaching requirements and to help you compile your job interview presentation portfolios. Begin now!

chapter 8

Effective Planning Strategies to Promote Student Learning

"The hardest part of student teaching is the PLANNING! I hate planning. I hated it when I first started, and I hate it now. However, it is the single-most important thing (followed by organization). There were days when I did not have time to plan. Those days were awful. The anxiety that came along with the knowledge that I had not planned was stifling, and the classes were chaotic. I hated those days. . . . I hated them more than I hated planning.

Student Teacher

The ability to plan high-quality lessons that engage students in learning experiences that promote thinking and understanding is the essence of good teaching. Designing curriculum is an important task for teachers and one that is becoming increasingly more important as student performance and outcomes are used to assess success in schools. High standards and clear expectations for what students should know and be able to do is currently a main focus of education. Classroom planning needs to reflect these high expectations and standards.

Teachers need excellent planning and preparation skills. Knowledge of the subject matter that integrates the content with other disciplines, being able to build on students' existing knowledge, and the proficiency to teach for understanding are skills expected of all new teachers. In addition, teachers need to understand who their students are by understanding the many aspects of their students' age group, interests, and ability levels. Planning also requires a clear articulation of the goals and objectives that teachers are trying to achieve. Finally, good planning and preparation require that teachers know what materials and resources are available and how to use them to create a positive learning experience for all students.

Student teachers often view planning as an isolated activity related to the lesson they are teaching and as a necessity of meeting their requirements for student teaching. In reality, planning is a critical component of instruction and it connects teaching to all aspects of the school day. Good lesson planning can promote positive classroom management and lessen behavior issues. The objectives in your lesson plan should relate to the learning outcomes you expect from the students. A cycle of plan, teach, assess, and reteach becomes the model for moving through curriculum objectives. Assessments, whether formal or informal, must relate to the plan. The ultimate goal for planning and assessment is student learning. Do your plans promote understanding and accomplishment, or are they just telling students what to do?

Teachers use both long-range and short-term planning. Yearly and quarterly planning are long-range planning skills. This provides an opportunity for the teacher to view the curriculum and align it with system and state frameworks. Some school districts have created their own curriculum plans that provide teachers with frameworks for teaching. Check with your cooperating teacher to see whether your school has developed these plans. Short-term planning includes unit plans, weekly plans, and daily lesson plans.

During your student teaching experience, you most likely will participate only in short-term planning. Ask your cooperating teacher to share her planning strategies with you. Ask how her plans are reviewed by her department chair or principal. This chapter will provide a variety of daily lesson-plan formats. Select one that meets the needs of your classroom or design a format of your own. You *must* do lesson plans and share them with the cooperating teacher and university supervisor. Create a system for having your plans reviewed prior to teaching. For example, unit plans can be reviewed prior to teaching any of the lessons in the unit. As you teach the unit, daily plans will be created to meet the objectives you have stated. Weekly plan-book plans should be shared the week before you teach. These are short overviews mapping out the whole week indicating what you will be teaching and when. They typically do not include goals, objectives, or materials. Daily plans are the one-page sheets that include a more detailed script of the lesson and materials that you will need.

As you begin your practicum, all lessons you teach should be planned using the daily lesson-plan form. Use the model plans in this chapter, samples from your college courses or create your own template with your cooperating teacher. All plans serve as an outline for your lesson and can be shared with your cooperating teacher prior to teaching the lesson. The plan allows you to think about your objectives for the lesson before you teach. As you move through the semester, your cooperating teacher will give you more teaching assignments and you will become more comfortable in understanding the components of a lesson.

Student teachers often ask, "How many one-page daily forms do I have to do?" "Do I have to write a full-page plan for every lesson I teach?" "Do my plans have to be typed?" "When can I stop full plans and just complete plan-book style plans?" The answers to all these questions depend on the college requirements for obtaining a teacher license, the ability of the student teacher to think about and implement lessons, and the number of classes the student teacher is actually teaching. Daily lesson plans may not have to be typed unless they are being used in a unit that is being presented as part of your exit requirements. Make multiple copies of any of the forms from this chapter and simply handwrite your plan when you are working with your cooperating teacher. If the supervisor requires a typed copy for midterm and final observations, type those lessons. Talk with both your cooperating teacher and university supervisor to meet the lesson plan requirement for your student teaching program.

Student teachers often think that every lesson in their student-teaching binder has to be their own originally created lesson. This may not be the case. You may be coplanning lessons with your cooperating teacher, using plans designed by the textbook company, or following a fairly structured guide that has little room for change. You still need to write out the daily lesson plan for yourself so the plan does not simply say "Read Chapter 2 as the learning objective," but rather, it must state exactly what you are looking for as an outcome from reading Chapter 2. All lessons handwritten or typed, along with weekly plan books and units, should be labeled, dated, and placed in your student-teaching binder to be shared with your university supervisor on a regular basis.

Remember that plans *are meant to be revised, reworked, redesigned, and adjusted to meet the needs of the learners.* The plan itself is not the goal, but rather you are striving to create a plan that promotes "teaching for understanding and student learning." Writing the plan is not the end result.

What's Your PLAN for Learning?

Directions for getting the most out of this section: The PLAN section provides you with some "big ideas" for lesson planning as well as two Key Questions to think about. What do you already know about lesson and unit planning? Find those sample plans you created in coursework and pre-practicum experiences and review them now. Can you use any of them? Planning formats vary from school to school and university to university. Review the planning templates in this chapter, and use them as models that can be adjusted to meet your needs. Remember, an effective plan minimizes student distraction and maximizes learning. How will you design a plan to meet your needs during the practicum?

Key Questions:

1. **What is planning?** The *Plan* ACTivities on the ACT pages will provide you with specific strategies for thinking about planning.
2. **What are some effective models for daily lesson planning?** The *Lessons* ACTivities in this chapter offer you grade-level options for long-form planning templates.

PLAN to Discuss Professional Standards

inTASC Standards

Instructional Practice

Discuss this standard with your cooperating teacher and/or your university supervisor.

Standard #7: *Planning for Instruction.* The teacher plans instruction that supports every student in meeting rigorous learning goals by drawing upon knowledge of content areas, curriculum cross-disciplinary skills, and pedagogy, as well as knowledge of learners and the community context.

How does this professional standard relate to the Key Questions in this chapter? How is your cooperating teacher supporting students to meet learning goals?

Source: The Interstate New Teacher Assessment and Support Consortium (InTASC) standards were developed by the Council of Chief State School Officers and member states. Copies may be downloaded from the Council's website at **ccsso.org.** Council of Chief State School Officers and Interstate Teacher Assessment and Support Consortium. (2011, April). *InTASC Model Core Teaching Standards: A Resource for State Dialogue.* Washington, DC: Author, 2011.

CONNECT

CONNECT is a resource page with ideas and suggestions to support you during student teaching. Select and complete any CONNECT items that will enhance your experience in the classroom.

CONNECT with People

- Student teachers and your cooperating teacher and supervisor: Ask them to share copies of lesson plans they have found successful.

CONNECT with Readings and Resources

- Books and authors to explore on the Internet or at your local library:

  Rethinking Homework: Best Practices That Support Diverse Needs, by Cathy Vatterott (Association for Supervision and Curriculum Development [ASCD])

  Productive Group Work: How to Engage Students, Build Teamwork, and Promote Understanding, by Nancy Frey, Douglas Fisher, and Sandi Everlove (ASCD)

  An Educator's Guide to Block Scheduling: Decision Making, Curriculum Design, and Lesson Planning Strategies, by Mary M. Bevevino (Allyn & Bacon)

  Active Learning: 101 Strategies to Teach Any Subject, by Mel Silberman (Allyn & Bacon)

  Teaching and Learning Through Multiple Intelligences, by Linda Campbell, Bruce Campbell, and Dee Dickinson (Allyn & Bacon)

CONNECT Technology to Teaching

- Need lesson plans?

  Ask ERIC Lesson Plans (askeric.org/Virtual/Lessons/)

  Lesssonplans4teachers and search best lesson plans for more sites

- Check out other websites to see what works for you:

  school.discovery.com/schrockguide/index.html

  mrsp.com

  onemorestory.com

  en.childrenslibrary.org

  dawcl.com

  thelearningpage.org

ACT

Directions: ACT pages are designed to offer you options for planning lessons and units of study. The activities listed here relate to the Key Questions provided at the beginning of the chapter, and they are just suggestions. Review the strategies here and compare them to what you have learned in your seminar or courses. Implement the ideas that will be most useful to you.

Key Question Topic	ACTivity	Page	Check
Plan	8.1 Standards-Based Planning		
Plan	8.2 Planning with My Cooperating Teacher		
Plan	8.3 Five Important Planning Skills		
Plan	8.4 Unit Planning		
Plan	8.5 Planning Effective Lessons		
Plan	8.6 Planning for Student Understanding		
Plan	8.7 Writing Teaching Objectives		
Plan	8.8 Ineffective Lesson Planning		
Plan	8.9 Time and Planning		
Lessons	8.10 How To Complete a Daily Lesson-Plan Form		
Lessons	8.11 General Guide to Planning		
Lessons	8.12 Sample Early-Childhood Format		
Lessons	8.13 Sample Elementary and Middle School Format		
Lessons	8.14 Sample Secondary Format		
Lessons	8.15 Design a Plan of Your Own		

ACJivity 8.1 Standards-Based Planning

Key Question: What is planning?

Standards are being used in states and school districts to determine whether successful learning has taken place. These measures, or "outcomes," of students may determine funding or resources for schools. The federal No Child Left Behind Act (NCLB) stresses standards.

Standards apply to all students in a school, but all students may not be able to achieve or demonstrate the standard in the same way. This is why teachers need a variety of instructional strategies to meet the needs of diverse learners.

Directions: Interview your cooperating teacher about state standards that students are expected to know and be able to do. If you are planning to move to another state after student teaching, this is a good time to look at that state's standards. Compare them to those of your student teaching state.

1. What are the standards or frameworks this school/teacher is using? How are they reflected in her planning? How are they impacted by her instructional strategies?

2. How does your cooperating teacher integrate school and/or state standards in her classes/ classroom?

3. How were the standards that are established being used? Are they fair? Will all students be able to meet these standards?

4. How is preassessment used in lesson planning to reveal prior knowledge?

5. How is data-driven instruction informing your lesson planning?

How will this information assist you in getting hired for your first teaching position?

ACTivity 8.2 Planning with My Cooperating Teacher

Key Question: What is planning?

Directions: What do you already know about lesson and unit planning from the courses you have taken? This is the time to review and select the appropriate formats for your success in student teaching. The samples and templates in this chapter will expand your knowledge of planning or reinforce what you already know. It is one thing to write an "ideal" plan in a course and other to actually write a plan that you have to teach!

Prior-Knowledge Assessment—Rate your planning skills. Are you ready to plan lessons on your own and implement your plans?

1. What do you already know about lesson planning?

2. Did your college preparation program provide you with a planning template?

3. Do you know how to plan a unit? If yes, where did you learn? If no, who will help you?

4. Who will assist you in developing daily lesson plans?

5. What are the elements of a good plan? List them here.

6. If you have a required format from the university, share it with your cooperating teacher. How does her format differ or conform to what you know about planning?

PLANNING WITH YOUR COOPERATING TEACHER

At the beginning of your student teaching, the cooperating teacher will often suggest you teach part of a class or continue with a plan she may have already created. Student teachers quickly notice that cooperating teachers often don't have a LONG plan like those listed in this book. They ask if they must write a long plan or if could they just model what the teacher is doing. During student teaching it is highly recommended that you do as many detailed lesson plans as possible (especially when you are being observed by your supervisor), to ensure you understand the planning process. Shorter plans are for more experienced teachers who have internalized the components of the plan and understand how to implement a lesson.

How will you use this information in your portfolio?

ACTivity 8.3 Five Important Planning Skills

Key Question: What is planning?

Directions: As a teacher, you will always be planning curriculum and designing lessons. As a student teacher, you may not participate in all aspects of planning because the cooperating teacher has probably completed much of the long-range planning. Interview your cooperating teacher or department chair to determine how yearly and quarterly plans are designed and implemented. Take notes for future reference so you will be prepared to plan curriculum for your own classroom next year. Discuss the Long-Range Plans questions listed here with your cooperating teacher so you will understand this information for your first classroom.

Use the examples in this chapter to guide your planning for student teaching and your first classroom.

LONG-RANGE PLANS: YEARLY PLANNING

Purpose:

How were plans created?

What guides the plans?

    City/school system

    School or state curriculum guides

    Department

What does the plan look like?

LONG-RANGE PLANS: QUARTERLY PLANNING

Purpose:

How were plans created?

What guides the plans?

    City/school system

    School or state curriculum guides

    Department

What does the plan look like?

(continued on next page)

(continued from previous page)

SHORT-TERM PLANS: UNIT PLANNING

Short-term planning includes units, weekly plans, and daily lessons. It supports the goals of the long-term plans and puts into action these goals on a daily basis. Interview your cooperating teacher, department chair, or other teachers in the building to discover how they organize their short-term planning.

Units may be organized around themes or subject areas. Some units are interdisciplinary and use a variety of knowledge content areas. Units have a beginning and an end.

- Review examples of "model" units from your school of education. How are they organized?

- Ask your cooperating teacher to share units she has completed. What do you notice?

SHORT-TERM PLANS: WEEKLY PLAN-BOOK PLANNING

Teachers commonly complete weekly plans in a plan book distributed by the school system. These books are often available in office supply stores, and you may want to purchase one to document the lesson you will be teaching during the week.

Another option is to copy a page from your teacher's plan book. Make multiple copies and place them in a three-ring binder to use as your own plan book. This will give you a complete documentation of all lessons you have taught.

- How is your cooperating teacher's plan book organized?

- Is it color coded? Could it be?

- How will you organize your plan book?

SHORT-TERM PLANS: DAILY LESSON PLANNING

Daily lesson plans stem from long-range planning and short-term planning goals. Examples of daily lesson plans are located in this chapter.

- Does your cooperating teacher ever have a need for a daily plan?

- How did he do his daily plans when he was student teaching?

- What is the value to the daily plan in the scheme of long- and short-term planning?

How will your knowledge of short term planning help you in a job interview?

ACTivity 8.4 Unit Planning

Key Question: What is planning?

A unit is an organized group of lesson plans with a beginning, various activities, and a culmination. The unit may be subject based, interdisciplinary, or thematic. It can last as long as a semester or as short as a week. It has overarching themes and concepts to be learned through daily lessons. Teachers typically organize their instruction in teaching units according to skills, for early-childhood level; by subjects or themes, for elementary and middle grades; or by subject area topics, at secondary levels. Units are organized around books students have read, historical wars, science themes, topics, or anything you can think of that relates to knowledge.

A unit will have a general outline or plan for implementation as well as the daily lesson plans that demonstrate in detail how the unit is to be implemented in the classroom. Lesson plans are created *as you move through the unit,* not ahead of time, because the original plan often changes.

Directions: Review some unit plans that your cooperating teacher has created so you understand how units are developed. Also refer back to units you have created in teacher education courses. Consider the following questions when reviewing unit formats:

- What is the purpose of the unit?
- How much time will the unit require? How many lessons?
- What do students already know?
- What would students like to learn or know?
- How will the unit be introduced?
- What are the key questions that need to be answered?
- Is prior knowledge necessary?
- Will the unit have a theme?
- Will the unit cross disciplines? Is team teaching involved?
- Will any special activities be part of the unit?
- Will I need special materials or audiovisuals for this unit?
- Will guest speakers or field trips be part of the unit?
- Other?

UNIT ORGANIZERS

Unit organizers are valuable ways to map out your unit. Ask your cooperating teacher and university supervisor to share examples of unit organizers with you, which can serve as models for your unit outlines. Another way to organize is a learning web. Adapt this example to web the key ideas in your content unit.

What units do you already have that you can use as models?

ACTivity 8.5 Planning Effective Lessons

Key Question: What is planning?

Directions: Ask yourself the following questions and engage in a discussion with your cooperating teacher and supervisor so you stay on track while planning lessons.

- **Why am I teaching this lesson? What is the learning standard? Is data driving my instructional plan? Where did this data come from?**
  Required curriculum? Student interest in topic? Your interest in topic?

- **What do I hope to accomplish? Is there a preassessment required?**
  Skill to be developed? Concept to be discussed for understanding? Product to be produced?

- **Who are the students in this classroom?**
  Range of abilities? Range of ages? Ethnic diversity and varying cultures?

- **What is the time frame for teaching this lesson?**
  Part of a unit? One period or block schedule? Isolated lesson?

- **How will I begin the lesson to capture student attention?**
  Story, anecdote? Relevance to their lives? Props or visual displays?

- **Will I need other resources to teach this lesson?** Audiovisual or technology? Student handouts?
  Manipulatives or visual displays?

- **How will students spend their time during the lesson?**
  Small-group discussion? Individual? Large group? Hands-on activity or experiment? Taking notes or observing?

- **Should I anticipate any student-behavior issues?**
  Are there students on behavior plans? Are the materials I distribute safe?

- **How will this lesson be assessed?**
  Formal? Quiz or test? Informal? Observation of learning? Open-ended questions? Written? Verbal?

- **How will I close the lesson and close the class period?**
  Review and summary? Collecting papers? Giving next assignment? Allowing time for homework or questions?

- **Will there be homework or enrichment activities offered?**
  How will I collect later? Is it required or extra? Will it count? What is cooperating teacher's policy? How will I grade it?

- **How will I know whether I succeeded in teaching the lesson?**
  Self-assessment? Response of students? Cooperating teacher input?

- **How will the next lesson relate or build on this one?**

How will my answers to these questions help me design more effective lesson plans?

ACTivity 8.6 Planning for Student Understanding

Key Question: What is planning?

A teacher knows he has a good plan when, at the end of the lesson or unit, there is evidence of student understanding or skill development. An effective teacher, like an architect, designs a plan that will create a solid foundation for creative and original thinking. Teachers present information not just to be memorized for the weekly test, but so it is understood and integrated into a student's thinking. This is not an easy task, but one that should be kept in your awareness as you begin to plan lessons.

Directions: Review the five questions listed here and see how they relate to your thinking as you plan lessons with your cooperating teacher. What do you want students to know, understand, and be able to do *as a result of your lesson?*

1. *How will you think about breadth or depth as you design your lessons and units?*

   Are you aiming for breadth in your lessons (i.e., being able to connect this concept to other concepts or relevant experiences)?

   - Students explain why or why not.

   - Students extend the concept to others.

   - Students think about and give examples of similar concepts.

   Are you aiming for depth in your lessons (i.e., looking at the detail about this idea)?
   - Students question the information.

   - Students analyze the facts.

   - Students prove something.

2. *How will you set priorities for assessing student growth in lessons and units?*
   What do you expect all students to be familiar with?
   - To be able to do in this class?

   - To really understand for lasting learning?

3. *How will you select measurement tools to determine student understanding?*
   How will you know students understand?
   - What do *all* students have to know? How will you know they understand?

   - What do *most* students have to know? How will you know they understand?

   - What will *some* students have to know? How will you know they understand?

(continued on next page)

(continued from previous page)

4. *How will you create meaningful learning experiences that engage and support learning (not just busywork)?*

   - **Motivate** Have you included a "hook" to gain attention and provide relevance?

   - **Questions** Do you have key questions that promote discussion and thinking?

   - **Practice** Do you have time for students to practice and engage in activity?

   - **Self-Assessment** Do you allow students time to reflect on their work and set goals?

5. *How will you reflect on what you are doing?*

   What are your expectations for student behaviors in your classroom?

   If you stand at the front of the room and lecture using the board or a podium . . .

   ...the students will be expected to sit quietly and listen to you speak. An observer would see your students taking notes, answering questions if called on and would hear the teacher talking.

   If you engage your students in cooperative activities such as partners and small groups . . .

   ... the students will be expected to talk to their partners or share ideas in a small groups. They may be taking notes, sharing work, reading to each other, or completing a project together. An observer would hear student voices and see the teacher walking around the room interacting with small groups or partners.

   Both types of teaching are important to student success. Think about how you will design lessons that balance your teaching strategies. Always think about what the students are "expected" to be doing and if that expectation is doable. Expecting elementary students to sit and listen to a lecture for 30 minutes is not doable. So a lesson plan with that strategy is doomed to failure because the teacher does not have an understanding of the audience. Plans need to be designed for the student age group you are teaching.

   How does what you do impact how students respond?

ACTivity 8.7 Writing Teaching Objectives

Key Question: What is planning?

Students should be clear about objectives before they begin the lesson so they know what is expected of them. Objectives should be written as one sentence.

Use verbs to write your lesson plan objectives. In the table, see that *Bloom's taxonomy* organizes the verbs by levels of understanding. beginning with basic knowledge and moving up through comprehension, application, analysis, synthesis, and evaluation. Higher level thinking is expected for verbs at Levels 5 and 6. These verbs indicate *what the student should be doing.* This taxonomy is applicable to all grade levels.

Directions: Practice writing objectives using Bloom's taxonomy. State the objective in clear, understandable terms that can easily be understood by students and parents. Be sure to vary the levels of complexity in your lessons by using higher order thinking for your objectives.

Examples:

Name the planets, in order from the Sun.
Predict the ending to this story.
Explain the reasons for the start of the Civil War.

Level of Thinking	Verbs
6 Evaluation	Choose, conclude, evaluate, defend, rank, support, rate
5 Synthesis	Construct, create, formulate, revise, write, plan, predict
4 Analysis	Analyze, classify, compare, contrast, debate, categorize
3 Application	Apply, demonstrate, draw, show, solve, illustrate
2 Comprehension	Describe, explain, paraphrase, summarize, rewrite
1 Knowledge	Define, identify, label, list, memorize, spell, name

How can you use this taxonomy to write learning objectives that challenge your students?

ACTivity 8.8 Ineffective Lesson Planning

Key Question: What is planning?

Directions: What are you thinking as you design your plans? Read these lists and make sure you are on track with the purpose of planning.

If you are thinking . . .

How can I keep the students quiet?

What should I do today?

What can I use from the teacher's edition?

How can I get through this period?

What can I use for busywork?

Should I show a movie this period?

. . . you are not creating lessons for learning.

If you are only creating lessons such as . . .
Read Chapter 2 silently.

Complete this worksheet.

Do the problems on page 65.

Write a paragraph on _____.

. . . you are not teaching and planning lessons for student participation.

This kind of thinking and lesson planning without other types of interaction leads to frustration and poorly designed assignments. Assignments should state what the student will accomplish or achieve when the assignment is *complete*, should not be an activity simply to keep the classroom quiet.

What is your personal experience of ineffective lesson planning?

ACTivity 8.9 Time and Planning

Key Question: What is planning?

One of the biggest concerns teachers have about teaching is that they don't have enough time in the day to accomplish all there is to do. The majority of the time in class should be spent on teaching the curriculum that you have planned, not on making announcements, collecting lunch money, passing out materials, getting students into groups, or cleaning up. However, these tasks do need to get done.

A class period is your "allocated teaching time," but it also needs to include housekeeping activities. "Instructional time" is the time when students are actually engaged in learning activities. Your lesson plan is the way to organize your thinking so that most of the allocated time is spent engaging students in learning and checking for understanding.

Directions: Review the chart and decide how much time you need for the different components of a class period. Write how much time you think you will need in the boxes.

How much time?	Start of class period: Housekeeping activities	• Required tasks • Collection of homework
Time?	Beginning lesson: Introducing or connecting to previous day	• Motivation/relevance • Overview • Directions • Purpose of lesson
Time?	Middle:	• Objective • Key questions • Students engaged in learning • Activity • Knowledge • Student sharing • Informal assessment and checking for understanding
Time?	Closing:	• Wrap up • Review of key points • Collection of materials/papers
Time?	Ending class period: Housekeeping activities	• Required tasks • Collection of class work

Use this as a guide and include *time* as a factor in designing your lesson plans. When you have a particularly complicated lesson with many materials or if you need to move students into groups, take that into consideration and think of ways to prepare and set up so you don't take away from teaching time.

How will planning your time for sections of your lesson help you to stay on track?

ACTivity 8.10 How to Complete a Daily Lesson-Plan Form

Key Question: What are some effective models for daily lesson planning?

Directions: Review this planning guide and compare it to one you will be using.

LESSON PLAN TITLE: Write the name of the topic or class here

DATE: Day you teach lesson **SUBJECT:** Content

TIME OF CLASS: Period of time **LENGTH OF PERIOD:** How much time to teach

PURPOSE OF LESSON: Why are you teaching this lesson? What is the goal you are seeking to reach?

STANDARDS AND OBJECTIVE(S): Bloom's taxonomy verb—what the student will achieve or accomplish

THEME OR UNIT # ___: Is this an isolated lesson or part of a bigger curriculum unit? Number it as to where it fits in the sequence. If there is an expectation that students need prior knowledge to complete the lesson, how will you handle this with new students or those who have missed prerequisite information?

KEY QUESTIONS: The questions you will introduce to the students to guide the discussion, and activities of the lesson should be broadly designed to encourage discussion and critical thinking. (Questions should not be designed for yes-or-no answers.)

PROCEDURE: Note that the class period includes other housekeeping activities, such as collecting papers from the night before, announcing future school activities, or collecting lunch money. These need to be incorporated into the lesson plan to avoid running out of teaching time.

CLASSROOM MANAGEMENT NOTES: Effective planning ensures efficient teaching with a minimum of classroom-discipline issues. Note any problems you foresee as you implement this lesson. For example, if you are using many supplies and students need to leave their seats, you need to be prepared to supervise this movement to avoid problems.

ASSESSMENT TOOL: What are you planning to use to check for understanding? List it here. Does it need to be collected?

FOLLOW-UP: Are there any ending details that need to be put on the board or announced at the end of class, such as homework assignments, extra credit options, or enrichment activities?

STUDENT TEACHER SELF-ASSESSMENT: What is your impression of the lesson and what would you do differently next time you teach it? Write your response on the back of the lesson plan.

SAMPLE PROCEDURE FOR USE OF ALLOCATED CLASSROOM TIME

Directions: Fill out the typical behaviors you will be doing and the students will be doing in each part of the class. Discuss what these behaviors might be with your cooperating teacher.

Time	Classroom Lesson	Teach Behaviors: What Will You Be Doing?	Expected Student Behaviors: What Will the Students Be Doing?
5%	Starting class period	Housekeeping	Listening Passing in homework
10%	Beginning lesson	Introducing objectives, vocabulary, and key questions	Showing interest Participating Listening
70%	Middle of Lesson	Facilitating a variety of activities and formative assessments for student learning	Collaborating Thinking, discussing Responding to key questions
10%	Closing lesson	Summarizing, reviewing, and evaluating lesson objectives. Setting goals for next lesson.	Answering key questions Self-assessing
5%	Ending class period	Housekeeping	Passing in materials

What can you do to ensure you are spending most of your class time on the middle of the lesson?

ACTivity 8.11 General Guide to Planning

Key Question: What are some effective models for daily lesson planning?

Refer to ACTivity 8.10 for help filling out this form.

Directions: Copy this guide and handwrite your notes for lessons you will teach. Type the lessons if needed. The planning process requires you to think about your answers to these topics.

Lesson Plan Title: _____

Date: _____

Time of Class: _____

Length of Period: _____

Subject: _____

Purpose of Lesson: _____

Standards and Objective(s): _____

Theme(s) or Unit #: _____

Key Questions:
1. _____
2. _____
3. _____

Key Words:
1. _____   4. _____
2. _____   5. _____
3. _____   6. _____

Procedures: _____

_____

Anticipated Classroom Management Issues: _____

Formative Assessment and Summative Evaluation Tools: _____

_____

Follow-Up/HW: _____

Self-Assessment: After the lesson, complete these questions.

How did the lesson go?

What will I do differently next time?

Tomorrow I need to_____.

ACTivity 8.12 Sample Pre-School and Early Childhood Template

Key Question: What are some effective models for daily lesson planning?

Directions: Discuss planning practices for pre-school and early childhood classroom. How do teachers know when to move forward?

Date: _____

Subject: _____

Unit Lesson #: _____

Standards and Objectives for Lesson

1. _____

2. _____

Skills	Materials	Assessment
		What will *all* students learn?
		What will *most* students learn?
		What will *some* students learn?

ACJivity 8.13 Sample Elementary or Middle School Template

Key Question: What are some effective models for daily lesson planning?

Directions: Make copies of this template and use it to guide your thinking as you plan your lessons.

Why Am I Teaching This Lesson?_____

Lesson Topic:_____

Standard(s):_____

Subject:_____

Date:_____

Behavioral Objectives: (What do you expect students to know and be able to do?)

1. _____
2. _____
3. _____

Key Vocabulary		Key Questions
1. _____ 4. _____		1. _____
2. _____ 5. _____		2. _____
3. _____ 6. _____		3. _____

Materials/Resources/Technology

Procedure (beginning, middle, closing)

Assessment (How will I know students learned?)

Classroom Management Notes/Lesson Modifications

Homework/Follow-Up/Enrichment

Teacher Self-Assessment of Lesson:

What would I do differently? (Write here or attach.)

ACTivity 8.14 Sample Secondary Template

Key Question: What are some effective models for daily lesson planning?

Directions: Make copies of this template and use it to guide your thinking as you plan your lessons.

Why Am I Teaching This Lesson?_____

Date: _____ Period: _____ Time: _____

Standards: _____

Subject: _____ Block: _____

Textbook: _____ Pages: _____

Material/Handouts: _____

Objectives	Key Questions
1. _____ _____ 2. _____ _____ 3. _____ _____	1. _____ _____ 2. _____ _____ 3. _____ _____

Vocabulary
_____ _____ _____ _____ _____ _____ _____ _____ _____ _____ _____ _____

Introduction	Overview (Purpose of lesson) (What do I expect students to know and be able to do?):
Mini-lecture	Key points
Student pairs, group work, or way in which students are engaged	Activities and formative assessments
Closing	Summary

Assessment

Homework

ACTivity 8.15 Design a Plan of Your Own

Key Question: What are some effective models for daily lesson planning?

Directions: Create a model like this on the computer and fill it in with your own topic areas. Be sure to include "anticipate" so you can look ahead to possible student behavior that may occur as a result of this lesson. Standards and objectives should be clearly defined. Play with all kinds of formats so you will be ready for your first classroom planning process.

Date: _____ **Subject:** _____

REFLECT and SET GOALS

Think about . . .

Directions: Review the two Key Questions for this chapter and respond to the additional "Reflect..." questions that follow.

Key Questions:

1. What is planning? (ACTivities 8.1–8.9)
2. What are some effective models for daily lesson planning? (ACTivities 8.10–8.15)

Reflect . . .

How does your ability to plan effectively impact your students' learning?

How will you integrate students' prior knowledge into your planning?

SET GOALS: Possible Next Steps . . .

Create and Collect Portfolio Artifacts from Chapter Activities

If you are creating an e-portfolio, format your documents appropriately.

✓ Create samples of three long-lesson plans for your portfolio.

✓ Take photos of the students while they are completing the lessons.

✓ Include a photo of you teaching the three lessons.

These artifacts can be used to meet final student teaching requirements, to help you compile your job interview presentation portfolios, and will be useful as you prepare for your first classroom.

Completing the Practicum, the Job Search, and Your First Classroom Experience

Completing the Practicum, the Job Search, and Your First Classroom completes your practicum journey and moves you in the direction of your first teaching position. Chapter 9 provides you with ways in which you can complete your portfolio for the practicum, and includes suggestions for using a portfolio during the job search and interview processes. Options for the electronic portfolio and a teaching brochure are given to get your creativity flowing. The activities in this chapter have all been tested and used by student teachers with successful results. Chapter 10 provides a concrete checklist of what to expect as you wind down your student teaching experience and complete your requirements. Skim these chapters to see what will be most useful to you.

Are you prepared for the job search? Chapter 11 offers a compilation of practical information relating to the job search; these resources are included to alleviate the burden of having to pull all these essentials together for yourself. The links and books will be helpful as you map out where you want to teach.

Finally, your journey from student teacher ends and you begin your first teaching job! Chapter 12 assesses your needs in your new setting (unless you are able to secure a job in your student teaching setting!) and provides you with ideas to get started. The activities offer a range of topics and suggestions to assist you in your first year.

This book is designed to be a resource for you during your transition from student to student teacher, and finally to teacher. If you use this book effectively by recording notes in the margins, completing the activities that are meaningful to you, and practicing your skills to learn what works with students, you will be on the road to success. Don't attempt to reinvent the wheel your first year. Use what you have learned during your practicum and college preparation program to become the best first-year teacher you can be. Success is the quality of your journey. Make your journey into teaching one that is more joyful than stressful by using what you have learned.

9

Designing a Portfolio: Where Do I Begin?

"Focus on the students.

Student Teacher

An important tool for documenting your learning is your portfolio. A teacher's portfolio is sometimes known as a *professional portfolio*, an *interview portfolio*, an *employment portfolio*, a *standards portfolio*, a *presentation portfolio*, a *reflective portfolio*, or a *certification competency portfolio*. It doesn't matter what you call it, it matters what your purpose is for creating one. You may be required to complete a portfolio as part of your teacher preparation for state certification or to complete your teacher education program, if so, use this chapter to help you meet that requirement. If this is not a requirement, use the suggestions to prepare a portfolio for your job interview process.

If you are not applying for teaching positions right away, you should still complete your interview portfolio upon completion of student teaching while the experience is still fresh in your mind. The focus of your interview portfolio should be what you have done for students. How can you demonstrate in your portfolio that you are a teacher who is worth being hired because you can help students learn and be successful in school and in life?

Hopefully you have been using the suggestions at the end of each chapter to collect artifacts throughout your student teaching experience. If you have not done so, review the last page of each chapter now. A portfolio, what ever its purpose, should provide clear evidence of your teaching skills, abilities, and other attributes that you bring to the profession.

You may choose to prepare a hard-copy version of your portfolio or an electronic portfolio; or, you may consider doing a combination of both. The collection of work you present is a visual display that illustrates your organizational skills and creativity, whether you are displaying artifacts to verify that you have met the standards or you are showcasing your work to a prospective employer.

Keep in mind, a hard-copy portfolio should not be overwhelmingly large, nor should it hold all your teaching lessons. Rather it should be a *selective* representation of lessons and activities that highlight your strengths in a streamlined format. This practice also applies to an e-portfolio. Don't feel you have to put everything you have ever done into your portfolio. But you may use any information from pre-practicum, full practicum, and teacher-education courses and readings to highlight your skills as a prospective teacher.

Your portfolio is also a valuable professional development tool to maintain throughout your years of teaching. It is a place for you to collect and record your accomplishments as you move through your professional career. It can be shared with peers, parents, and principals. It can be displayed on Open House nights to let new parents and students get to know you. The benefit of a hard-copy portfolio is that you can easily open it and share photos, reflections, artifacts, and examples of your teaching without the use of a computer or other device.

As a beginning teacher, you may even be required to maintain a professional portfolio in addition to undergoing the formal evaluation process conducted by the principal. Evaluation is an important aspect of rehiring and obtaining professional status in your school district, and your portfolio can be useful in sharing what you are currently contributing to the school district.

For a hard-copy portfolio, you may choose to use an artist's case, a book bag, or a large easel pad to display your skills. Choose the presentation style that best reflects your grade level and subject area of teaching as well as your creative style. Pre-school, early childhood, and elementary teachers may prefer to create interactive portfolios that hold manipulatives they have designed for their students. High school teachers may want to create a binder that reflects their subject area and target age group. Purchase a portfolio that allows you to insert additional pages so you can add new information during your beginning years of teaching.

You may choose to create an e-portfolio in addition to or instead of a hard-copy presentation binder. This will highlight your technology skills and you can easily include video clips, audio clips, and photos of yourself teaching, to enhance the impact of your presentation.

The portfolio is an "outcome" that is the result of a process of gathering artifacts, thinking about why they represent your skills, and displaying them in a meaningful way. It represents learning and growth over time. Standardized tests for teacher competency measure one aspect of knowledge. The portfolio is an additional, authentic assessment that allows the reviewer to gain an inside perspective of your thinking and development. Ask yourself, Why am I creating this portfolio? Who is the audience?

If you are looking for a teaching position, the process of creating an interview portfolio prepares you to share your teaching experiences in a thoughtful way at an interview. Some student teachers have mentioned that they were not even asked to share their portfolio at the job interview. This, of course, disappointed them after having put so much work into creating the product. Read the ACTivity in Chapter 11 to learn how to integrate your portfolio into the job interview to avoid this situation. Be assured that the process of creating the portfolio will help prepare you for your teaching interview because you will be able to respond confidently to the interviewer's questions even if they don't ask to see your portfolio.

The portfolio is a prop. It is not a teacher. You are the teacher. Use any type of portfolio to share who you are, verify what you have learned, or illustrate how you can contribute to the school district to which you are applying. Create something that represents you well.

What's Your PLAN for Learning?

Directions for getting the most out of this section: The PLAN section is designed to give you the "big ideas" for this chapter in the form of Key Questions. Schedule time to skim the chapter to see which activities will be most relevant to your purposes. Read the Key Questions and assess your understanding of them. Do you already know some of the answers to these questions or is this unfamiliar territory for you?

Key Questions:

1. **What should I include in my interview portfolio?** The *Artifacts* activities on the ACT pages in this chapter will provide you with lists of ideas on what to include. A sample table of contents for either a hard-copy portfolio or an e-portfolio is included here.

2. **How should I organize my artifacts?** You will have so much to share it can get overwhelming. The *Organization* activities on the ACT pages will provide you with suggestions for hard-copy portfolios and e-portfolios.

3. **What are some alternatives to a traditional hard-copy portfolio?** A hard-copy portfolio, even a small one, is always beneficial because it can be easily accessed and shared without relying on technology. However, it is appropriate in this age of technology to also provide the prospective employer with an electronic option. The *Alternatives* activities on the ACT pages will provide you with several options for documenting your practicum and sharing your knowledge, skills, and disposition for teaching and learning.

PLAN to Discuss Professional Standards

inTASC Standards

Review and discuss all 10 standards with your cooperating teacher and/or university supervisor. Refer back to page 9 in Chapter 1 for the complete list.

Source: The Interstate New Teacher Assessment and Support Consortium (InTASC) standards were developed by the Council of Chief State School Officers and member states. Copies may be downloaded from the Council's website at **ccsso.org**. Council of Chief State School Officers and Interstate Teacher Assessment and Support Consortium. (2011, April). *InTASC Model Core Teaching Standards: A Resource for State Dialogue.* Washington, DC: Author, 2011.

CONNECT

CONNECT is a resource page with ideas and suggestions to support you during student teaching. Select and complete any CONNECT items that will enhance your experience in the classroom.

CONNECT with People

- Teachers who have created portfolios: Talk with teachers in your school or district who have completed portfolios for professional development or during inservice training. Ask them to share their portfolios with you.

- Student teachers who have created portfolios: Seek out student teachers who completed portfolios last semester. What advice can they offer as you begin the process of putting yours together?

- Administrators: Interview administrators and ask them which type of portfolio they would prefer to see. Make sure you ask a number of people about their preference. You may receive a wide variety of responses, so don't ask just one person's opinion.

CONNECT with Readings and Resources

- Books and authors to explore on the Internet or at your local library:

  How to Develop a Professional Portfolio, by Dorothy M. Campbell, Pamela Bondi Cignetti, Beverly J. Melenyzer, Diane H. Nettles, and Richard M. Wyman, Jr. (Allyn & Bacon)

  Creating Portfolios: For Success in School, Work, and Life, by Martin Kimeldorf (Free Spirit Press)

  Teacher Portfolios: Literary Artifacts and Themes, by Sheri Everts Rogers and Kathy Everts Danielson (Heinemann)

  The Teacher Portfolio: A Strategy for Professional Development and Evaluation, by James E. Green and Sheryl O'Sullivan Smyser (Technomic)

  The Digital Teaching Portfolio Handbook: Understanding the Digital Teaching Portfolio Process, by Clare R. Kilbane and Natalie B. Milman (Allyn & Bacon), also the workbook by the same authors.

CONNECT Technology to Teaching

- Search the Internet:

  Type "how to create a teacher portfolio" into your browser's search box and review **annikeris.com** for ideas.

  See **teachnet.com** for the ultimate teaching interview portfolio.

  Portfolio*Gen* will show you how to make a web page in minutes.

  Lisa Spenser's site will step you through an electronic portfolio.

- Search and surf to find what fits your needs and personality.

<u>ACT</u>

Directions: ACT pages are designed to offer you options for preparing your interview portfolio. The activities listed here relate to the Key Questions provided at the beginning of the chapter. Select the activities that apply to you and complete them on your own or in your seminar.

Key Question Topic	ACTivity	Page	Check
Artifacts	9.1 Student Teaching Portfolio Final Checklist		
Artifacts	9.2 Writing My Philosophy Statement		
Artifacts	9.3 Possible Artifacts: What Did You COLLECT?		
Organization	9.4 How will you SELECT?		
Organization	9.5 REFLECT to Making Meaning		
Organization	9.6 Table of Contents and Page Layout		
Alternatives	9.7 Creating a Mini-Portfolio Brochure		
Alternatives	9.8 PowerPoint Portfolio		
Alternatives	9.9 Digital Portfolios		
Alternatives	9.10 Tips for Completing an e-Portfolio		

ACTivity 9.1 Student Teaching Portfolio Final Checklist

Key Question: What should I include in my interview portfolio?

Directions: If your portfolio is required to complete student teaching and to demonstrate your competencies, use these guidelines to assist you. If your portfolio is not required as a summation of your college practicum, you should consider making one for the job interview.

1. Did I complete all university requirements for the portfolio?

   Ask yourself:
   How does this portfolio represent my growth as a teacher?

   Where did I grow the most?

   Where do I still need to focus my efforts?

2. Use the portfolio to gain feedback about your teaching before you submit it.

   Ask other student teachers, your cooperating teacher, and university supervisor:
   What did you like about my teacher portfolio?

   What do you see is "missing"?

   Do you have a compliment for me?

   How can I improve my portfolio?

Read someone else's portfolio and answer the same questions for them. Be sure to share your portfolio with someone! You have done lots of work and it is important to be acknowledged!

ACTivity 9.2 Writing My Philosophy Statement

Key Question: What should I include in my interview portfolio?

In the first chapter, you completed a form that started you thinking about your disposition, assumptions, and beliefs about teaching ACTivity 1.2. Reread what you wrote and compare it to what you believe now.

Directions: Write a one-page "philosophy statement" that will be placed as the cover page of your hard-copy or digital portfolio. This statement is the foundation of your portfolio. All artifacts and examples will stem from this platform statement. Remember that your statement will be unique and will represent who you are as a teacher and how you see yourself.

A FORMULA FOR WRITING A BRIEF PHILOSOPHY STATEMENT

Paragraph 1. Who You Are Select three words that describe you as a teacher; they should highlight your unique skills. These words will be ones you have chosen or they could be words others have used to describe you.

Paragraph 2. What You Believe Two beliefs you have about teaching and learning and why you believe them.

Paragraph 3. Your Contribution What you will bring to the teaching profession and the school. Cite examples of what you have done in student teaching as evidence of your performance that relates to either your two beliefs or the three words you used to describe yourself.

It is one thing to believe something and another to actually put that belief into action in a classroom. What you did during student teaching matters. It is the evidence that shows you have the potential for success as a beginning teacher. The artifacts you select should all relate to the philosophy statement you wrote. They make your statement come alive. For example, if you selected the word *enthusiastic* and describe yourself that way, one or more of your artifacts should show you being enthusiastic and getting your students to be enthusiastic. The point here is to have your written statement and then be sure the rest of your portfolio actually backs it up. Your artifacts should not just be a random set of things you have done. They should add up to become supporting evidence for your philosophy statement. That is why you should always write your philosophy statement *before* you select your interview portfolio artifacts!

ACTivity 9.3 Possible Artifacts: What Did You COLLECT?

Key Question: What should I include in my interview portfolio?

Directions: After you write your philosophy statement you are ready to SELECT the artifacts that will illustrate who you are as a teacher. You can use one artifact in multiple ways. If you describe yourself as *organized* you may choose the floor plan of your classroom and photos of your room to illustrate how you manage a classroom effectively. If you believe in creating colorful learning environments, you could use the same floor plan and photos to articulate that belief. YOU create the portfolio to highlight your strengths! Check-off the artifacts you collected and could consider using from the following list.

_____ ACTivity pages in this book that you completed (especially from Chapter 3)

_____ REFLECTions and ideas from the end of each chapter

_____ Diagram of classroom (i.e., floor plan, photos, or both)

_____ Lesson plans highlighting any original work created

_____ Unit plans integrating subject areas, including the arts, thematics, etc.

_____ Cooperative-learning techniques you implemented

_____ Classroom management and discipline strategies you used

_____ Samples of student work: include each subject area, advanced work, work adapted for diverse needs, homework, tests, artwork, performance assessment

_____ Audiorecordings of students in groups, recordings of you introducing a lesson

_____ Videorecordings (permission slip required) of students during a lesson, documentary of classroom

_____ Materials from pre-practicum that may be highlighted

_____ Photographs of classroom, bulletin boards, group lessons (appropriate permissions from students)

_____ Documentation of any honors or awards

_____ Appreciation letters, notes from parents, notes from students

_____ Evaluations from others: cooperating teacher recommendation, supervisor evaluation

_____ Professional profile (third-person bio page) to go with resume

_____ Books and articles read, including description of how they helped you to be a better teacher

_____ Inspirational writings, poems, etc., which may serve as titles for pages or cover

_____ Other?

ACTivity 9.4 How Will You SELECT?

Key Question: How should I organize my artifacts?

Directions: Review the ideas on this page to organize your artifacts.
The portfolio is not a scrapbook or a complete documentation of your student teaching. Your student-teaching binder should include all the requirements for student teaching, and the teacher portfolio should be a showcase of your work and reflections. Select a few examples or artifacts that illustrate your competencies. You don't need to display a lesson plan for every artifact in your portfolio—one or two are enough to demonstrate that you know how to plan and implement an effective lesson.

GUIDELINES FOR SELECTING ARTIFACTS

1. Use your philosophy statement as a guide to selecting the examples that you feel best represent who you are as a teacher. Determine what *must* be in your portfolio based on how you described yourself in your philosophy statement.

2. Use professional standards to guide you. InTASC Standards cross state lines, so if you are applying to teach in another state you may consider organizing your work around them. Other standards may be from your university or state teaching licensing boards. Demonstrating your competency as a beginning teacher is a key purpose to organizing your portfolio.

Select artifacts that will let the reader know you have met professional standards and are a competent and caring teacher. For example, one way to organize your portfolio could be around five teaching competencies:

To illustrate your content knowledge you may consider using...

> a copy of your transcript, state test scores, or summary of content workshops you have attended.

To illustrate your ability to plan and design lessons and units you may consider...

> sample lesson plans, units, and curriculum you have designed to demonstrate what you have done during student teaching. Include assessments and ways you would use technology in your lessons.

To illustrate the way you deliver Effective Instruction you may consider...

> samples of lessons you actually taught, along with examples of student work. Photographs of yourself in action with students will help illustrate your skills. List specific ideas here.

To illustrate the way you manage classroom climate and create a productive learning environment you may consider...

> samples of your classroom routines as well as ways in which you work with students to keep them motivated and engaged. Ways you worked with parents to keep communication open are also important.

To illustrate the ways in which you Promote Equity you may consider...

> samples of ways you thoughtfully organized your classroom for all learners.

To illustrate the ways in which you Met Professional Responsibilities you may consider...

> your professional commitment to teaching through books you have read, meetings attended, and how you participated in your community of learners at the college or at your assigned school.

You decide how you want to organize your artifacts. What works best for you?

ACTivity 9.5 REFLECT to Make Meaning

Key Question: How should I organize my artifacts?

Directions: Read the ideas on this page to guide you as you write your own reflections for your portfolio. Reflection is what defines your portfolio and makes it different from a scrapbook. How you create meaning for the reviewer is essential to matching your philosophy statement to your actual practice.

Write a short description and reflection for each artifact you select. Review the artifacts and cluster them into themes of evidence. For example, if you have three artifacts that all relate to your classroom management strengths, you will put them together on one page. See the sample page layout on the next page for ideas.

Each page in your portfolio should have a clearly defined title with a description of what is on the page so the reader knows what its purpose is and how it is represents you.

Each artifact should have a short description AND a short reflection. Reflections can be one sentence. Note: A reflection is not your caption or description, but rather your thinking about teaching that tells the reviewer what you learned from teaching the lesson you are illustrating in your example, what you would do differently, what worked, and so on.

Example: A photo of you teaching a science lesson holding a model you created

Caption: Ms. Costa sharing science model with fifth-grade students

Reflection: I like to create models to show the students because it helps them see a concrete example of what I expect them to do in class.

Artifacts should be clustered in an organized way to tell a story of who you are as a teacher. The titles of the pages should be clearly marked with standards you have met, or teaching qualities you bring to the professions. What is your story? How will you present yourself to a prospective employer?

Optional: You may want to put a *Final Page* at the end of your portfolio that serves as a book end to your opening page philosophy statement. This page could summarize what you learned and what you look forward to in your own classroom.

ACTivity 9.6 Table of Contents and Page Layout

Key Question: How should I organize my artifacts?

Directions: Review the ideas on this page to assist you in organizing your portfolio.

_____ Philosophy Statement (one page)

_____ Professional Profile (third person; one paragraph)

_____ Highlight your professionalism, additional activities, and strengths by including a professional profile in the portfolio. Like a biography, this narrative will provide your readers with highlights of your best features: include the languages you speak, places you have traveled, sports you play or coach, and skills you bring to teaching. Review your student teaching profile and resume for ideas. Use an author's description on a book jacket to guide you.

_____ Your Instructional Practice

This will be the major portion of your portfolio. It should be organized by competencies and/ or themes with captions and reflections so the reader knows what you are showing.

_____ Artifacts (photos, lesson plans, etc.)

_____ Diagrams

_____ Audio and video with a written explanation of what is on the CD or DVD.

_____ Samples of student work

_____ Appreciation notes: public appreciation (from parents, teachers, students)

If you saved notes that people have written to you that were positive, include them on a page titled "Appreciation." If they relate to a particular lesson, you may include them on the page where you highlight that particular lesson.

_____ Evaluation Reports (from supervisor and cooperating teacher)

_____ Final Reflection (book end summary that matches your philosophy statement see ACTivity 10.4 for directions)

_____ Guest Register (last page)

The Guest Register is a place for reviewers to sign and date when they read it. Space for one brief comment from each guest should be included.

(continued on next page)

(continued from previous page)

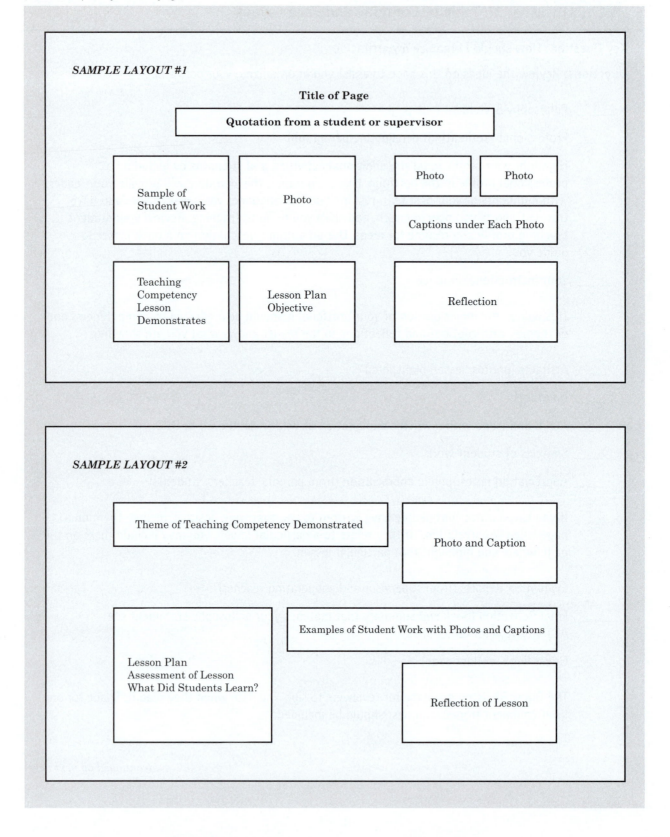

SAMPLE LAYOUT #1

Title of Page

| Quotation from a student or supervisor |

Sample of Student Work

Photo

Photo

Photo

Captions under Each Photo

Teaching Competency Lesson Demonstrates

Lesson Plan Objective

Reflection

SAMPLE LAYOUT #2

Theme of Teaching Competency Demonstrated

Photo and Caption

Lesson Plan
Assessment of Lesson
What Did Students Learn?

Examples of Student Work with Photos and Captions

Reflection of Lesson

ACTivity 9.7 Creating a Mini-Portfolio Brochure

Key Question: What are some alternatives to a traditional hard-copy portfolio?

Directions: Read the ideas on this page and make a decision to create your own brochure. It has been proven to capture employers' attention. Many student teachers say it got them interviews where they could share their larger portfolio.

Many student teachers have created one-page (two-sided) trifold brochures. They mail them with their applications and bring them to interviews. This small document is easy to carry and distribute, and it highlights key strengths quickly, colorfully, and easily.

Make sure the first fold (the cover) includes your name, physical mailing address, email address, and phone number so you can be reached for an interview! Most student teachers include photos, which can be of you alone or in your classroom with students. An inspirational quote or testimony from a student will add to create an eye-catching cover. Remember, you want the reader to OPEN the brochure and read all about you. Think about how you want your brochure to open and what you want the reader to see first, second, and third.

The other five panels in your brochure can include a variety of information. Here are some things student teachers have used:

- A brief summary of your philosophy statement using key words or quotations

- Photographs with students in the classroom

- Testimony from others who have worked with you

- Standards with evidence of something you have done to meet the standard

- Your goals for teaching

- A letter to the reader

- Graphic designs that are school related

Review brochures from the business world to see layout options. Keep your brochure visually pleasing and colorful with lots of white space to catch the reader's attention.

Note: *This brochure can easily be reformatted as an introduction letter to be mailed to the parents of the students in your first class. Be sure to save one side of the trifold for the mailing address!*

ACTivity 9.8 PowerPoint Portfolio

Key Question: What are some alternatives to a traditional hard-copy portfolio?

Directions: An easy way to create an electronic portfolio to present at an interview is to use PowerPoint. Select key points and design a short presentation that represents who you are and demonstrates your competency. Use the ideas for the portfolio and mini-portfolio brochure to give you ideas. Remember this is a visual display so you need to limit your narrative because you will be talking about the slides during your presentation. This e-portfolio will necessarily be short because time will be limited! You may need to bring your own laptop to show it. Be sure that everything you require to present your e-portfolio is organized *before* the interview (laptop, extension cords, etc.)!

Sample PowerPoint Portfolio for an Interview

1. Your name and photo with inspirational quote	2. Why you want to teach in this district	3. Your qualifications: *degree and license specifics*	4. Your philosophy in bullet form
5. Experience in the classroom: *list school(s)*	6. Evidence of success tied to standard	7. Evidence of success tied to a standard	8. Evidence of success tied to a standard
9. Goals you have for your first classroom	10. Why you would like to be considered for the position	11. Closing quote that inspires you or testimony from students	12. Contact information

Add graphics, photos, and voice to slides to enhance the presentation. Incorporating the voices of your students and cooperating teacher or supervisor will give you more credibility!

ACTivity 9.9 Digital Portfolios

Key Question: What are some alternatives to a traditional hard-copy portfolio?

Directions: Review the ideas on this page and talk with other student teachers who have created digital portfolios to see if this approach is for you.

Digital portfolios can be called, webfolios, e-portfolios, e-folio, multimedia portfolios, or electronic portfolios. They contain much of the same content of a hard-copy traditional portfolio but present the artifacts in digital format. You have options to use word processing software, audio recordings, video, and graphics to enhance your presentation. You can store your portfolio on a server at the university, on a CD, a flash drive, or a file server. You may create a portfolio on your computer using your own program software or you may purchase space to create and store your work. The options are limitless, but that means you need to research so that you learn what options are workable for you. The learning curve may be high or you may be very familiar with the technical terms associated with these options. Your employer is not concerned with your technical skills as much as your teaching skills.

ADVANTAGES TO DIGITAL PORTFOLIOS

Fun to create! You can use many resources and ideas to create a unique presentation.

Easily accessible! They are easy to copy to disk, attach to an email, or upload to a server. Instead of carrying bulky materials for show and tell, photos of classrooms and samples of work can easily be viewed.

Demonstrate your technology skills! This lets the employer know you are current and can use these skills with students and other teachers.

CHALLENGES WITH DIGITAL PORTFOLIOS

Knowledge and skill are required to learn how to actually create a digital portfolio. The learning curve is often high and the language and technical skills can be confusing. Coordinating all the programs and equipment is a specialty area and it keeps changing constantly.

Equipment and programs can be expensive. Laptops, InFocus machines, document viewers, interactive whiteboard, audiorecorders, and video and still cameras.

Time and energy. Creating the digital portfolio can actually take longer than assembling a hard-copy version because the you have to create the portfolio AND then put it in digital format.

The digital presentation may actually detract from the message. Your real accomplishments and competence may not be as noticeable if the bells and whistles of your portfolio overshadow its content.

Your goal is to present your competence in a way that can be easily viewed by a prospective employer. Decide whether a digital format is right for you at this time.

ACTivity 9.10 Tips for Creating an e-Portfolio

Key Question: What are some alternatives to a traditional hard-copy portfolio?

Directions: If you have decided or are required to submit your portfolio electronically, these guidelines may help you avoid some common pitfalls that some student teachers have experienced.

1. Be familiar with the online platform that you will be using to upload your work! Don't wait until the last day to learn how to use the technology. Ask for help if you need it.

2. Select lesson plans and photos that are visually pleasing to illustrate your work in the classroom. If you select student work, erase the names before scanning.

3. When scanning artifacts, actually look at them on the site before you submit them. Sometimes scanned documents are upside down, sideways, or are out of focus. Select another artifact to represent yourself if the one you choose will not display properly.

4. In the digital age more is not always better. Don't upload your entire photo album with hundreds of photos and expect the reviewer to know which ones you think are important. Select a few key photos and write your reflections next to them so the reader is clear about what you are demonstrating.

5. If you are using a web page or other format (i.e., PowerPoint portfolio) text your site and layout for visual impact. Less text and more samples usually have more impact on the viewer.

6. The portfolio should impress interviewers with your competency in teaching, not overwhelm them with the razzle-dazzle of sound and visuals. Make sure the technology you use doesn't overpower your message!

REFLECT and SET GOALS

Think about...

Directions: Review the three Key Questions for this chapter and respond to the "Reflect . . ." questions that follow.

Key Questions:

1. What should I include in my interview portfolio? (ACTivities 9.1, 9.2, 9.3)

2. How should I organize my artifacts? (ACTivities 9.4, 9.5, 9.6)

3. What are some alternatives to a traditional hard-copy portfolio? (ACTivities 9.7–9.10)

Reflect...

What am I most proud of as I create my portfolio?

What is challenging for me as I put all of this together?

SET GOALS: Possible Next Steps...

Just Do It!

If you are creating an e-portfolio, format your documents appropriately.

✓ Make a list and follow it until you are done

✓ Proofread before submitting your work! (Or have a peer proofread it for you!)

✓ Review your artifacts for evidence that focuses on students!

All of these artifacts can be used to meet final student teaching requirements and job interview presentation portfolio requirements.

10

Completing the Practicum: What Needs to Be Done?

"Congratulations! You have just completed one of the most serious

and challenging experiences of your college career.

Student Teacher

As you complete your student teaching experience, you should feel a sense of satisfaction. You have participated in an intense experience that has prepared you to become a teacher. Whether you completed a full semester or a whole school year, you have had the opportunity to be in a classroom in the role of the teacher. You made it! Do you remember reading the quote at the beginning of Chapter 1? *"Don't blink; it will be over before you know it!"*—well, it is over!

Review all the REFLECTs and CONNECTs you wrote throughout the semester. How have you grown and changed in this short time? How have these new relationships affected you as a teacher and as a person? What has this experience given you that you will bring to your own classroom?

Take time to acknowledge the people and the students who have worked with you as you developed your teaching skills. Elaborate gifts are not expected. Simple handwritten thank-you notes with your appreciative comments mean the most to teachers. How will you leave this school and the students?

As you complete this practicum course, two important summative actions must be taken at the end of the semester.

1. **A Grade Submitted for Your Transcript.** Grading procedures vary. Be sure you are clear on how on your grade is being determined. If self-evaluation is a component of grading, be sure to complete your self-evaluation and submit it on time. Typically, the university supervisor submits the grade after gaining input from the cooperating teacher. Remember, the grade includes *all* requirements that needed to be completed during this time, such as your journal and student-teacher binder.
2. **Recommendation for Teacher Certification.** A certificate of teaching is a license that will be sent to you after you formally apply to the state. Procedures vary from state to state, so you need to work closely with your college certification officer and field office or Office of Practicum Experiences to follow your state's procedures. If your college program has been officially approved by the state, you will receive an endorsement, usually placed on your transcript. Your cooperating teacher may also be asked to write a letter of recommendation for certification as well as signing other state forms.

This is not the end of your teaching experience. Completion leads to new beginnings, and by completing student teaching you are *opening the door to the teaching profession.* Complete the activities in this chapter and look forward to Chapters 11 and 12, which will guide you through the *new door* by assisting you in the job search and settling you into your new classroom.

What's Your PLAN for Learning?

Directions for getting the most out of this section: The PLAN section is designed to give you the "big ideas" for this chapter in the form of Key Questions. Schedule a meeting with your university supervisor to discuss the content of the chapter and see what applies to you. Remember requirements vary and you need to be clear what is expected of you. This chapter is just a guide to your completion.

Key Questions

1. **How do I reflect on my entire experience?** The *Closure* activities on the ACT pages in this chapter will provide you with some suggestions for reviewing your entire student teaching experience. Rereading your journals and writing some final thoughts will provide you with closure and a summary of what you learned. These activities can easily be integrated into your portfolio.

2. **How will I acknowledge the people who have supported me?** The *Acknowledgment* activities on the ACT pages in this chapter will provide you with suggestions for thanking your cooperating teacher and students. A survey from the students will assess your teaching and acknowledge you for what you have done.

3. **What closing paperwork can I expect to complete?** The *Paperwork* activities on the ACT pages will provide you with examples of typical paperwork assignments so you will know what to expect at the end of your practicum. Your university program may also have additional requirements.

$\mathcal{P}$LAN to Discuss Professional Standards

inTASC STANDARDS

Review and discuss all 10 standards with your cooperating teacher and/or university supervisor. Refer back to page 9 for the complete list.

1. How have you met these standards or you own state standards during this experience?

2. How are you demonstrating your competence with evidence of completing the standards?

3. How are you referring to the standards in your portfolio?

Source: The Interstate New Teacher Assessment and Support Consortium (InTASC) standards were developed by the Council of Chief State School Officers and member states. Copies may be downloaded from the Council's website at **ccsso.org.** Council of Chief State School Officers and Interstate Teacher Assessment and Support Consortium. (2011, April). *InTASC Model Core Teaching Standards: A Resource for State Dialogue.* Washington, DC: Author, 2011.

CONNECT

CONNECT is a resource page with ideas and suggestions to support you during student teaching. Select and complete any CONNECT items that will enhance your experience in the classroom.

CONNECT with People

- Favorite people: Personally acknowledge all the people who helped you through the semester. It does "take a village" to educate students, and you had the opportunity to work with many knowledgeable people along the way. Ask them for final thoughts and advice.

- Cooperating teacher: What do you need to talk about that you haven't already taken time for? Take the opportunity now or schedule a time after student teaching is over to reconnect.

CONNECT with Readings and Resources

- Books and authors to explore on the Internet or at your local library:

  Digital Portfolios in Teacher Education, by Laurie Mullen, Jody Britten, and Joan McFadden (Jist Works)

  Developing a Professional Teaching Portfolio: A Guide for Success, by Patricia M. Constantino, Marie N. De Lorenzo, and Christy Tirrell-Corbin (Allyn & Bacon)

CONNECT Technology to Teaching

- Check out this website:

  (atozteacherstuff.com) for lots of ideas

ACT

ACT pages are designed to offer you options for completing the practicum.

Directions: Skim the activities listed here and the following pages and select the ones that apply to you.

Key Question Topic	ACTivity	Page	Check
Closure	10.1 Self-Assessment: What Have I Learned?		
Closure	10.2 Reflection Summary of Journals		
Closure	10.3 Advice to Future Student Teachers		
Acknowledgment	10.4 Student Survey		
Acknowledgment	10.5 Sample Thank-You Letters and Gifts		
Paperwork	10.6 University Requirements		
Paperwork	10.7 Cooperating Teacher Recommendation for License		
Paperwork	10.8 Application for State Teacher License		

ACTivity 10.1 Self-Assessment: What Have I Learned?

Key Question: How do I reflect on my entire experience?

Directions: Compare your current knowledge, skills, and disposition for teaching with where you were at the beginning of the semester. Read the questions that follow, and take some time to assess your progress and acknowledge what you have learned. All of this information can be used in your teaching portfolio in some way to demonstrate your learning and progress over time.

What did you learn from observing? Review all of the observations and discuss or write a short summary that includes the themes and patterns you've noticed. What are the overarching ideas for your learning? What did you take away from these observations that you can use in the future? Topics you learned may include the ways in which effective teachers manage classroom routines, ways in which they interact with students, unique motivational strategies, ways to minimize off-task behavior, and so forth.

What did you learn from audiotaping and videotaping yourself? Was one assignment easier than the other? How has your practice changed as a result of doing either of these assigned reflections?

What did you learn from reflecting on your teaching? The self-assessment forms in Chapter 3 provided you with an opportunity to evaluate your own effectiveness as a teacher. As you review all of your assessments, do you notice some common themes?

What challenged your thinking during student teaching? Did you face a dilemma? (Did you find yourself asking, "Do I teach to the test, or try to create a meaningful hands-on lesson?" "Do I stick to the book, or do I bring in other curriculum that may be controversial?")

ACTivity 10.2 Reflection Summary of Journals

Key Question: How do I reflect on my entire experience?

Directions: Reread all of your journal entries or REFLECT activity responses and write a final impression of your thinking (two pages) as it has evolved during this practicum.

What themes have emerged?

What do you notice about your development as a teacher?

What did you write about most often?

What were your challenges at the beginning, middle, and end of the practicum? Were they different?

What else do you notice about your reflections?

Use this rubric to assess your writing and thinking. Where are you in each area?

Category	Beginning	Emerging	Applying	Mastery
Organization (grammar and spelling, 2-page length)	Some organization lacking and not 2 pages	Fairly well written with 2 pages	Well organized and written with 2 pages	No errors and met requirement for 2 pages
Development of Ideas (with evidence to back them up)	Ideas not well developed and no evidence cited from writing	A few ideas with some evidence listed	Ideas are stated and most evidence is clear	Full development with evidence
Connection to Standards and Teaching Practice	A little connection with minimal reference to standards	Beginning to notice standards and relate reflection to actual teaching	Makes relevant connections to teaching and standards	Standards and teaching practices are clearly articulated
Professional Disposition for Teaching and Learners	Personal opinion and judgments override professionalism	Professional attitude emerging	Confidence and professionalism articulated	Examined issues objectively and seeks to solve problems

ACTivity 10.3 Advice to Future Student Teachers

Key Question: How do I reflect on my entire experience?

Directions: Write a letter and give it to a prospective student teacher.

Sample Letter

Dear Future Teacher,

I have just completed my student teaching and I am exhausted. It has been the most important experience of my college preparation. I was able to take my course work and methods classes and actually put them into action with real students! It was so exciting and also very tiring. I didn't realize how hard teachers worked until I had to teach full-time all day for 3 weeks in a row. I don't know how my cooperating teacher does it all year every day!

What I also didn't realize is how many disruptions and distractions are possible during one class period. Just getting everyone's attention so I could give directions was a challenge. By observing other teachers regularly, not just at the beginning of the semester, I slowly started to see what effective teachers did to gain attention and motivate students. It is complicated because you have to do so much at the same time!

I wish I had kept all of my work from my methods courses more organized so I could just retrieve what I needed and use it in my classroom. Sometimes I was trying to find things I had done and ended up having to re-create them, and that took too much time. My advice is to stay organized and save things in a file on your computer or in hard copy or both!

What I wasn't prepared for was the fast pace of the day. Copying papers, moving from class to class, assigning homework, doing hall duty and bus duty, and going to meetings. I just couldn't keep up all the time and had to make sure I went to bed early each night.

All in all, I LOVED the experience and can't wait to have my very own classroom. Observing other teachers, interviewing students, and reflecting on my practice regularly have given me so much more confidence than I had when I started.

Good luck!

Completing Student Teacher

ACTivity 10.4 Student Survey

Key Question: How will I acknowledge the people who have supported me?

Directions: The students are the purpose for teaching. They are the barometer of an effective teacher and can clearly tell you how well you have accomplished your goals. Take some time to develop a survey to distribute to all of your classes. You may suggest the students write their advice in the form of a letter to you. If you teach young children, you may choose to interview them or create a visual survey. If you really want honest answers, don't ask for names.

Possible questions for your survey or topics for letters to you:

How do students support the success of teachers?

Which lesson did you most enjoy that I taught?

How do you learn best?

What could I do better in my teaching?

Do you think I was fair to all students? Why or why not?

What do you like most about school? About this classroom?

What advice do you have for me as I enter my own classroom?

Is there anything else you would like to say to me?

ACTivity 10.5 **Sample Thank-You Letters and Gifts**

Key Question: How will I acknowledge the people who have supported me?

Directions: Write a personal note to your cooperating teacher. Even though a gift is not required, the suggestions here could engage your students in the process! You may also want to write a note to the class or to any other people in the building who have given you special time or support.

Sample Letter

Dear Room _____,

Saying good-bye is never easy. It has been hard for me to think about leaving your classroom. From the first moment I met all of you, I knew this was going to be a positive experience.

I am giving you a plant for the classroom because both you and I have done a lot of growing this term. I have learned so many wonderful things from your teacher and from each of you that I will be able to bring to my own classroom. I will always hold a special place in my memories for this class. Be good, study hard, and take care of this plant and watch it grow!

Sincerely,

Ms. Costa

OTHER GIFT IDEAS

You could give a book that you have signed with the date and year for the school or class library, a plant for the classroom, a bouquet of flowers, a cake in a special shape or decorated in the theme of a unit you taught, a special unit that you developed that you copy and leave with the teacher, a collection of the students' writings put together in a book format, supplies for the classroom, photographs displayed in a poster or scrapbook, a gift certificate, a PowerPoint presentation with all the students' photos, an audio-message card or book from you, a classroom video that you made with them, or one of your own ideas!

ACTivity 10.6 University Requirements

Key Question: What closing paperwork can I expect to complete?

Directions: Review the possible evaluation options that may be required and ask your supervisor what else you need to do to complete the program.

COMPLETION OF REQUIREMENTS

Review the university syllabus requirements and check for completion.

Did I do everything I was asked to do?

_____ Textbook and article readings

_____ Required observation forms

_____ Products that need to be complete (e.g., samples of lesson plans, unit plans, teaching binder)

_____ College-related requirements (e.g., attendance on campus for seminar or other required events)

_____ Journals

_____ Classroom competencies (state standards required for licensing)

_____ Other requirements _____

_____ List any extra credit completed during the semester

_____ Did I complete all university requirements on time and present them clearly and free of error?

ACTivity 10.7 Cooperating Teacher Recommendation for License

Key Question: What closing paperwork can I expect to complete?

Directions: As part of some state certification procedures, the cooperating teacher is often required to write a letter of recommendation stating your competence as a beginning teacher. If that is the case, you may use this list as a guide. If a letter is not required for the state, you may use this as an opportunity to invite your teacher to write a reference letter for your job-interview application packet. Copy this list and share it with your cooperating teacher. Also give another copy of your resume and student teaching profile from Chapter 1 to your cooperating teacher to assist her in highlighting your specific skills and strengths.

The letter may include the following...

- The statement that you are recommended for state ____ certification

- An example(s) of work you have done that demonstrates your competencies

- The date and semester you student taught

- A brief description of the school and type of classroom(s) in which you worked

- Your cooperating teacher's experience as a classroom teacher and why she is recommending you for this license

- Why your cooperating teacher thinks you would be a good teacher

What else would you like your cooperating teacher to include in your recommendation letter?

ACTivity 10.8 Application for State Teacher License

Key Question: What closing paperwork can I expect to complete?

Directions: You will apply for state certification or license in the state in which you complete student teaching. This certification can then be fairly easily transferred to other states in the United States. Check the certification procedures in your teacher education program to ensure a smooth application process. Find out if you need to complete a "credential file" in your state.

LICENSURE WHERE YOU COMPLETED STUDENT TEACHING

_____ Complete all final paperwork with your university supervisor and receive your grade.

_____ Meet with the university certification officer or director of teacher licensure to follow university and state procedures.

_____ Complete application and mail to State Department of Certification.

_____ Register for and successfully pass any state teacher test mandated for certification.

OUT-OF-STATE TEACHING LICENSE

_____ Review a reciprocity procedure. *Reciprocity* means that your college preparation is acceptable to another state and is considered to be comparable. It does not mean you are "automatically" certified in another state, nor does it mean you won't have any additional requirements for that state.

_____ Request an application and verification of completion of student teaching. Usually, the state will send you a form that needs to be completed by your college certification officer indicating that you completed an "approved program" in that state.

_____ Contact the state or review the state website for most current regulations.

REFLECT AND SET GOALS

Think about...

Directions: Review the three Key Questions for this chapter and then respond to the "Reflect..." questions that follow.

Key Questions:

1. How do I reflect on my entire experience? (ACTivities 10.1, 10.2, 10.3)

2. How will I acknowledge the people who have supported me? (ACTivities 10.4, 10.5)

3. What closing paperwork can I expect to complete? (ACTivities 10.6, 10.7, 10.8)

Reflect...

How are you feeling at the end of this experience? What is the biggest change in your perspective of teaching?

How have the students influenced you as a teacher?

Who will help you complete all of this paperwork?

SET GOALS: Possible Next Steps...

Review Activities as Potential Portfolio Artifacts from Previous Chapters

If you are creating an e-portfolio, format your documents appropriately.

✓ SELECT the best artifacts to demonstrate your skills

✓ Less is more—and remember to write a REFLECTion for each artifact. Why is this an important artifact to illustrate your skill?

11

The Search for a Teaching Position: Where Do I Begin?

"Organize! Organize! Organize!

Student Teacher

As you complete your student teaching experience, you will begin your search for your first teaching position. Integrate your job search activities through the course of your student teaching practicum by beginning your portfolio, writing your resume, finding out what services the career center offers, and creating your own personal time line for teaching in a classroom of your own. When you complete student teaching, you can more actively submit letters of application, participate in interviews, and demonstrate your teaching to prospective employers.

The job search is an exciting and stressful time for a beginning professional. If you are willing to relocate to parts of the country that have many teacher openings, your search may not be as difficult. If you are only interested in staying in your hometown or state, you may have more of a challenge if openings are not available. The international job market, private schools, and charter schools are all other possible places to seek teaching positions. The question you must ask yourself is "Where would I like to teach?" Set your goals for positions where you see yourself being personally and professionally satisfied.

There are resources to assist you in your search. You should seek out the career center or job placement office located on your college campus. This office will provide information for you as you design a plan for seeking employment. These offices may offer meetings to help you write resumes and cover letters and complete applications. Another service may be to provide on-campus recruiting for local area towns that are seeking new teachers. Take advantage of all the services this office provides. Your own personal relationships and the connections you have made during student teaching are also valuable resources. Finding out where the openings are and when they will be posted is important as you devise your personal time line for employment.

If you graduate from your teacher preparation program in May, you most likely will be looking for a job that will start in September. School districts typically hire in the summer when the school budgets have been approved and when teachers have made final decisions about retirements. Some new teachers are hired as late as the first day of school. However, with the trend toward needing teachers in some specific subject areas, you may notice that jobs are being posted earlier in the year.

If you graduate in December, you may still be seeking a full-time job for the next year, but you have a chance to review the options and perhaps substitute teach in districts where you feel employment may be forthcoming. Your time line has to match your life's objectives. When do you want to be in a classroom? When will districts be hiring? How long do you wait? Are you willing to teach as a substitute if a full-time job is not available?

Organizing and implementing an effective job search will offer you more choices for teaching positions. Selecting where you will start your professional career is an important life decision. Use these pages to guide you.

What's Your PLAN for Learning?

Directions for getting the most out of this section: The PLAN section is designed to give you the "big ideas" for this chapter in the form of Key Questions. Schedule time to skim the chapter to see which pages make most sense for you to complete. Read the Key Questions and assess your understanding of them. Do you already know some of the answers to these questions, or is this unfamiliar territory for you?

Key Questions

1. **Where do I want to teach?** The *Where?* activities on the ACT pages in this chapter will provide you reflective questions to focus your search.

2. **What is the application process?** The *Application* activities on the ACT pages will provide you with specific suggestions and models for preparing a solid application packet. It will also include a template for keeping track of where you have applied so you can follow up.

3. **How do I prepare for an interview?** The *Interview* activities on the ACT pages will provide you with practical suggestions and real interview questions. A demonstration-lesson guideline is also included.

4. **How do I accept a teaching position?** Use the *Contract* activities to give you general guidelines for signing a contract.

Plan to Discuss Professional Standards

inTASC STANDARDS

Review and discuss all 10 standards with your cooperating teacher and/or university supervisor. Refer back to page 9 in Chapter 1 for the complete list.

Source: The Interstate New Teacher Assessment and Support Consortium (InTASC) standards were developed by the Council of Chief State School Officers and member states. Copies may be downloaded from the Council's website at **ccsso.org.** Council of Chief State School Officers and Interstate Teacher Assessment and Support Consortium. (2011, April). *InTASC Model Core Teaching Standards: A Resource for State Dialogue.* Washington, DC: Author, 2011.

CONNECT

CONNECT is a resource page with ideas and suggestions to support you during student teaching. Select and complete any CONNECT items that will enhance your experience in the classroom.

CONNECT with People

- Administrators in the school and district: Talk with the principal at your student teaching site to gain advice about the job search in the district and the surrounding towns. Ask for her advice in the job search.

- Personal networks: Review all the people you know who may have a "connection" to a school. Call to find out where the jobs are, and ask whether they will give you a positive word.

CONNECT with Readings and Resources

- Check with the career planning office to find the most current books on this topic.

- Read the latest issue of AAEE, published by the American Association for Employment in Education, 947 E. Johnstown Road #170, Gahanna, Ohio, 43230.

CONNECT Technology to Teaching

- Check out these websites and use your browser to make CONNECTions:

    (teacherjobs.com)

    (teachers–teachers.com)

    (proteacher.com)

    Also check your state's Department of Education job employment matching website.

    Search your local school district postings on the Web.

    Search domestic and international job postings.

ACT

Directions: ACT pages are designed to offer you options for learning about the job search. The activities listed here relate to the Key Questions provided at the beginning of the chapter. Select the activities that will help you find a job and complete them alone or with another student teacher.

Key Question Topic	ACTivity	Page	Check
Where?	11.1 Selecting a District That's Right for Me		
Where?	11.2 Teaching Positions: Where to Find Them		
Application	11.3 The Application Process		
Application	11.4 Your Cover Letter		
Application	11.5 Your Resume		
Application	11.6 Follow-Up		
Interview	11.7 Preparing for the Interview		
Interview	11.8 Closing and Follow Up to the Interview		
Interview	11.9 Teaching a Demonstration Lesson		
Contract	11.10 Professional Ethics and Signing a Contract		

ACTivity 11.1 Selecting a District That's Right for Me

Key Question: Where do I want to teach?

To be successful as a teacher and to remain in the profession, you need to have your personal and professional needs met. The position you select may become your teaching position for many years to come. It is important to select a school system that is a good match for you and not to jump into a job just because it was offered to you.

Directions: Even if you don't have a choice of positions, you should ask yourself the following questions to determine whether the one you've been offered is a good fit.

WORKING CONDITIONS

Is there positive support for teachers in the school?

How do teachers relate to parents?

Would you have a mentor teacher assisting you?

BENEFITS

Salary   Sick days
Job security   Medical insurance
Promotion opportunities   Dental insurance
Schedule   Professional development
Vacations

MATCH FOR YOUR PERSONAL GOALS

Does the school/district match your goal for type of school: public, private, international?

Does the district/school support the success of beginning teachers?

Does the district/school match your teaching philosophy?

All three areas are important, and there is no one way to analyze your answers. If the district is a 100% match for you, you will be very lucky, but often there will be areas that are not up to your needs. For example, one district may pay less than another but it provides more-positive working conditions. You are the only person who can decide which will meet your needs in the long run and support your staying in the profession.

Analyzing the answers to these questions will be important. A key question is, "Does the district provide a mentor teacher to support you during the first year?"

If you have more than one choice, make a list of each school's advantages and disadvantages. Then think about the "intrinsic" rewards that you are looking for. Does this choice match your philosophy? Good Luck!

ACTivity 11.2 Teaching Positions: Where to Find Them

Key Question: Where do I want to teach?

Directions: Review the information on this page and check the suggestions you will explore.

You need to put a conscious systematic effort into discovering where teaching jobs are being posted. You may want to teach in your own hometown, but there may not be any immediate openings. You have options: You could opt to substitute teach to get your foot in the door and wait for a teaching position, or you could branch out and teach in a neighboring district and transfer into your own town when openings become available. Remember, openings for teaching positions are created by (1) teachers retiring from existing positions and (2) growing districts adding new schools and teachers. Read the newspaper and real estate guides to see where towns are growing or where there are numbers of retiring teachers.

PLACES THAT CAN POINT YOU TO JOB OPENINGS

_____ The university's career center or job placement office, upcoming job fairs, resume matches, job listings on the website

_____ Websites and newspapers

_____ Sunday newspapers usually list openings for positions in the geographic area

_____ State Department of Education and Bureau of Teacher Certification list openings on the website for schools or on the Department of Education list of towns where new schools are being built

_____ State Employment Office and federal government, positions teaching in correctional institutions, Bureau of Indian Affairs, other government agencies related to education

_____ State Teachers' Union and Teachers' Retirement Board may have a job-matching system that shows where openings are due to retirement

_____ U.S. Department of Defense (DOD) schools

_____ Office of Overseas Schools in Washington, DC

_____ Real estate groups (realtors will have information about area schools and where new ones are being built)

_____ Personal networks (ask your parents, your friends who are teachers, the school you attended, where you student taught, and any others you can think of)

ACTivity 11.3 The Application Process

Key Question: What is the application process?

Directions: Reflect on your goals for teaching, and review the options listed here.

WHAT ARE YOU LOOKING FOR IN A TEACHING POSITION?

_____ Public school? Urban? Suburban? Rural?

_____ Independent school?

_____ Religiously affiliated school?

_____ International school?

You need to find out how the positions are being posted. Are they listed by the central office, by the superintendent of schools, or by the building principals who actually do the hiring? Do they require a letter or an application? Do private schools have a different procedure for application? Your university career center may be able to guide you in learning about the districts and schools in which you are most interested.

APPLICATIONS FOR POSITIONS MAY BE COMPLETED BY...

1. Responding to an official opening posted in the newspaper for a specific position needed: Specific details and job requirements will be listed. See how closely you match the description and respond if you fit the bill or if you come close.

2. Attending on-campus recruiting sessions with districts that are in need of teachers: Typically, school personnel arrive on campus and spend a day doing short interviews. This screening process allows districts to see a large number of student teachers and allows a student teacher to interview with a variety of districts in a short time. Usually, resumes are sent to the districts through the career center and the districts select students to be interviewed. After the initial interview at the college, school personnel call back students they would like to have come to the school site for a second interview.

3. Exploring in a district, region, or state where you would like to teach by viewing postings on the Web. This could be in your own hometown or in a geographic area in the state that you have decided on. Focus on towns and areas that have retiring teachers or that are building new schools.

4. Mailing applications or letters of interest to towns that have not posted a job, but where you would like to teach, is also a strategy. Often positions don't get posted in a timely way. If your application is on a principal's desk when an opening occurs, you could be invited to an interview. Lots of positions are last minute and in the summer because districts have no way of knowing how many openings they will have in the fall.

ACTivity 11.4 Your Cover Letter

Key Question: What is the application process?

Directions: Review the information about cover letters here and then write your own cover letter.

Your cover letter is perhaps the most important piece of your application packet because it is the first impression you give to the hiring committee. Every resume you send should be accompanied by a cover letter. The purpose of the letter is to introduce yourself, arouse the reader's interest, and persuade the person reading the letter to interview you. If you are responding to an official job posting or advertisement, state that clearly. If you are writing a letter of inquiry about possible jobs, state that. Sample cover letters should be available in your college career planning and placement office. If the application process is online, there may not be a place to attach a cover letter. Mailing a hard-copy letter to the appropriate office or to the building principal may give you an edge because they will have more information about you. You may also consider sending an email to the building principal to ensure he sees your hard copy application package. The process will vary from district to district. You will need to be proactive and investigate the hiring procedures as well as other ways to get your name to the appropriate people.

TIPS FOR SUCCESSFUL COVER LETTERS

- Personalize the letter.
  Use the name of the district and person who is doing the hiring whenever possible. If you use parts of the letter as a template, be sure to review it carefully and change the names from previous letters!

- Proofread for perfect grammar and spelling. Have someone else read it!

- Limit the cover letter to one page.
  Emphasize your teaching experiences, special interests, and the reasons that you are the best candidate for the district!

- Include your *permanent* mailing address, phone number, and email.
  You may be in transition, so make sure the address you list is one that you would consider permanent. Change your voice mail or answering machine greeting if it is inappropriate for potential employers to hear.

- Refer to your teacher portfolio.
  At the end of the letter, state that you have a teacher portfolio and would be happy to share it at an interview. This is a "hook" to create interest to gain an interview.

SAMPLE OUTLINE FOR A COVER LETTER

Paragraph 1	• Why you are writing this letter (i.e., responding to a posting or exploration of possible position that may open in the near future). If it is a response to a posting, *clearly identify the position.* • What you already know about the district via the Internet or other connection and why it is a match for you.
Paragraph 2	Your interest in becoming a teacher (i.e., beliefs about teaching).
Paragraph 3	Teacher preparation program, qualifications, and student teaching experience.
Paragraph 4	Request interview, refer to enclosed resume, refer to portfolio available at interview, and include a thank you.

Go to the Web to see sample resumes and cover letters for all subjects and levels.

Resumes-for-teachers.com will give you some A+ samples.

ACTivity 11.5 **Your Resume**

Key Question: What is the application process?

Directions: Review the ideas suggested here and write your resume. If you already have a resume, refresh it with some of these tips.

Your resume should be no more than two pages and should be printed on either white or off-white paper. Design a resume format that is uncluttered and easy to read. There are many templates available in computer software programs and on the Web. Remember, you may be one of hundreds applying for a position and you want to have your material read. A clear and concise style is always better than a wordy narrative. Look for the "white space" in your resume to see how your layout appeals to the eye. Review sample copies of resumes available in your career center or practicum office. Ask administrators what kind of format they prefer to see when they are reviewing a prospective teacher's resume.

POSSIBLE HEADINGS FOR AN EDUCATION RESUME

Name and current address are the most important elements to your heading. Don't use your dorm address if you are moving home during the summer.

Email address and cell phone number are also important so you can be reached easily for an interview.

Website (if you have one) should be listed up at the top under this information.

Select the headings that you would consider for your resume after you have reviewed the following samples.

_____ Professional objective

_____ Education (undergraduate, graduate)

_____ Teacher preparation courses (highlight special ones that may make you stand out)

_____ Teaching experience (pre-practicum, full practicum, other)

_____ Related experience

_____ College activities

_____ Leadership skills

_____ Volunteer experience

_____ Language proficiency

_____ Honors and awards or achievements

_____ Computer skills

_____ Portfolio (link to electronic portfolio or reference to portfolio available at interview)

_____ References available upon request

- *Don't* include personal data, such as your age, height, family status, or a photograph on your resume.

- *Do* list experiences in reverse chronological order.

  Go to the Web to see sample resumes and cover letters for all subjects and levels.
  Resumes-for-teachers.com will give you some A+ samples.

ACTivity 11.6 Follow-Up

Key Question: What is the application process?

Some school districts require candidates to complete the district's own application in addition to sending in a resume and cover letter. If the position is posted in the newspaper, it may instruct you to call for a paper application or request you complete it on-line. If it does not state that there is a district application, you can assume a cover letter and resume is sufficient.

Directions: Keep a record of the districts to which you have applied and what specific materials are required. Create this table on your computer and update it regularly. Write the date in the box when you send the material.

District/ School	Contact Person	Application Date sent	Cover Letter and Resume Date sent	Interview Date Scheduled	Summary Portfolio or Brochure Prepared	Demon- stration Lesson Required?	Follow Up Completed

After you have mailed your materials to a school district or principal, you will be anxious to hear from them. If you mailed your materials using a return receipt, you will know exactly when it was received. However, you won't know when the committee will meet to review the qualified candidates and set up subsequent interviews.

Wait a few weeks and if you have not heard what the selection procedure will be, you may want to place a courtesy phone call to the district secretary. There is no need to talk directly with the principal or superintendent because they may not be part of the process at this time. The secretary or the human resources department in larger districts usually takes care of the details for setting up interviews and is aware of the hiring time lines in a school. If the voice-mail system is automated and you find you cannot connect with a live person, you may want to ask for the person who signed your return-receipt slip.

When making this call, be clear, cheerful, and short. Ask if the packet has been received, if any other information is needed, and when you might expect a call or letter regarding an interview. If the person does not know, thank him for his time and ask whether there is someone you should be talking with instead. The goal is just to get a time frame and a procedure that you can expect. If the school is not interviewing for 2 more months, you can relax for a while!

Typically, the larger the district, the longer the process will be. If you are working through the process in a city with a human resources division that is taking applications for hundreds of schools, you can expect delays. On the other hand, in a small school where the principal does the hiring directly, the process could move more quickly.

ACTivity 11.7 Preparing for the Interview

Key Question: How do I prepare for an interview?

Congratulations! You have made it through the first hoop, and you have been invited to be interviewed at the school. Either you mailed your materials directly to the school or you participated in an on-campus recruiting session, and the district wants to know more about you.

Directions: Read the guidelines suggested here to help you prepare for your interview. Practice the questions with a colleague so you will be ready. Role playing will help.

DO YOUR RESEARCH

- Research the school on its website.
- To gain some insights, talk with students from your college who are already teaching.
- Attend an interview workshop if one is available on campus.
- Find out who will be at the interview (e.g., one person, a committee, and/or parents).
- Review and role-play potential interview questions (audiotape or videotape).
- Review your philosophy statement, your portfolio contents, and your resume.
- Plan your interview attire (suit or dress with jacket).
- Think about questions you would ask them.
- Prepare packets for people who will be at the interview so they have something to keep (refer back to Chapter 9).

THINK LIKE AN INTERVIEWER

Remember
Interviewers are looking for teachers who . . .

- Will fit into an existing school-system culture
- Will be enthusiastic about teaching
- Will go the extra mile for the students
- Can relate to parents and other teachers
- Will be contributing members of the school

. . . so make sure you demonstrate these qualitites when you are being interviewed!

(continued on next page)

(continued from previous page)

PRACTICE SAMPLE QUESTIONS

1. What do you consider are your strengths as a teacher?

2. How would you plan a lesson for _____ (subject)?

3. How do you engage students in learning?

4. How do you assess student learning?

5. What procedures do you use for classroom management and discipline?

6. Describe two mistakes in teaching you have made and how you solved them.

7. What three words describe you as a teacher?

8. What do you believe about teaching and learning?

9. Describe your content strengths.

10. Why should we hire you?

11. What are the reasons for your college success?

12. Why do you want to work at this school/in this district?

INTEGRATING YOUR PORTFOLIO INTO THE INTERVIEW

Some student teachers prepare portfolios and the interviewers never ask to see them. This is frustrating because so much time and energy is spent on this task. One way student teachers have managed to work parts of the portfolio into an interview is to use them in response to a question that is being asked. For example, if one of the questions asked of you is, "How do you engage the students in learning?" instead of just responding to the question, you could turn to one of the pages in your portfolio that actually demonstrates that you can visually engage students. This is an instance when a hard-copy portfolio is an advantage. You can use the portfolio for two or three questions to highlight your answers visually. This contextual approach to using your portfolio is more effective than flipping through page by page and "showing and telling" what you have done.

To integrate your portfolio as a response to questions means you must be very familiar with what you have in your portfolio and be comfortable practicing which question response matches which page in your portfolio. Remember, you will not show your entire portfolio, so think about which three pages you would most like to share, and see how you can make them fit with the questions being asked. Practice! Practice! Practice!

THE DAY OF THE INTERVIEW

If your interview will be face to face, you need to make sure you know where you are going. Driving to the school before the day of the interview and then locating the room may not always be possible, so be sure you allow enough travel time to arrive a bit ahead of schedule.

Your interview may be via Skype or by telephone if you are applying for a position abroad or one that is a great distance from where you live. Phone interviews may be conference calls with a committee or one on one. Depending on the type of set up, you may need to call in to a central number or someone may call you. Skype is used by some districts. If you have not used this technology, practice first with a friend, so you can see yourself on the computer. Check the background of your room so you can be sure it presents as a professional setting and not simply as your bedroom, if possible.

Suggestions for Interviews

- Practice a Skype interview.
- Check the backgroud in your room if you are participating in a Skype interview.
- Dress professionally—a suit is best.
- Shake hands as you meet administrators and teachers or greet them online.
- Make eye contact throughout the interview. Computer cameras can distort so check your height and seat for the best view of you.
- Be yourself—smile, be positive, be passionate about teaching.
- *Listen carefully* to the questions before responding.
- Ask for clarification if you don't understand a question.

EXPECT THE UNEXPECTED

- A writing sample may be requested on the spot. Samples are often related to a scenario of how to handle a teaching situation.

PREPARE TWO QUESTIONS YOU WOULD LIKE TO ASK

1. What are you most proud of in your school/district?
2. What types of assessments are required for students?
3. How is teacher professional development encouraged?
4. How are new teachers oriented and mentored? This is an important one!
5. Which curriculum areas/classes/grades would I be hired to teach?
6. When will the decision be made?

If you do have a hard-copy portfolio and you have not been able to successfully integrate it into the interview, you could simply say, "May I share two pages from my portfolio that highlight my strengths as a teacher?" Do not go page by page; select two pages maximum unless the committee asks to see more. You can also leave the entire portfolio and pick it up the next day if you feel there is interest from one or more members of the committee.

Leave the interview site confidently as soon as you have finished. Do not stay and talk with candidates who are waiting to be interviewed.

ACTivity 11.8 Closing and Follow Up to the Interview

Key Question: How do I prepare for an interview?

Directions: Review the Summary Portfolio suggestions that you could leave at the close of the interview or consider emailing them to the committee if they prefer electronic copies. Read Follow up Reflections to plan your next steps.

CLOSING SUMMARY PORTFOLIO

This would be a packet or file folder with a few materials to leave with the committee, or several attachments that relate to the interview that you want to be remembered.

Consider including:

- Cover letter written to this committee thanking them for the opportunity to be interviewed
- Your philosophy statement or brochure (see Chapters 1 and 9)
- ONE lesson plan and a reflection on how you taught it
- A photograph (you in your classroom with students, if possible)
- A resume
- **Optional:** You may want to create your own educational business card. Don't forget to include your email address. Add the card to your resume and cover letters when applying for positions and include it in your portfolio and executive summary portfolio. Create a logo and have your portfolio match! Be creative!

Do not put too much in this summary portfolio. It should be placed in a slim colorful cover with your CURRENT address and phone number so you can be reached easily.

Remember to bring enough copies for all members of the interview committee and leave the brochure or summary portfolio for them to keep!

FOLLOW UP REFLECTIONS

- Evaluate the interview. Your notes and reflections of what happened at the interview are important. As soon as you leave, write as many questions as you can remember in an interview notebook. Each interview you participate in helps you to gain confidence and skills in sharing yourself.

- Write a short thank-you note. If you want to write to all members of the committee, call the school secretary the next day to obtain correct names with titles and spellings. There are two schools of thought about whether your note should be emailed or handwritten. Discuss this with your peers and advisors and do what makes most sense for you.

Letters or phone calls from the district/school indicate your next steps. A phone call is usually positive, and you may be asked for a second interview or a demonstration lesson. Rejection usually comes in the form of a letter or perhaps an email.

If you are rejected, think about what you learned from the experience and *move on to the next interview.* You may want to talk with the principal or committee chair to ask how you could improve your presentation.

After each interview, note the questions you were asked. What questions do you recall? Write them down immediately so you will be prepared for your next interview.

ACTivity 11.9 Preparing and Teaching a Demonstration Lesson

Key Question: How do I prepare for an interview?
As part of the interview process prospective teachers may be asked to demonstrate their teaching skills. This process allows the principal or interview committee to see how the teacher candidate interacts with students. If you have a sample of yourself teaching (perhaps a video that was recorded during student teaching) you may offer that to the committee as an option to a live lesson.

Directions: Review the checklist included here and PRACTICE a lesson to prepare yourself for the demonstration.

PREPARING FOR A DEMONSTRATION LESSON

- Ask the committee/principal what type of lesson they would like to observe. If there is a choice, choose a lesson that you have already successfully implemented.

- Prepare a long lesson plan (use one of the templates in this book or from your university) to show the committee/principal your planning skills. Pace the lesson for the time frame offered—don't pack in too much. Make sure you have 5 minutes for the closing of the lesson to demonstrate your ability to summarize and informally assess what the students learned.

- Integrate strategies for diverse learners.

- Ask if you can have the names of the students or name cards before you teach.

- Ask if there are any particular student needs or issues that you should prepare for.

WHAT TO DO AT THE SCHOOL SITE

- Show off what you can do!
    Use visuals.
    Use technology.
    Engage students.

- Arrive early at the site and view the room organization.

- Meet the teacher and committee and share your plan. Have extra copies for all viewers.

- Teach the lesson!

- Clean up your materials.

- Have a follow-up conversation with the committee. Ask if the committee has any questions.

Note: Sometimes the school wants to videotape these demonstration lessons for members of the committee who can't be there. Don't be nervous—smile and share your skills!

ACTivity 11.10 Professional Ethics and Signing a Contract

Key Question: How do I accept a teaching position?

Directions: Read this page and think about how you will decide to sign a contract with a school district. List the pros and cons for each district if you have more than one choice. Don't be afraid to ask questions if you need clarification.

Public school employees in most states have contract agreements with their local school boards that list their salaries and benefits. Ask for a copy of the contract when you are asked to sign your agreement. If you seek employment in private or international schools, there may be other forms of agreement required such as a requirement to teach in the school for 2 years.

Review contracts before signing them. If you are not sure about some language or wording, ask if you can take it home to review it. *DO NOT SIGN if you are not sure* or if you have other offers pending. Be open and tell the district or school you are waiting to hear from another district, and ask if you may have a few more days.

Ethics are involved in making and keeping an agreement. When you sign a contract, you are stating to the school district that you have made a commitment to the students in the classroom to which you will be assigned. Breaking a contract is a serious matter. Breaking a contract because another job comes along that pays a higher salary or offers other benefits is an ethical issue. Think of the agreement in reverse: How would you feel if the district came back to you several months later and said they had found a stronger candidate and were letting you go?

Be sure your commitment is with this district before your pen touches the paper.

How will you decide whether you will sign a contract?

REFLECT and SET GOALS

Think about . . .

Directions: Review the four Key Questions for this chapter and respond to the "Reflect . . ." prompts that follow.

Key Questions:

1. Where do I want to teach? (ACTivities 11.1, 11.2)
2. What is the application process? (ACTivities 11.3–11.6)
3. How do I prepare for an interview? (ACTivities 11.7, 11.8, 11.9)
4. How do I accept a teaching position? (ACTivity 11.10)

Reflect . . .

What is my biggest challenge in the job search?

How will I know which position is right for me?

SET GOALS: Possible Next Steps . . .

Methodically Apply to as Many Districts as Possible

Use a large white envelope when mailing materials so your packet stands out.

Maintain an accurate list of the districts where you have sent materials and follow-up in a timely way to check on the status of your application.

12

Your First Classroom!

"Jump into your long awaited first year with both feet and hands,

an open mind, a loving heart, and your entire soul.

Student Teacher

This is it! Your very first classroom! You will be solo teaching, perhaps for the first time and it will be exciting, and also a bit scary. You will experience a range of emotions as you begin and some new teachers quickly move into survival mode if there are challenges they are unfamiliar with and did not practice during student teaching.

The key to successful entry into the profession is solid mentoring from an experienced teacher in a supportive school environment. If you find you are "on your own" a bit too much, you may want to read and use another book written specifically for beginning teachers, *The First Year Matters: Being Mentored in Action* (Pearson, 2009). It is a companion book to *Mentoring in Action* (Pearson, 2006), which is used widely by mentors. You are being inducted into the teaching profession just by being in your first year. How well your induction program supports you depends upon your district and school vision and resources. That is why it is important to ask if there is a mentoring program when you are hired. If you have the choice between two districts, the one with a support program for you will be more beneficial to your development as a teacher.

Teaching is difficult and rewarding work. As a beginning teacher, you will face the realities of children and families every day. The first year can be very isolating, because you are alone with the students without a cooperating teacher to guide you. Coping with the stresses of your daily schedule, taking care of yourself, and participating in your continued professional growth and development are important to your well-being and retention in the profession.

Many teachers leave the profession within the first 3 years because they feel unsupported and overwhelmed. Think about what you require for support and ask for assistance. Experienced teachers are there to help. You also need to think about ways in which you can actively create a support network of beginning teachers in your school or district. It can be fun to meet weekly and share ideas and to support each other through the growing pains.

You will move through many stages as a teacher. The beginning years serve as your induction into the profession and may be the most difficult for you. As you struggle with your classroom management, new curriculum, and working environment, remember the difference you are making in your students' lives. Setting high standards for learning and maintaining your vision are valuable contributions to the profession. You bring enthusiasm, dreams, and new ideas to the schools.

Don't give up if you don't reach all your goals the first year! Work with the experienced teachers, listen, learn, and reflect on the ideas you bring. This chapter will provide you with an overview of the resources available to teachers. Participating fully in every aspect of your professional career means continuing to learn, grow, and reflect on your own practice. Welcome to the profession! You *do* make a difference.

$\mathcal{W}$hat's Your PLAN for Learning?

Directions for getting the most out of this section: The PLAN section is designed to give you the "big ideas" for this chapter in the form of Key Questions. Read the Key Questions and assess your understanding of them. PLAN to read and complete the pages that will help you. What do you already know about organizing your first classroom? How can this book and this chapter help you transition smoothly into your teaching position?

Key Questions:

1. **How will I organize my first classroom?** The *Organize* activities on the ACT pages in this chapter will provide you with some ideas to consider.

2. **How will I integrate into the school culture?** The *Integrate* activities on the ACT pages will provide you with suggestions that will enhance your first months of school.

3. **How will I continue to learn?** The *Learn* activities on the ACT pages will list some options for you to consider.

4. **How will I know I am effective?** The **Reflect** activities on the ACT pages will list some topics for your review.

$\mathcal{P}$LAN to Discuss Professional Standards

inTASC STANDARDS

Review and discuss all 10 standards with your cooperating teacher and/or university supervisor. Refer back to page 9 in Chapter 1 for the complete list.

Compare the inTASC standards to the district or state standards where you will be working.

How are they alike?

How do they differ?

Source: The Interstate New Teacher Assessment and Support Consortium (InTASC) standards were developed by the Council of Chief State School Officers and member states. Copies may be downloaded from the Council's website at **ccsso.org.** Council of Chief State School Officers and Interstate Teacher Assessment and Support Consortium. (2011, April). *InTASC Model Core Teaching Standards: A Resource for State Dialogue.* Washington, DC: Author, 2011.

CONNECT

CONNECT is a resource page with ideas and suggestions to support you during student teaching. Select and complete any CONNECT items that will enhance your experience in the classroom.

CONNECT with People

- Community members: Talk with people in the town to learn about the school through their eyes.

- Teacher-education faculty and field-experiences office: Let us know where you are! We want to support you and connect with you! You are alumni now!

- Principals and department chairs: Seek out ways in which you can participate in the school (club advisor, coach, honors clubs, yearbook, drama).

CONNECT with Readings and Resources

- Professional-development centers in your state

- Books and authors to explore on the Internet or at your local library:

  Tips from the Trenches: America's Best Teachers Describe Effective Classroom Methods, by Charles M. Chase and Jacqueline E. Chase (Technomic Publishing)

  Being Mentored: A Guide for Protégés, by Hal Portner (Corwin Press)

  Surviving Your First Year of Teaching: Guidelines for Success, by Richard D. Kellough (Merrill)

  A Handbook for Beginning Teachers, 2nd ed., by Robert E. MacDonald and Seán Healy (Longman)

  Your First Year of Teaching and Beyond, by Ellen L. Kronowitz (Pearson/Allyn & Bacon)

  What Keeps Teachers Going, by Sonia Nieto (Teachers College Press)

  The First Days of School: How to Be an Effective Teacher, by Harry K. Wong and Rosemary T. Wong (Harry K. Wong Publications)

  The Unauthorized Teacher's Survival Guide: An Essential Reference for Both New and Experienced Educators!, by Jack Warner, Clyde Bryan, and Diane Warner (Jist Works)

CONNECT Technology to Teaching

- Create your own web page for parents and students to read!

- Check out these websites:

  Help for new teachers, student teachers, and mentors (**inspiringteachers.com**)

  Tips and strategies from first-year teachers (**teacherweb.com**)

  For 100 websites that you'll find interesting, check out (**teachingdegree.org**)

  For professional resources and conferences (**newteachercenter.org**)

ACT

ACT pages are designed to offer you options for learning. The activities listed here relate to the Key Questions provided at the beginning of the chapter.

Directions: Skim the activities listed here and select the ones that will support you in your first classroom. Invite your mentor or another colleague to discuss some of these pages with you.

Key Question Topic	ACTivity	Page	Check
Organize	12.1 Assessing My Needs		
Organize	12.2 My Classroom Design		
Organize	12.3 Letters to Students and Parents		
Organize	12.4 Revisiting Your Survival Packet		
Organize	12.5 Beginning the School Year Successfully		
Integrate	12.6 Meeting My Mentor		
Integrate	12.7 What Will the School Expect from Me?		
Learn	12.8 Creating My Professional-Development Plan		
Learn	12.9 Being Evaluated and Rehired		
Learn	12.10 What Is Professional Development?		
Learn	12.11 Professional Organizations		
Learn	12.12 New Teacher Leadership Roles		
Reflect	12.13 When My Teaching Fails		
Reflect	12.14 Teaching as a Career Choice		
Reflect	12.15 Maintaining My Passion		

ACJivity 12.1 Assessing My Needs

Key Question: How will I organize my first classroom?
You have accepted your first teaching position, and now it is time to organize your very own classroom. Before you do that, you need to know what to expect.

Directions: Review the following checklist and complete the activities that apply to you.

A CHECKLIST

_____ **Visit the school.**
- Introduce yourself to all the important people (see your list from this text).
- Ask for school handbooks, curriculum guides, and policies (same as student teaching).
- Ask how you will receive materials and supplies.

_____ **Meet with the principal/department chair.**
- Make an appointment to talk.
- Ask when school begins.
- Ask when you can be in the building.

_____ **Meet with Human Resources to sign paperwork and receive benefits information.**
- Ask if there are required meetings.
- Receive a school calendar.

_____ **Meet the teacher union representatives.**
- Ask about membership.
- Ask if there is a new-teacher orientation.
- Obtain a contract.
- Ask for a list of other benefits.

_____ **Meet your mentor teacher.**
- Find out whether she is assigned or is a volunteer.
- Exchange phone numbers.
- Ask details of the support program.

_____ **Add other things to your list as needed.**

ACTivity 12.2 My Classroom Design

Key Question: How will I organize my first classroom?

Directions: The space in which your teaching takes place can affect your ability to create a successful community of learners. Visit your classroom and follow the reflective prompts here to get started. Record your thoughts in a beginning-teacher journal that you can easily reference. Keep your ideas in one place. Refer back to the chapters in this text that relate to this topic to remind you of what you have learned during your practicum.

1. Assess the condition of the room. What does the space look like? How is it organized? How do you feel when you enter this room? How are the desks organized? Are they movable? Is the room old or new? Take a photo of the space from several angles so you can start to think about how you want to organize it. Where will you put your desk?

2. Inventory what is actually in the room. Are there materials from a former teacher that need to be removed? Are there supplies for you? How will you know what to do with what is in the room?

3. Do you have to share your space? Will you be moving from one room to another or will you be team teaching in this classroom? Will you have a paraprofessional teacher in your room or an instructional aide? How will you provide space for that person?

4. Think about "creating the space for learning" in this classroom. Where will you hang student work? Where will the students sit? Where will you place your inspirational posters or quotes? How will you put yourself into the space of the room? For example, how will the students know who you are? Will there be personal photos, or samples of things you like to do?

5. Are you allowed to enhance your space with color or bring things in to make the room more comfortable? Find out how you can do this.

ACTivity 12.3 Letters to Students and Parents

Key Question: How will I organize my first classroom?

Directions: One important way to introduce yourself is to write a letter. Review what you wrote when you were a student teacher and modify it for your first classroom. You may also take the brochure you developed for the job search and adapt it to be a more colorful introduction of who you are and what you bring to teaching.

Sample Letter to Students

Dear Class (or individual student's name),

I am looking forward to meeting you on the first day of school. I have heard that you are a terrific group of students! We will be working together to learn math and it is my favorite subject. I studied math at Anytime College and completed my student teaching last spring. My students told me they loved to work in groups and create interesting projects so I will be continuing to do those things with you this year.

I expect excellence and effort from each one of you and I will be motivating you to do your best each day. Effort is a must and it shows your character. There is no quitting in math. Homework is going to be fun this year! Yes fun! I will give you activities that will help you learn and achieve in this class. Effort and homework stars will be posted to show your success.

A few things you need to do to succeed are to come to class prepared with a writing utensil (pen or pencil) and your notebook. If you are absent you can collect makeup work that is placed in a bin at the front of the room. You may also talk with a friend who will help you to catch up. I will offer makeup classes after school too. These are routines to help you succeed if you have to miss school for any reason.

My classroom will be a "math talk" only classroom and it will be a place you can learn about famous mathematicians and talk the language of math. We will also ask ourselves, "What would mathematicians do?"

I can't wait to begin! See you soon,

Ms. Costa

Note: A modified version of this sample letter could be sent to the parents.

ACTivity 12.4 Revisiting Your Survival Packet

Key Question: How will I organize my first classroom?

Directions: Review Chapter 2 activities and see how they relate to your new school. If you have been hired at the same school where you did your student teaching, you can skip this activity.

1. Learning about my school: Creating a profile. You may not have time for a scavenger hunt, but you will need to know the answers to the questions if you want to succeed! See how many questions you can answer!

2. Take some photos of the school. Photos allow you to see where the parking lots are and where you will enter the building.

3. Getting to know the school district and the neighborhood. Follow the observe/research model to note what is important for you to succeed in this school or district. Is this unfamiliar territory for you? If it is, get some support immediately so you will be successful.

4. Review all other activities in Chapter 2 and apply them to this new context. Are there any new buzz words you need to know?

5. What is your general feeling for the school? The main entrance? The hallways?

6. Make sure you know the secretary and the custodian!

ACTivity 12.5 Beginning the School Year Successfully

Key Question: How will I organize my first classroom?

Directions: Review the following categories before the first week of school and decide how you will address them. Refer back to the chapters in Section 2 that relate to demonstrating your teaching skills. This will remind you of what you have learned during your practicum and what you need to know for your first classroom.

_____1. **Getting to know your students.** Create a survey or interview to find out who they are and what they need. Refer back to your student teaching experience for ideas. Take photos and have a place to post them along with student names the first week. This becomes an instant bulletin board and provides an easy way to learn their names.

_____2. **Create a plan for organizing your students.** Will you create teams based on colors or topics? Will you place students in pairs? Will you have time for student sharing each day—even for 2 minutes? What did you do in student teaching that you can use here?

_____3. **Review learning-styles literature** and be prepared to create lesson plans that have options for different types of learners.

_____4. **Establish your routines!** This is extremely important! List all of the routines you need to create: opening the classroom, responding to students being late, walking to another classroom, bathroom passes, lost pencils, collecting work, absent students, and so forth; decide now what you would like to do. Write out these routines and hand them out to the students on the first day of school.

_____5. **Rewards and consequences** need to be decided now. Students will expect you to be consistent. What worked during student teaching? What didn't? Now you need to establish a system for management. You don't want to wait to ask the students. They know what they are supposed to do, they want to know if YOU know and whether you have the courage to manage the room effectively.

_____6. **Procedures** for fire drills and/or other building protocols. Find out now! Ask, if the principal has not supplied this information. Often, if you are the only new teacher in the school, they forget to tell you these kinds of things!

_____7. **Find out how to sign out books from the library,** use equipment, get school supplies, access student records, and call in if you are sick are important systems to learn now.

_____8. **Find out where to make photocopies** and where to take your breaks. You will need these two things every day!

What else should you add to the list?

ACTivity 12.6 Meeting My Mentor

Key Question: How will I integrate into the school culture?

Working with an effective mentor will help assist your integration into the school culture. You will have many questions—and your mentor will be able to help you find the answers. Sometimes mentors are not assigned early and you may find yourself asking the "teacher next door" to help you figure out what to do. These informal mentors are really an asset, as they help you navigate your day-to-day operations. The key to effective mentoring is SCHEDULING TIME to meet regularly. Don't wait until you *need* the mentor. Find a common time before or after school where you can talk uninterrupted for at least 15 minutes or more per week. You will be "mentored in action" throughout the school year!

Directions: Read the following suggestions to get the most out of the mentoring experience. Review Chapter 3 in this textbook because the cooperating-teacher experience is similar to that of having a mentor. The one main difference is that now you are colleagues!

Building a Relationship Through Listening

When you meet your mentor you will have some first impressions (just like you did with your cooperating teacher). Refer back to your activities in Chapters 2 and 3 to see how you will build this new relationship. Listening to your mentor will help you understand the culture of the school. Even though you will not be completing formal observations of other teachers, like you did in student teaching, you are encouraged to observe other teachers in your new school context. You are also encouraged to interview your mentor and other teachers. Compare and share your beliefs and experiences to begin your relationship with your mentor. Share who you are and show all of the materials you prepared for the job interview. Be a confidential colleague to maintain a trusting relationship with your mentor.

The School as a Learning Community

The days of going into your classroom and closing the door to the rest of the school are over. That is not how to build a relationship with others or to model collaboration for your students. You will miss opportunities if you do not reach out. Other teachers in the building will also provide support for you in different ways. Don't just stay in your room! Get out and meet people and see how they can help support your work as a teacher. Integrate yourself into the faculty. Create a new support group.

New-Teacher Support Group

New teachers have stated that they love to meet in new-teacher groups even if they teach different content areas and/or grade levels. You will find groups like this to be very supportive, but you may find that your school may not offer this type of peer group organization. This might mean you will need to form a group yourself. A coffee and conversation group with new teachers from the school or district can rotate from one classroom to another and provide a place where you can support each other. Try it!

Going Beyond Your Mentor!

Remember the mentor is ONE person and cannot meet all of your needs. Try to create a support team of people outside of school who can help you. During student teaching you created a support team; now you need to do it again.

ACTivity 12.7 What Will the School Expect from Me?

Key Question: How will I integrate myself into the school culture?

Directions: Read this page to discover what might be expected from you this year.

Experienced teachers expect you...

To share new knowledge and methods, to put your best foot forward, to have questions and to ask them, to fit in, to be receptive, to be professional, to respect their time constraints.

Other new teachers expect from you...

Camaraderie and support, sharing materials, sharing ideas, a shoulder to lean or cry on, feedback, a sense of humor!

Administrators expect from you...

Professionalism; control of class; good lesson plans with objectives; good judgment with discipline; effective communication with parents; up to date on education reform and professional development; positive attitude with staff, children, and parents.

What You Can Expect in Your First Year of Teaching

1. **How tiring it is** to teach all day long! When the student taught they could take breaks and coteach, and now they need to be "on" all day!

2. **Paperwork!** There is so much of it, and at the beginning of the year the school office required so many forms! Be sure to complete any forms the department chair, principal, or elementary coordinator requires, immediately. It will be noticed if you do not complete school paperwork on time.

3. **More duties** and you'll find it more difficult because you will not be sharing them with your cooperating teacher. So find out the duty schedule and don't complain about doing your part!

4. **Meetings after and during school** take a lot of time out of the day, which means later nights to meet requirements for planning and correcting assignments. Things do get better when you have a routine. The first year is challenging until you understand the culture of the school and the expectations for meetings. Most meetings are required by contract, so don't miss them.

5. **Speaking up** when a teaching situation may not be right to you or seems to be unfair. As a beginning teacher, you may be uncomfortable at times and not know how to respond. Talk with your mentor to decide the best course of action before speaking up at a public faculty meeting. Public meetings have cultures of their own and you want to successfully integrate into the staff before you speak.

Learning about the school culture is key to integrating into a school. Integration does not mean you are invisible. It means you are learning through observation and listening so you can contribute to the school.

ACTivity 12.8 Creating My Professional–Development Plan

Key Question: How will I continue to learn?

Districts often require a professional-development plan to document your goals and objectives for professional growth. Self-directed study may be a part of your professional plan; it allows you to choose the topics in which you are most interested. For example, an elementary teacher has to teach all subject areas, but you may particularly love teaching math and science. Your professional goal for the first year could be to focus on these areas because you find them fun! A secondary major teaching history may really love the Civil War, and that could be the focus of her professional development.

Self-directed study could result in a product, such as a curriculum unit, developed from a trip you took, other published materials, software packages, masters' theses, work in some kind of business, or in a community-service learning activity. For instance, you might develop a plan for having your students work with the elderly and design a unit around this.

Sometimes teachers are involved in study groups or teacher-research groups as part of their personal self-directed study. Others may conduct workshops for teachers or join reading groups in which all members read books and journals related to classroom practice.

Directions: Write your professional plan with your district mentor and also review the requirements for recertification in your state.

My Professional–Development Plan

Include the following in your plan:

Dates—the date you begin the plan and when you will review it

Your goals for the school year

How goals relate to student learning

Evidence of meeting your plan

Professional Plan Activity Schedule

Activity	Description	Started Date	Completed Date

RECERTIFICATION

Many states require teachers to recertify every 5 years or less. This means that teachers may have to take courses or complete independent projects to renew their teaching licenses. Your professional-development plan may even be required for recertification in your state. Check with your state's Department of Education to receive a list of recertification requirements.

ACTivity 12.9 Being Evaluated and Rehired

Key Question: How will I continue to learn?

Directions: Talk with your mentor, union representatives, and administrators to find out how you will be evaluated. Use these questions as a guide to what you need to know.

1. When will I have my first formal observation? Who will observe me?

2. How many observations will I have this year? Is there a schedule? Are there any unannounced observations?

3. How should I prepare for that observation?

4. Is a preconference and postconference required for the observation? Is the feedback formative and summative?

5. May I see a sample observation form and how the protocol the observer will use to document my classroom practice?

6. Is a formal lesson plan required for observation?

7. Are there other evaluation tools or checklists used for teacher evaluation that I should be aware of?

8. When will I know if I am rehired for next year?

9. Are there other evaluation dates or requirements I need to know about?

10. Is there any paperwork I need to sign to be rehired?

Your mentor and other teachers in the building will be able to guide you in this process. Have your mentor observe you while you teach so you will become more comfortable with the process. Refer back to the forms and templates in Chapter 3 to remind you of the supervision process you used in student teaching. Many of the observation processes you used may be similar to what you have learned already.

ACTivity 12.10 What Is Professional Development?

Key Question: How will I continue to learn?

Technology has brought educators closer to new information by way of the Internet. But the Internet alone will not provide you with enthusiasm and connections to people who make a difference. That is why you should continue to read, take courses, and participate in summer institutes.

When you were student teaching you participated in *preservice* education, which means "before teaching." Now that you are a full-time teacher in your own classroom, *inservice* education programs will assist you as you continue to learn how to be a more effective teacher. The term used in schools is *professional development*.

Directions: Talk to your mentor or other teachers in the building to discover what professional-development options are available to you.

Professional-Development Options to consider:

New teacher professional development

When are workshops offered and do I need to attend—or are some optional?

School-based professional development

Is it after school? Am I required to attend?

During school? Do I need a substitute teacher?

Are there topics related to curriculum I am teaching?

Is professional development offered in groups or for individuals?

Districtwide professional development

Will I be with teachers at my grade level/subject level or is it a mixed-level program?

Professional workshops and conferences

Are they face to face or online?

Am I eligible to attend? Perhaps with my mentor?

Graduate courses or a master's degree program

Am I interested in enrolling in a graduate course? How will taking a course enhance my salary?

Do I have time for a course this year or would next year be better?

Writing about teaching practice: Article? Book? Or blog?

Have I maintained this reflective guide in a way to tell a story for other new teachers?

Do I have something to share? A kit? An idea?

Because teaching is dynamic and always growing and changing along with education reform mandates, professional development in schools and districts is also changing yearly. Staying current is critical to being an effective teacher. Even though you just completed your student teaching and feel you are up to date, the district may be using curriculum or programs that you are not familiar with. There is a constant flow of information, new programs, literature, and strategies you need to learn as you are teaching.

ACTivity 12.11 Professional Organizations

Key Question: How will I continue to learn?

As you begin your professional career, you must remember to stay updated about new teaching methods, new information in your subject area, and new ways to work with your students.

Directions: There are many organizations for teachers today, ranging from early childhood education to secondary content areas. These organizations have local, state, and national conferences and workshops. Most have a professional journal that keeps you updated on current research and practice. Search the Web or ask your mentor or your school librarian to find out which organizations the school may already be a member of and which journals are in the library for your use. Join the organizations that relate to your area of teaching.

Professional Organizations

ARTS EDUCATION

National Art Education Association (NAEA)

naea-reston.org

BILINGUAL EDUCATION

Nation Association for Bilingual Education (NABE)

nabe.org

EDUCATIONAL TECHNOLOGY

The Education Coalition—Distributed Learning Systems and Services

tecweb.org/index.html

International Technology Education Association

iteaconnect.org

ENGLISH EDUCATION

The National Council of Teachers of English

ncte.org

The International Reading Association

reading.org

The Great Books Foundation

greatbooks.org

National Institute for Literacy

nifl.gov

(continued on next page)

(continued from previous page)

HISTORY/SOCIAL STUDIES EDUCATION

National Council for the Social Studies

socialstudies.org

The Organization of History Teachers

historians.org

The National Council of Economic Education

ncee.net

MATHEMATICS

Association of Teachers of Mathematics

atm.org.uk

National Council of Teachers of Mathematics

nctm.org

National Council of Supervisors of Mathematics

ncsmonline.org/OtherResources/listserv.html

MODERN LANGUAGES

American Association of Teachers of French

frenchteachers.org

American Association of Teachers of German

aatg.org

American Association of Teachers of Spanish and Portuguese

aatsp.org

American Council on the Teaching of Foreign Languages

actfl.org

Computer Assisted Language Instruction Consortium

calico.org

National Network for Early Language Learning (NNELL)

nnell.org

MUSIC EDUCATION

The National Association for Music Education

menc.org

The Kennedy Center Arts Edge

artsedge.kennedy-center.org

PHYSICAL EDUCATION
National High School Coaches Association

nhsca.com

National High School Athletic Coaches Association

hscoaches.org

SCIENCE EDUCATION

National Association of Biology Teachers

nabt.org

National Center for Improving Student Learning and Achievement in Mathematics and Science

wcer.wisc.edu/NCISLA/index.html

National Science Teachers Association

nsta.org

American Association of Physics Teachers

aapt.org

TALENTED AND GIFTED EDUCATION

Center for Gifted Education

cfge.wm.edu

Professional Training for Teachers of the Gifted and Talented

5.kidsource.com

California Association for the Gifted

cagifted.org

Council for Exceptional Children

cec.sped.org

National Association for Gifted Children

nagc.org

ACTivity 12.12 New Teacher Leadership Roles

Key Question: How will I continue to learn?

Joining committees at your school, taking on a leadership role in the teachers' union, joining a professional organization, or collaborating with other beginning teachers are ways in which you can be a part of the profession.

Teacher leadership requires courage and time to contribute beyond classroom teaching. You may think this is impossible your first year and perhaps it is. Your ability to contribute to the professional community is an important way to influence the culture of the school and to impact the students. Leadership is required of teachers of the 21st century. You are a leader.

Directions: Review the topics listed here and decide how you can contribute to the school in some small way in your first year. Who is a leader you admire? Put a photo or quote from this person on your desk for inspiration. How will you model teacher leadership?

How will you demonstrate your leadership this year or in future years?

_____ 1. Participating in schoolwide meetings

_____ 2. Volunteering to lead a club, advise the yearbook staff, or coach a sport (choose one you love)

_____ 3. Leading a committee at the school

_____ 4. Designing a new curriculum and sharing it with other teachers

_____ 5. Joining a professional organization and reading the journal

_____ 6. Attending professional-development workshops and sharing with your mentor

_____ 7. Inviting other teachers to join a new-teacher support group

_____ 8. Become a National Board Certified teacher (NBPT standards are available online)

_____ 9. Become a teacher's union representative

_____10. Collaborate with another teacher to create a unit

_____11. Peer-coach another teacher

_____12. Mentor or be a cooperating teacher (in a few years)

What other leadership ideas will empower you in your workplace?

ACTivity 12.13 When My Teaching Fails

Key Question: How will I know I am effective?

I was so stressed when I started and then I realized I didn't need to be a perfect teacher; I needed to be a good teacher. I tried to teach the best I could every day and to learn from my students. I knew that I would get better at this next year.

FIRST YEAR TEACHER

Stress is very real, and first-year teachers feel it! It will be a different kind of stress than what was experienced from student teaching. Your desire to do well and to do right by your students may increase your stress level. How do *you* cope with stress? Are you trying to be perfect? What are your survival skills?

Directions: Review the two topics on this page to discover ways to minimize your stress.

LEARNING FROM YOUR MISTAKES

A book you may find supportive when you feel stressed is, *Oops: What We Learn When Our Teaching Fails* (Power & Hubbard, 1996). It includes essays written by real teachers about the mistakes they have made in the classroom. Some of the essays are humorous, like, "I Wonder If Real Teachers Have Problems?" and "New Teacher Blues: How I Survived the First Year." What are your "oops" moments? How can they inform your teaching? When you articulate these moments and learn how to talk about them you can begin to solve your own problems. Refer to the Problems to Possibilities activity in Chapter XX. Perhaps you may even consider publishing your own "oops book" for new teachers. (Refer to Leadership Options in ACTivity 12.14.)

UNDERSTANDING PHASES OF TEACHING

There are also phases of teaching that you will experience during your first year. They can't be ignored. Ellen Moir (New Teacher Center, Reflections (2001), p. 1) calls them "attitudes toward teaching" and says new teachers move from anticipation in the first month through survival, disillusionment, rejuvenation, reflection, to anticipation for year 2. Where are you right now? Is it causing you stress?

Some new teachers say they move through those phases each day! Recognize the phases so you will know where you are and that these feelings are natural to new teachers. You are not alone in your feelings, but you may need to seek out other teachers to get some support.

ACTivity 12.14 Teaching as a Career Choice

Key Question: How will I know I am effective?

Directions: Read about the options on this page to think about your future.

LEADERSHIP OPTIONS

You may have come to teaching with another goal in mind. Perhaps you have always wanted to be an administrator or a curriculum director and you knew some time in the classroom would help you achieve that goal. You don't have to make the decision to leave the classroom now. Teach and learn what it takes to be an effective teacher before you move on to other education-related positions.

Some education roles that are available to consider include

Administration—principal or headmaster or assistant roles

Department chair or content coordinator

Specialist—technology, reading, special education, content coach, or director

Higher education professor—teaching teachers' courses or practicum

OTHER EDUCATION RELATED OPTIONS

In their first year of teaching most new teachers say, "I can't do this, I am leaving," at one point or another. Most teachers don't mean it. They are just experiencing a phase of disillusionment. However, some teachers actually do leave the classroom in the first year. Leaving the profession before thinking about other education alternatives could be a mistake. Some teachers who struggle with whole-class engagement become excellent one-on-one tutors. If you are struggling and find you are not effective with whole-class or large-group instruction, consider the alternatives of smaller classes and tutoring environments. Another alternative is curriculum development and school-based materials, perhaps with a publishing company.

ACTivity 12.15 Maintaining My Passion

Key Question: How will I know I am effective?

Directions: Reflect on your experiences in the classroom and find your joy. Acknowledge what you are good at and where you still need to grow. Read this page to guide your thinking.

Only you will know if you are truly happy in the teaching profession. You know in your heart what gives you joy and what you are really good at. This doesn't mean you are perfect in your first year of teaching—far from it. There is a steep learning curve and you are on it. New teachers reveal that it takes them 5 years to feel comfortable in teaching. Be patient with yourself.

At a recent gathering, a third-grade teacher close to retirement stated, "I just don't want to leave. I love teaching! I have always loved it and I will really miss the kids." The other teachers at the table groaned. Many were counting the days to retirement after serving for more than 30 years in teaching at the same grade level. What makes some teachers race to the door, and others not want to leave? Passion is difficult to describe but easy to see. Can you find your passion after the 1st month, the 5th month? At the end of year 1?

Teaching is filled with challenges. Even the most experienced teachers will admit this. With new students each year, new situations every day, and new reforms every year, this dynamic profession requires energy, dedication, and diligence. Both beginning and veteran teachers agree that the first year is the most difficult. Only you know whether you have the passion or the "fire in your belly" to do what it takes—on a daily basis—to contribute to America's future. You "touch the future" each and every day with your students. That is how you know you are an effective teacher, by being there for your students.

Optional: Map out your career in a visual format starting from when you first decided to become a teacher up to now. Honestly assess your personal joy and your moments of challenge. Mark them on your map. Remember, challenge leads to growth.

REFLECT and SET GOALS

Think about...

Directions: Review the five Key Questions for this chapter and respond to the "Reflect . . ." questions that follow.

Key Questions:

1. How will I organize my first classroom? (ACTivities 12.1–12.5)
2. How will I integrate into the school culture? (ACTivities 12.6, 12.7)
3. How will I continue to learn? (ACTivities 12.8–12.12)
4. How will I know I am effective? (ACTivities 12.13, 12.14, 12.15)

Reflect...

What are my goals for this year? Write three in your own hard-copy or online journal?

Where do I see myself in 5 years? In 10 years?

Do I still have a passion for teaching (in spite of my challenges)?

SET GOALS: Possible Next Steps...

Document Your First Year!

✓ Take a photo of yourself on the first day of school.
✓ Take photos throughout the school year.
✓ Keep a journal by your desk to note your stories and learning.
✓ Share your portfolio with the students and parents.